THIS GROUND IS HOLY

"Do not come near; remove your sandals from your feet, for the place on which you are standing is holy ground."

Exodus 3:5

THIS GROUND IS HOLY

Church Sanctuary and Central American Refugees

IGNATIUS BAU

Paulist Press
New York/Mahwah

Library of Congress
Catalog Card Number: 85-60406

ISBN: 0-8091-2720-2

Published by Paulist Press
997 Macarthur Boulevard
Mahwah, N.J. 07430

Printed and bound in the United States of America

CONTENTS

Foreword   1

Introduction   5

1. **The Provision of Sanctuary**
   for Central American Refugees   9
   The Development of a Sanctuary Movement   10
   A Ministry of Hospitality   12
   A Ministry of Social Justice   14
   Religion and Politics   16
   Protest and Civil Disobedience   19
   A Turning Point: A Week in Tucson   21
   Tensions in Solidarity   29

2. **United States Immigration Law**
   Concerning Refugees   38
   Current United States Refugee Policies in Context   38
   History   40
   United States Refugee Policies   44
      Early Legislation   44
      International Obligations   48
        The United Nations Convention and Protocol   48
        Nonrefoulement in Other International Instruments   52
      Application of International Law to United States
      Refugee Policy: The 1980 Refugee Act   55
      Asylum Under the 1980 Refugee Act   60
        Procedures   60
        Access   62
        Standard of Proof   66

3. **The Confrontation Between Church and State**   75
    Federal Prosecution of Sanctuary Workers   75
        United States v. Stacey Lynn Merkt   76
        United States v. Philip M. Conger   79
        United States v. John ("Jack") Elder   80
        United States v. Jack Elder and Stacey Merkt   82
        United States v. Aguilar, Clark, Conger, Corbett,
        Emery, Espinosa, Fife, Flaherty, Hutchinson, LeWin,
        MacDonald, Martel-Benavidez, Nicgorski, Priester,
        Quinones, and Waddell   83
    The Future   87

4. **Legal Implications for Sanctuaries
    and Sanctuary Workers**   90
    Sanctuary Under United States Law   90
    Unlawful Harboring and Transportation of
    Undocumented Aliens   92
    Defenses   101
        Sanctuary Activity Outside the Statute   101
        Lawful Refugees Are Not "Illegal Aliens"   102
        Equal Protection Under the Employment Proviso   108
        Humanitarian Transportation Not in Furtherance
        of the Aliens' Violation of the Law   109
        First Amendment Free Exercise of Religion   111

5. **The Ancient Tradition of Sanctuary**   124
    Old Testament Cities of Refuge   125
    Old Testament Altar Sanctuary   127
    Greek and Roman Sanctuaries   129
    Early Christian Sanctuaries   130

6. **The Law of Sanctuary in England**   134
    The Anglo-Saxon Period   134
    Three Types of Sanctuary   140
    The Late Anglo-Saxon and the Norman Periods   140
    The Plantagenet Period   143
    Abjuration of the Realm   144
    The Demise of Sanctuary in English Law   150
        Abuses by Debtors   150

London Sanctuaries   151
Ecclesiastical and Judicial Regulation   152
Henry VIII   153
Final Abolition   156

7. **Sanctuary in United States History**   158
The First Colonists   158
The Underground Railroad for Fugitive Slaves   160
Sanctuary During the Vietnam War   161
    In the East   161
    In the Universities   164
    In the West   167
    Analysis   169

8. **Application of the History of the Sanctuary
    to Central American Refugees Today**   172
From Holy Places to Communities of Faith   173
A Movement of Common People   174
A Theology of Liberation   176
Accountability and Liability   180
The Future of Sanctuary   182

Appendix: Numbers 35:6–34   184

Notes   186

Bibliography   259

Epilogue   286

ACKNOWLEDGEMENTS

The words of acknowledgement that follow are poor compensation for the spirit of sharing that has nurtured this work. I thank those who have shared with me the gifts of knowledge: Professor John Noonan, whose seminar on the Religious Sources of American Law at Boalt Hall School of Law provided the inspiration for this work; Carolyn Patty Blum, who has guided me in immigration law and who has always been generous with her time and wisdom; Fernando Villa and Howard Simon, who shared their unpublished papers with me; and all those at the Immigration Project of Catholic Social Service in San Francisco who gave me practical insight and experience in the immigration system.

I am deeply grateful to all those in the sanctuary movement who have shared with me and who have lived out and done that which I can only write about: Rev. Gus Schultz, Eileen Purcell, Stacey Merkt, Jim Larson, Kathleen Purcell.

I also wish to thank Fr. George Fitzgerald and the staff at Newman Hall/Holy Spirit Parish in Berkeley, who have given me a community of faith for the past six years and who helped me get my manuscript to Paulist Press. Don Brophy of Paulist Press has been an extremely patient and supportive editor.

Thanks also go to Vickie Parker, who stayed up late nights and long hours typing the manuscript. Most of all, I am grateful to Lillian Howan, whose companionship and careful editing sustained me throughout the months. This book would not be what it is without her support and contributions.

May our lives and our hearts be sanctuaries for each other and for our God.

FOREWORD

"We were the land's before the land was ours." Land that owns us. Land that we own. Land that we love. Land that is ours. The sense of possession is very strong. The/"me first" and "mine" of childhood graduates to the dignity of "us" and "ours," no longer narrowly egotistic but broadly encompassing all our fellow citizens. It is our land, our turf, our foundation of national identity. We don't have to share it with anyone.

The people of Israel were once told that their God "loves the alien who lives among you, giving him food and clothing. You too must love the alien, for you once lived as aliens in Egypt." We too, or our ancestors, once lived as aliens in this land that is ours. Recollection of that experience may enhance our ability to empathize with the aliens in the land today. Worshipers of the God of Israel—Jews or Christians—we may suspect that that God has not changed his compassion for the alien living amongst us. These thoughts, religious in origin, humane in implication, may temper the primitive passion, the fierce territorial zeal with which we assert the land is "ours."

When the alien comes to our land not because he or she wants to immigrate, but because he or she has been persecuted at home—beaten, tortured, put in fear of death—then that alien has a right to life that presses upon our right to our land. By accident of birth we the citizens occupy this territory. By accident of birth they the aliens have been subjected to terror. They come to our territory because they do not know where else to come. "Home is the place where, when you have to go there, they have to take you in."

But is this their home? Do we *have* to take them in? The questions lead to another question: Is the land really ours? Religious teaching holds that no human ownership of property is absolute. We are stewards, that is, economic managers only. God is the owner. We must answer the questions as his agents.

1

Territorial integrity, our right to our land and the culture we have built in it, on the one hand; religious and humane impulses to befriend the stranger and the right to life of each person on earth, on the other hand—these competing considerations swirl in our minds. By law we have created a compromise—a statute on immigrants that rations the number that may enter, that gives special protection to the persecuted, that as administered is grudging, almost hostile to the persecuted who flee from Central America.

Religious and humane impulses push beyond the compromise of the law and its Kafka-like operation. At this point an idea half-religious, half-legal occurs: sanctuary. Sanctuary, it is proposed, should be extended to the alien fleeing persecution.

Sanctuary is shocking to the secular mind. How can there be any place within the confines of a nation that the law does not operate? How can religion claim a privilege to say it is beyond the law? How can the law stultify itself by acknowledging that in certain places the law ceases to hold sway?

Religious history teaches otherwise. An ideal institution of Israel consisted in "the cities of refuge," specially designated areas where an unintentional killer would be safe from the kinsman whom the law permitted to avenge the death the killer had caused. The altar of Israel's God also operated as a sanctuary for suspects subject to capital punishment. The notion that God himself limited the scope of human justice was nourished.

The idea became part of the Christian inheritance from Israel. In England, for example, in Alfred the Great's day every church had the right to offer sanctuary to fugitives for a period of a day. Eventually certain shrines were recognized by the king as being able to give immunity from arrest to those within their territorial limits.

Violent men did not always respect these privileges. The murder of Thomas Becket by agents of Henry II in the archbishop's own cathedral at his own altar was a sensational demonstration of how power could push aside the sacred and wreak its will. But the circumstances of Becket's death at the altar made his martyrdom memorable, the proclamation of his sainthood inevitable, and scourging of the repentant king an element of the atonement required for the outrage.

The original Jewish use of sanctuary had incorporated the idea of the sacred into the law to limit the severity of strict law. Catholics understood sanctuary not literally but analogically and brought forth the institution that church law, civil law, and popular custom converged to uphold—sanctuary from violence or arrest within a church. In the nineteenth century, churches fathered another analogical variant: churches were to be used as safe places for slaves who had fled their masters in slave states. Fugitive property in the eyes of the law, these black human beings were subject to summary recapture. Those who obstructed their recapture were felons under federal law. Here sanctuary was not incorporated into the law to limit the law but operated in bold defiance of the law. Nonetheless the ancient idea of the special character of a holy place was at work. Somewhere on earth, it was believed by religious people, the hunted should be beyond their pursuers. Where should this refuge be if not in a Christian church?

American law has not changed since the days of the Underground Railroad. It is a federal felony today to hide, harbor, or shield any alien "not lawfully entitled to reside within the United States." Yet religious people have not hesitated to offer their churches and themselves at the risk of being found guilty of violating this federal law.

American law is not without respect for the sacred. Sacred days—Sundays and Christmas—are observed in a special way throughout our land. Sacred property, that is, property dedicated to the worship of God, is everywhere immunized from taxation. Sacred duties imposed by conscience, such as the duty perceived by some not to fight in war, are recognized by statute. But no statute acknowledges a church's right to accord sanctuary. Sanctuary in America does not have the standing Scripture accorded sanctuary in Israel and canon law accorded sanctuary in Catholic England. Sanctuary in the United States is beyond the law although not necessarily beyond the conscience of the citizen.

A conscientious citizen of course obeys the law. But the law cannot be the sole measure for his or her conscience. The fallacy of that position was exposed in the Nuremberg Trials. The German judges who cooperated with the Nazis had been meticulous in obeying the Nazi laws. Nonetheless they were condemned for crimes against humanity. The law of their land was no defense for their conduct.

The relationship of law and conscience had been pondered far earlier by Thomas More. Imprisoned in the Tower for failure to take the oath required by law acknowledging the king's supremacy over the Church in England, he admitted to the Archbishop of Canterbury that he would not condemn those who took the oath. The archbishop observed that he must then be in doubt himself; and if he were in doubt, he should resolve the doubt by obeying the king, for he had a clear duty to obey. More, as he wrote his daughter Margaret, was greatly troubled by this argument and tempted to accept it. But he then thought: If the argument is valid, whenever there is a doubt in theology, there is an easy way to resolve it. We will ask the king, and whatever he decides will decide our question. This result was a *reductio ad absurdum*. The king or the law could not so easily resolve a doubt of conscience. Each person, More realized, must decide such doubts within his own conscience; and obedience to one's conscience could, as his did, lead to losing one's life for one's disobedience to the law.

All these matters—their history, the present system of statutory and criminal case law that affects sanctuary today, the issues before us as law-abiding conscientious religious persons—are the subject matter of Ignatius Bau's book. Different consciences will respond differently to the invocation of sanctuary today. In a secular society it embodies the sacred, setting a limit to the law. For reasons of humanity, for reasons of religion, its special role requires our attention and response.

John T. Noonan, Jr.
Berkeley, California

INTRODUCTION[1]

Stacey Lynn Merkt is not an ordinary felon. On May 12, 1984 Stacey was convicted of three federal felony indictments: two counts of aiding and abetting the unlawful transportation of undocumented aliens and one count of conspiracy to transport undocumented aliens. In June she was sentenced to a ninety-day suspended sentence and two years of probation. In December 1984 she was indicted and arrested again. On February 21, 1985 Stacey was acquitted of two counts of unlawful transportation but convicted of one count of conspiracy. On March 27, she was sentenced to an 18-month prison term for the conspiracy conviction. The risks of arrest, criminal prosecution and imprisonment that have faced Stacey Lynn Merkt are the same risks that have been taken by members of over two hundred churches across the United States as the churches have declared themselves public sanctuaries for Central American refugees.

Stacey's journey of faith is not complex, beginning from a small suburban community in northern California. She grew up as a Methodist, with faith in a "living and growing God." As she stood before the federal district court judge before her sentencing in June 1984, she proclaimed:

> First and foremost I have a belief in God. A God of life, and of love, and of people. I am a lover of life. I have deep respect for this land, this soil and the life she contains. I protect and nourish this earth. That's Stacey, the farmer. It pleases me to no end to spade and weed and harvest. I am one who belongs in the fields, especially as I see the connection between creation and people—food and sustenance.[2]

Stacey first began to become interested in Central America when she was at Bijou House in Colorado Springs, a Christian house of hospitality. She learned first from the news media and then

5

from the testimonies of Central American refugees who had found their way to Colorado. Finally, Stacey decided to journey to Mexico to learn more first-hand, and so in October 1983 she visited Mexico City and Chiapas for three months. The stories she heard and the people she met changed the course of her life. She had more to do; she had to get more involved. In Feburary 1983 Stacey went to San Benito, Texas in the Rio Grande Valley near the United States-Mexico border, to live and work with Jack and Diane Elder at Casa Oscar Romero, a house of hospitality for Central American refugees. The house is funded by the Roman Catholic diocese of Brownsville and other local church groups. Stacey had planned on staying at Casa Romero for only a few months—but her plans were changed.

"We are never in the wrong place at the wrong time," says Stacey. Where she was at 5 A.M., the morning of February 17, 1984, was in a car with a nun from Indiana, a reporter from the *Dallas Times-Herald*, and three Salvadorans. They were driving from San Benito to San Antonio but were stopped and arrested by the United States Border Patrol. The government has pronounced its verdict on Stacey: guilty of a federal felony because the Salvadorans in the car with her were "illegal aliens." The second series of indictments also focus on her work at Casa Romero, especially the transporting of and assisting of Central American refugees into the United States.

Stacey has another perspective: "First and foremost, I believe in a God of life and a God of love. And we are called to love, not just in words, but actively, in deed." She holds out one hand and continues, "I am called to extend my hand to those in need—to these Salvadorans—but I am also called to work for justice so that I don't need to extend my hand." Before her sentencing in June 1984 she declared to the judge:

> I'm no celebrity. I'm no martyr. And I'm no felon. I am a woman with a heart and mind. My faith commitment connects me to the people and to justice. I am a worker. You and me, we are co-creators of this earth inasmuch as we accept that responsibility standing for justice. We don't take that lightly.[3]

This reluctant celebrity, still uncomfortable before large crowds and with constant interviews, maintains a firm belief in her innocence before the law and before her God. What the government calls a crime, she simply names as her duty as a Christian: to extend her hand of hospitality, to work for justice. After her first arrest, while awaiting her trial, she reflected:

> I've spent the last couple of weeks stripping away layers in order to expose my core, then to remember all that makes me uniquely me. The core that sustains me is the still small voice. It is God whom I wish to hear. The small voice encourages me to live out my faith—the biblical mandate to love. I am not to love in mere words. I am to love by my actions—to put my body where my mouth is.[4]

Stacey's experiences and her beliefs are shared with humility, gentleness, warmth and patience. There is a calmness and peace about her. Even when challenged or questioned by a hostile member of one of her many recent audiences, she answers without raising her voice, without any anger.

Before her second trial, Stacey was asked what it meant to her to be indicted for sanctuary work. She responded:

> We as people of faith need to examine our fears in light of the stories of why the refugees come to us. If we don't take that small step and act regardless of our fears and regardless of whether or not we have courage, we'll never know what courage is. It is step by step and inch by inch that we struggle in our process to live out our faith.[5]

Stacey faces the possibility of imprisonment with the same faith that first brought her to Casa Romero:

> I've tried to get my fears into perspective. I don't fear going to jail or being imprisoned. My incarceration, if it comes to that, is nothing compared to the torture and death the refugees have seen or could face if deported. A Salvadoran friend has told me I will be representing her people if I go to prison.[6]

She faces the future with boldness:

> I don't want to fall into the illusion that I, or anyone else, am the world's savior. I'm not. But I want to live my life with truth,

integrity and love. For therein lies power and change. . . . I like
to quote Dorothy Day's remark, "Don't make me into a saint."
I'm just Stacey Lynn Merkt, who did what was right, what was
compassionate and what was legal.[7]

Today, hundreds of churchpeople across the United States face
risks of criminal prosecution similar to Stacey Lynn Merkt. Their
churches have declared themselves as sanctuaries for Central Americans, invoking the ancient privilege of holy places to provide protection to refugees. They open their doors as a sign of hospitality
and as a sign of protest against their government's immigration and
foreign policies. Some will observe that they have broken the law.
They humbly respond that they only seek to uphold the law. This
is their story.

CHAPTER ONE

The Provision of Sanctuary
for Central American Refugees

"This is the time and we are the people to reinvoke the ancient law of sanctuary, to say to the government, 'You shall go this far and no further.' This is the time and we are the people fleeing the blood vengeance of the powers that be in El Salvador. We provide a safe place and cry, 'Basta! Enough! the blood stops here at our doors.' This is the time to claim our sacred right to invoke the name of God in this place—to push back all the powers of violation and violence in the name of the Spirit to whom we owe our ultimate allegiance. At this historic moment we are the people to tell Caesar, 'No trespassing, for the ground upon which you walk is holy.' " [1]

> Rev. David Chevrier,
> Pastor of the Wellington Avenue
> United Church of Christ,
> Chicago, Illinois, July 24, 1982

The invocation of the privilege of sanctuary by a growing number of North American churches[2] which seek to provide refuge for Central Americans fleeing their homelands has raised many questions about the history and legal viability of sanctuary. As one examines the development of the tradition of sanctuary, it becomes evident that the concept has deep religious and historical roots. Similarly, the current manifestation of sanctuary has profound historical, sociological, legal and theological meaning. This book attempts to place the current sanctuary movement in the context of the rich

9

tradition of sanctuary and offers some reflections upon its implications for the churches, the legal institutions and the social structures of the United States.

The Development of a Sanctuary Movement

The national sanctuary movement was originally conceived by the Reverend John Fife of the Southside United Presbyterian Church in Tucson, Arizona, and Jim Corbett, a retired Quaker rancher. Fife's church was one of the first to publicly declare itself as a sanctuary, doing so on March 24, 1982, the second anniversary of the assassination of San Salvador Archbishop Oscar Arnulfo Romero. Corbett became involved with Central American refugees in May 1981 when a friend picked up a Salvadoran refugee hitch-hiking in the Nogales, Arizona area. When Corbett followed up on the refugee, who had been arrested by the border patrol, Corbett became increasingly involved in the complex immigration procedures concerning refugees. He was soon actively helping Central American refugees apply for asylum in the United States. Rev. Fife had been deeply affected by the plight of refugees when a professional "coyote" (the Spanish name given to those commercial smugglers who help aliens cross the United States-Mexico border for a fee) abandoned a group of Salvadorans in the Arizona desert in the summer of 1980. Half of the Salvadorans died of dehydration but the other half were placed in detention to be deported as soon as they were released from the hospital. Fife's church started a weekly prayer vigil for refugees (that still continues) but the prayer meeting also became a place for immigration lawyers and refugees themselves to come and discuss their problems. In the spring of 1981, the Tucson Ecumenical Council created a Task Force on Central America to respond to some of these needs. The Task Force began to raise money for bail to bond refugees out of detention and to fund paralegals to help them with the asylum application process. However, after close to $750,000 in bonds and up to $100,000 in legal expenses were raised, the TEC Task Force realized that their efforts were futile. Fife declares:

> So if you hear from INS that what those churchpeople ought to do is try to work within the law first, we did it. And we did it

with as much energy and imagination and creativity as we could.[3]

Jim Corbett began to challenge Fife and the rest of the TEC Task Force to do more than help the refugees after arrest. Corbett had already filled his own house and the houses of other Quakers with refugees; now he was asking Fife's church to do the same and thereby protect them from arrest. At first, refugees were introduced during the worship services at Southside United Presbyterian and members of the congregation would volunteer to take the refugees into their homes. However, members of the church were soon transporting the refugees away from the border, then from the border to the church, and finally, from across the United States-Mexico border. The decision to publicly declare sanctuary became inevitable. Rev. Fife reflects:

> We couldn't stop. We'd already made the decision when we got involved in that whole effort that the life-and-death needs of the refugees overrode any other set of risks that we might encounter here in the United States. The conclusion we came to is the only other option we have is to give public witness to what we're doing, what the plight of the refugees is, and the faith basis for our actions.[4]

Still, the church required a process of what Rev. Fife calls "Bible study, prayer, discussion, and agonizing" during December 1981 and January 1982 before finally deciding to declare sanctuary publicly. The church then wrote to other churches to propose joint declarations.

One of those churches that responded was the University Lutheran Chapel in Berkeley, California. University Lutheran had been a sanctuary church for war resisters during the Vietnam War (see Chapter Seven). In the fall of 1981, a group called the Sather Gate Churches, composed of Berkeley pastors from the churches near the University of California campus, began discussing the issue of Central American refugees in the San Francisco Bay Area. University Lutheran's pastor, Rev. Gustav Schultz, recalled his church's experience of providing sanctuary. As the presence and problems of the refugees from Central America persisted, the Berkeley churches decided to gather together to form the East Bay Sanctuary Covenant. In November 1981, St. John's Presbyterian Church in Berkeley secretly sheltered a refugee family. When Southside United Presbyterian Church in Tucson declared public sanctuary, University Lutheran Chapel publicly welcomed a refugee family into the church, as one of the five initial members of the East Bay Sanctuary Covenant.[4a]

From those first public declarations in March 1982, the movement has spread to the geographical boundaries of the United States—from Seattle, Washington to San Diego, California, from Weston, Vermont to Miami, Florida.[5] As of early 1983, there were forty-five public sanctuary sites, six hundred supporting congregations and religious organizations, and fifty local organizing committees involved in the movement.[6] By the end of the fall of 1983, at least twenty-four more churches had publicly declared themselves sanctuary sites, bringing the total close to seventy.[7] By the summer of 1984, the number of sanctuaries has grown to over one hundred and fifty, with thousands of individuals committed to the movement.[8]

It is difficult to estimate how many refugees have been aided by these sanctuaries. Fife estimated in 1982 that his church alone had brought into the country and harbored some sixteen hundred Salvadorans, including over two hundred families.[9] One estimate has listed the number of refugees aided by the national sanctuary movement as three thousand, including three hundred and fifty families.[10] Others estimate only several hundred.[11]

The individual and congregational motivations for participation in the movement are varied but seem to emphasize four themes: (1) the provision of physical security and services for the Central American refugees, (2) a new ministry of social justice by the churches, (3) an emerging role for the church in United States politics, and (4) a protest of the United States foreign policy in Central America.

A Ministry of Hospitality

In analyzing the sanctuary movement, it is easy to focus on its theory—its history, its legal implications, its impact on the church in the United States—and overlook the actual practice of providing sanctuary. Eric Jorstad, who has written extensively about the sanctuary movement, states:

> Sanctuary is, first, an act of compassion, an expression of the fundamental Christian concern to love one's neighbor . . . sanctuary is a way of expressing compassion in caring for our suffering neighbors from Central America. It is a way of providing for people in need, not only with social services, but also by giving them haven from the potentially disastrous consequences of deportation.[12]

Sanctuaries provide legal services (money for bail, legal assistance at deportation proceedings, preparation of applications for asylum), social services (food, shelter, medical aid) and evasion services (transportation, resettlement).[13] Many of the sanctuary churches have a long (or perhaps recently renewed) tradition of sheltering the homeless and feeding the hungry through soup kitchens, temporary shelters, inner city rescue missions, and other ministries of hospitality.[14] To these churches, is seems only natural that doors that are open to the poor of the United States should also be open to Central American refugees in the United States.

Some of the sanctuary churches had rich experiences with refugees after the close of the Vietnam War when there was a tremendous influx of refugees into the United States from Southeast Asia. Churches were active in resettlement efforts, either through the direct sponsorship of refugee families or through contributions to church-affiliated agencies working with the refugees. While one may argue that there are many differences between the refugees from Southeast Asia and those from Central America,[15] such distinctions are generally irrelevant to the churches involved. What is essential to these churches is that these persons have fled their home countries and now seek refuge in the United States. When such a refugee stands at the church door requesting assistance, there is no preliminary inquiry into the merits of one's claim to the status of refugee as defined by the United States immigration law. There is only an unconditional invitation and welcome extended to the person in need.

A Ministry of Social Justice

The church's ministry to the needy of society has generated great controversy within the church itself. In the early twentieth century there was much debate over the orthodoxy of the so-called social gospel in mainstream Christianity. While every pastor and priest, like the New Testament lawyer, knows that the greatest commandments are to love God and to love neighbor,[16] the simplicity of the biblical mandate continues to be confused in the process of implementation. Regardless of historical or denominational traditions, many churchpeople today are rediscovering a rich biblical tradition that seeks justice and peace as concrete elements of the kingdom of God.[17] The strongest and most articulate voices proclaiming a contemporary theology of liberation have emerged from third world churches.[18] Regardless of whether any or all of these contemporary theologies are ultimately adopted by the mainstream United States churches, their impact upon the nature of the church in the world is irreversible. In Latin America, the network of *communidades de base* have replaced rigid institutional structures as the manifestation of contemporary Christian faith. Simultaneously, a new understanding of what it means to be church has emerged.[19] With humble understatement, Jim Corbett eloquently explains his understanding of the meaning of the sanctuary movement for the North American church:

> Reports that we here in Tucson have built an underground railroad or established a sanctuary movement are false; we are simply in the process of discovering the church. In whatever measure the church is the church, it will protect the oppressed from organized oppression—which usually means protecting them from the state. The oppressed are often betrayed by clergy and congregations who give primary allegiance to the law and order of established powers. . . . [20]

In "discovering the church," many of the sanctuary churches have found their own institutional structures ill-suited for the ministry of public sanctuary. Thus, the decision to declare public sanctuary has often led to radical changes in the structures as well as the attitudes and self-perceptions of the church community. While there have been national networking and coordinating efforts, each local church has followed its own individualized process in deciding whether to become a public sanctuary. When pre-existing internal church structures are inadequate for such a major commitment, many churches have made bold changes. There is a new level of involvement and new priorities within the church. The use of the church building is often altered, either to directly shelter the refugees or to provide a forum for meetings, fundraisers and worship services. New channels of communication and cooperation within the church often result, bringing both lay professionals (lawyers, doctors, social workers) within the church community and even those outside the church congregation into the life and ministry of the church. There is a new urgency about being a genuine community; the person in the next pew is no longer a stranger but now a potential co-felon.

In all this development of a new ministry of justice called public sanctuary, there are some inevitable limitations and common restraints. Churches must also remain faithful to their more conventional activities and agendas. While sanctuary can become a rich subject for prayer, study, worship and action, it cannot be the exclusive activity of the church. Churches must decide to what degree of involvement they will commit themselves: either directly sheltering refugees within the church building, thereby requiring a twenty-four-hour ministry, or providing a lesser commitment of support. It is important to distinguish what degree of involvement each sanctuary church has undertaken. Some sanctuary churches have not actually physically sheltered refugees. These are sometimes termed "secondary sanctuaries" rather than "immediate sanctuaries."[21] In turn, some churches and many individuals have sheltered refugees without any public declaration. Secondary sanctuaries can provide a wide variety of support services: contributing money, food, clothing, or furniture, or providing transportation, volunteers, or the use of church facilities for educational and other gatherings. In the past year, it has become increasingly common to use a public caravan to bring refugees to sanctuary sites.[22] Such a caravan requires the cars and volunteers of many sanctuary churches, as well as the organization of waystations and receptions along the caravan route.

Once a sanctuary church does decide to shelter a refugee, other decisions become necessary. The first decision involves the length of time that the refugees will stay in the church building. Sometimes the refugees will appear in the church only for a welcoming service and then proceed immediately to the private homes of church members or even to a home of their own. In other cases, the refugees will actually live in the church building for either a brief or an extended period of time. Each sanctuary church, usually in cooperation with other neighboring churches, will also determine what degree of assistance will be provided to resettle the refugees. The sanctuary churches can also be committed to the support of the refugees should there be any arrests. Such support includes funds to bail out the refugees from jail and legal representation in any deportation proceedings. Often churches will provide a twenty-four-hour vigil to physically protect the refugees from any governmental intrusion.

The new activism and commitment that sanctuary demands establishes social justice as an essential part of the church's ministry. The churches take responsibility for all the needs of the refugees—physical, emotional, legal and economic. Providing sanctuary is a full-service, wholistic ministry of justice.

Religion and Politics

As the sanctuary movement produces new ministries and new identities for church communities, other forces also demand that the North American church reassess its role in society. In the United States, the current formulation of the issue focuses on the proper relationship between the church and the state. This issue becomes most crucial when organized religion participates in national partisan politics. In 1976 a new phenomenon burst onto the electoral scene of the United States: the Year of the Evangelical. Jimmy Carter's outspoken faith echoed the popular discovery and publicity of born-again Christianity. In 1976 few questions were raised about the First Amendment separation of church and state; there was no controversy similar to that which surrounded John F. Kennedy's presidential candidacy in 1960. Whatever the reasons—a new degree of religious tolerance, the emergence of an outspoken Protestant candidate rather than a Catholic one, or simply the post-

Watergate political climate desperate for a change and fresh directions—1976 marked a radical new degree of acceptance of religion into the public life of the United States.

The tolerance wore thin in 1980 with the surprising coup of the New Religious Right. The new marriage of religion and politics became a multi-million dollar and multi-million voter venture. Several liberal Senators and, perhaps ironically, even Jimmy Carter felt the new political clout of the Moral Majority, the Christian Voice, and, most importantly, the National Conservative Political Action Committee. Religion had clearly asserted itself as a force to be reckoned with in future elections.

The political activism of many churches in national and local elections has created a background for much debate and discussion about the relationship between church and state. In many ways, President Ronald Reagan's administration has heightened the tension. On the one hand, Reagan has called upon churches to help fill the holes in his so-called safety net as federal budget cuts have left thousands without jobs, food and shelter. At the same time, the Reagan administration has increased military spending and continued to pursue a nuclear arms race which has provoked an unprecedented degree of organizing, demonstrating and direct acts of civil disobedience by churchpeople.[23] Moreover, a significant response, extremely critical of current governmental policies, has emerged from the United States Catholic bishops in the form of pastoral letters on war and peace and on the United States economy.[24]

On the other hand, Ronald Reagan has also unabashedly made religious issues key elements of his domestic policies, especially in his second term. Abortion, prayer in public schools, diplomatic recognition of the Vatican, tax exemptions for religious schools that practice racial discrimination, tuition tax credits for parochial education, and a whole list of other issues have become part of the national political agenda. While the religious basis of Reagan's positions on many of these issues may be challenged,[25] the Reagan White House continues to invoke religious themes in establishing national public policy.

The issue of religion and politics emerged at the forefront of the 1984 presidential campaign.[26] One of the first public statements by Geraldine Ferraro after her nomination as a vice-presidential candidate challenged Ronald Reagan's practice of Christianity. Reagan fueled the controversy with a Dallas speech about the indispensability of religion in politics. Several Roman Catholic bishops joined the debate by challenging Ferraro's position on abortion. Members of both the political and religious right and left lined up to defend their positions. Regardless of what direct impact all this public discussion of religion and politics did or did not have on the ultimate outcome of the election, 1984 marked a campaign year when a significant portion of the United States church, including fundamentalists, Roman Catholics, Jews, and black churches, was far from apolitical.

As the church is called—or pushed—into partisan politics, it is necessary to articulate its proper role in the United States public life. The sanctuary movement must be understood as one strand of a larger movement within the church to identify the appropriate response of the church to these pressures to assert a position in national public policy. While the sanctuary churches themselves have probably not consciously decided to engage in sanctuary activity simply for the sake of exploring their theoretical role in society, it is evident that the sanctuary movement could not have grown as it has without this underlying pressure upon the church as a whole to become more public, more active, and more political.

The involvement of the church in politics inevitably raises questions of the separation of church and state. For the sanctuary movement, the issue is not so much one of separation as of survival. The danger of a political role for the churches is twofold. First, the church, generally unsophisticated in the way of politics, is vulnerable to being coopted by some pre-packaged political agenda. Second, the backlash against the churches can be severe—both from within its own ranks and from those outside the church. On the one hand, many traditional churchgoers chaff at the new activism and break ranks with their churches. The resulting exodus from these churches may cause division and the depletion of vital support. On the other hand, churches that find themselves on the wrong side of the political perspective currently in power may find themselves under unrestrained attack by the government and its supporters. The Catholic bishops have been called naive and irresponsible for their pastoral letter on war and peace, prompting a lay commission's rebuttal to their pastoral letter on the economy. The National Council of Churches has been subject to an exposé in the national news media, coordinated by the Institute for Religion and Democracy. It remains to be seen how tax exemptions, mail privileges and a whole spectrum of immunities will stand up when religious leaders and institutions begin taking public policy positions that openly defy the national government.

Many churches are discovering that the dangers of political involvement can be a double-bind: avoiding the first danger of being used by politicians can often dramatically increase the second danger of governmental attack. This realization presents the church with a fundamental ecclesiological question: Will the church of North America play the role of the king's court prophet, uncritically proclaiming blessing upon the ruling authorities, or will today's church follow the tradition of Nathan, Elijah, Elisha, Isaiah, Jeremiah and John the Baptist as the repentant prophet calling for the king's conversion?[27] While both religious right and left profess repentance for the national social sins of the United States, such repentance is often mingled with professions of patriotism. However, the test for the church must not be its loyalty to nationhood, but its faithfulness to the biblical vision of the kingdom of God.[28] The issue facing the sanctuary churches is not how to maintain the separation of church and state but how to remain faithful to their calling as a church in the face of contrary governmental policies. Eric Jorstad reflects:

> The situation of the Central American refugees challenges the self-understanding of the North America church, by asking that our practice conform to our principles. The question is not whether the church can or will take a stand, but with whom the church *is* standing.[29]

Protest and Civil Disobedience

The fourth theme that binds the sanctuary movement together is a growing consciousness of the implications of current United States foreign policies in Central America. The refugees seeking sanctuary incarnate the problems of Central America for the people of the United States in a way that the mass media never could. The stories of these Central Americans, now retold in churches and church communities all over the country, present a testimony of human suffering and of direct United States government responsibility for much of that suffering. Jorstad insightfully suggests that such testimony not only educates the churches about Central America but also empowers the refugees, giving them a political voice that can contribute to changes in United States policies that influence the futures of their home countries.[30]

Churchpeople have begun to listen to these stories and then have raised their own voices in protest. Many were shocked by the deaths of the four United States churchwomen in El Salvador, dramatically represented in the PBS documentary "Roses in December" and the December 1983 prime-time NBC movie "Choices of the Heart." The anniversary of those murders and the anniversary of Archbishop Romero's assassination have become focal points for church-based vigils, rallies, and demonstrations against United States policies in Central America.

Whatever one's ultimate conclusions and political analysis of the situation in Central America, it has become incumbent upon those concerned about the role of the United States in that region to voice their opinions. The sanctuary movement can never be divorced from its religious context. It is not politics in the conventional sense of registering voters, campaigning for candidates and issues, or even lobbying legislators and Presidents. It is a brand of political activity—or perhaps, more accurately, political dissent—that is rare, but not unprecedented, in the United States historical tradition. It is similar to the civil rights movement because it is nonviolent and church-based. It is similar to the anti-war movement during the Vietnam War because it is fundamentally a call for nonintervention and peace. However, it is perhaps closest to the Underground Railroad for fugitive slaves during the United States Civil War because it is a mass rejection of the presumptions and values of the status quo. The sanctuary movement is like the Underground Railroad because while it is inevitably a political act to break the law—an act of civil disobedience—law-breaking is not the primary motivation for sanctuary. One member of the sanctuary church explains the choice:

> We look down on those churches in Germany that allowed the
> Jews to be rounded up after they knew what would happen to
> them. . . . Now you know. If you believe that people are being

tortured and murdered in Salvador, and that we are supplying the guns and the bullets, then you know that we are standing behind the death squad member [who has] the gun and the knife. By offering sanctuary, we can at least stop supplying these death squads with their victims.[31]

Although there has always been a tradition of civil disobedience in the Judeo-Christian faith,[32] the sanctuary movement goes beyond civil disobedience. Jim Corbett explains:

. . . [S]anctuary also begins where war resistance played out, with community conversion. Civil disobedience is often understood (as Thoreau conceived it) to be individualistic resistance to state-enforced injustice, but the declaration of sanctuary is a different kind of civil disobedience that is intended to *do* justice. Individuals may resist injustice, but only communities can choose to do justice.[33]

A Turning Point: A Week in Tucson

A series of events took place in Tucson, Arizona on January 22 through 26, 1985 that will mark a turning point for the sanctuary movement. A two-day conference on the sanctuary movement was the only event originally scheduled, but the week became both a joyous celebration of two years of sanctuary work and a sobering challenge to the future of the sanctuary movement. The United States government had ironically provided a major contribution to publicity and attendance at the Inter-American Symposium on Sanctuary by its announcement of seventy-one indictments against sixteen sanctuary workers on January 16, 1985 (see Chapter Three). One source estimated that registration for the symposium had tripled since the indictments were announced.[34] The arraignments of the sixteen indictees were scheduled on January 23, the first day of the symposium. Meanwhile, the trial of Casa Romero director Jack Elder in Corpus Christi, Texas was also taking place. On the afternoon of the second day of the symposium, January 24, a tearful Stacey Merkt interrupted the panel discussion by announcing that the jury had acquitted Elder. The audience of over thirteen hundred burst into a standing ovation and cries of relief. Rabbi Marshall

Meyer of the University of Judaism in Los Angeles then led the entire gathering in an emotional singing of the chorus, "Gloria in Excelsis Deo."[35] The week continued with much evaluation, discernment and planning as the criminal proceedings added a new sense of urgency and importance to the sanctuary movement. Legal defense and fundraising strategies emerged from the week's meetings. A national consultation among sanctuary churches and communities was convened to take place after the symposium.

The week began with a benefit dinner on January 22 featuring Elie Wiesel, noted Jewish author and survivor of the Holocaust. While Wiesel refrained from becoming involved with what he perceived as political issues, he declared to the audience of some eight hundred persons, "How can I not be with you when I am one of you?" He castigated those who used the term "illegal alien," calling it an "antinomy" and asking rhetorically, "How can a human being be illegal?" Wiesel observed that the new person of this era is not a citizen but a refugee and noted how refugees were no longer welcomed but were now always unwanted. He therefore called for a new concept of sanctuary—not a place, but any human being. He declared that all human beings are dwellings of God and therefore sacred and inviolable. Finally, while admonishing his listeners never to compare human tragedies, Wiesel recalled that the few "righteous Gentiles" who assisted and protected the Jews from the Nazis did not do so because of any lofty political or religious motivations but only because "it was the right thing to do." Wiesel's prayer was that the people of the United States might have the same simple courage and vision.

The keynote speaker at the symposium, Rev. William Sloane Coffin, Jr. (who was one of the initiators of the sanctuary movement during the Vietnam War—see Chapter Seven), issued a call to link the Central American policy of the United States with its domestic problems. Coffin challenged the sanctuary movement to broaden its focus to include the poor and minority groups in the United States, pointing out the parallels in foreign and domestic policies that "make the rich richer, the poor poorer, and the military more powerful."[36]

Coffin began his address with a call to accountability: "The Reagan administration has blood on its hands but only because Congress and the American people have water on their hands like Pilate." He declared that revolution in El Salvador was "born and bred in local oppression" rather than being exported there since revolts occurred only where there were "revolting conditions." He called for an end to the "unexamined sloganism" of anti-communism, observing that by claiming the interventionist intentions of Havana and Moscow, the United States was able to design its own interventionism in Washington, D.C. Referring to the religious basis of the sanctuary movement, Coffin quipped that the "true leader" of the sanctuary movement "lies just beyond the reach of the INS," but warned the audience that "rarely will a good deed go unpunished." Yet he urged the members of the movement to remain loving and hopeful. [36a]

Other symposium speakers also denounced United States government policies relating to Central America and to Central American refugees. For example, Professor James Nickel from the University of Colorado advocated the following adaptation of a classic criminal justice axiom: better that a few "economic refugees" be allowed to remain in the United States than one "political refugee" be deported from the United States to persecution. Jim Wallis of the Sojourners community in Washington, D.C. denounced the increasingly lawless authority of the current administration and pointed out that the government had acknowledged that the United States church has become the key obstacle in implementing the current administration's foreign policy objectives in Central America. Professor Robert McAfee Brown from the Pacific School of Religion denounced the idolatry of the state that sought uncritical allegiance to the government. Brown called for "the FBI in our midst" to come forward to the stage in the temple and yield their recording devices as a sign of their repentance. Brown pointed out that most would like to think that they would have helped the Jews in Nazi Germany rather than remain silent or passive. He challenged the audience to make a similar choice concerning the Central Americans now in the United States. Rabbi Marshall Meyer, who had just returned from Argentina, questioned whether he was in the wrong country when he learned of the prosecution of sanctuary workers. He explained that he would not be surprised by such government actions in Argentina but was shocked to discover it in the United States.

Finally, the symposium provided a forum where a theology for the ministry of sanctuary (see Chapter Eight) could continue to grow and develop. In the symposium's opening invocation, a young Mexican priest, Fr. Antonio Garcia, humbly prayed for a new exodus to a promised land where human "documents" are not required for entry. Later, Salvadoran Rev. Marta Benavides called for a promised land not just flowing with beans and tortillas, or even milk and honey, but one filled with the prophet Isaiah's rivers of justice and righteousness. While gratefuly acknowledging the sanctuary movement, the Central American refugees who attended the symposium repeatedly pleaded for those in the United States to help create a sanctuary not in the United States but in all of Central America, to make their entire countries sanctuaries where they could return to live in peace and justice. The challenge was clear: if the sanctuary movement really wanted to help the refugees, it must eliminate the need for sanctuary in the United States.[37]

Felipe Excot, a Guatemalan who has found sanctuary at the Benedictine Priory in Weston, Vermont, spoke eloquently about doing justice as part of the ministry of the church. Felipe reminded the audience that Jesus opened the eyes of the blind, gave mobility to the lame and loosened the tongues of the mute. Are we not then, he asked, to open the eyes of the illiterate, give opportunity to the powerless, and speech to the voiceless? Joyce Hollyday from Sojourners related the testimony of Rev. Donovan Cook (pastor of the University Baptist Church in Seattle, Washington) before the federal judge presiding over the trial of Jack Elder. The judge, a Baptist, had acknowledged a Christian duty to feed the poor, care for the sick, clothe the naked, and visit prisoners but could not understand the basis for a Christian obligation to shelter and transport refugees. Rev. Cook humbly responded by reminding the court of the story of a man who found a stranger alongside a road and how he transported him on his donkey to the nearest inn, where he arranged for shelter and other care—the story of the Good Samaritan.[38]

Several critical themes emerged from the two-day national consultation among sanctuary churches that followed the symposium. A major theme which was continually repeated was that the sanctuary movement had to be a movement for the refugees, and not for the churches to experiment with social justice, not for the attorneys to test novel legal theories, not for political activists to broaden their coalitions of support. The refugees themselves emerged as the overlooked resource in the sanctuary movement. In Tucson, many of the Salvadorans and Guatemalans who had found sanctuary in the

United States were able to meet each other and share their experiences for the first time. The opportunity for the refugees to reaffirm and articulate their own commitment to the sanctuary movement became a challenge to the sanctuary churches to continue their work and to take even greater risks despite the threat of criminal prosecution by the United States government. In turn, the refugees also pledged to take greater risks—more travel, increased public visibility, and more communication among themselves—in order to offer their wisdom and insight.

The Central American refugees pleaded for more participation—a true partnership—in the ministry of the sanctuary movement.[39] They repeated their hopes of returning to their homes in El Salvador and Guatemala and denounced any direct or indirect insinuation that they wanted to resettle permanently in the United States. The refugees explained that they viewed the sanctuary movement as one of the few ways that they could help change the United States government policy in their home countries so that they could return to Central America. They pointed out that they could assist in the screening and preparation of refugees for sanctuary since they knew better than anyone else who would make the best spokespersons for their cause.

The refugees also offered themselves as consultants to the churches planning the future of the movement. For example, there is now a certain amount of fear and paranoia concerning government surveillance and criminal prosecutions among members of the sanctuary movement. However, for the Central American refugees who have just recently escaped the violence of death squads and entire armies, and survived perilous pilgrimages through hostile territory to come to the United States, any fear by the United States churchpeople must seem a little out of proportion. It is ironical that a movement that began to help Central American refugees may become a movement that now turns to those Central American refugees for assistance in future organizing and communication in the face of government attempts at infiltration and prosecution.

The refugees also warned against subtle forms of paternalism and condescension and asked for sensitivity and empathy. This warning had been well-articulated at the symposium by Yvonne Dilling, director of the Washington, D.C. office of Witness for Peace:

It is very difficult to maintain a sense of the worth of the individual when the word "refugee" replaces the word "person."
Persons are more easily seen as brothers and sisters, as equals in
the sight of God. Refugees tend to become inanimate objects toward which we direct pious acts of charity, for which, we think,
they should be exceedingly grateful.[40]

The Central American refugees did not directly criticize the
sanctuary movement but they clearly declared their opposition to
any attempts to make them mere objects of interest rather than persons with stories and experiences of much personal pain and suffering. While affirming their commitment to continue repeating their
testimonies as public witnesses of the suffering and human rights
abuses in their countries, the refugees asked that their hosts become
more sensitive to the emotional drain each retelling required of
them. They also asked for clarification of the sanctuary ministry,
citing the confusion that some of the refugees had experienced when
different sanctuary churches had different conceptions of sanctuary
and therefore different expectations of the refugees.[41] The Central
Americans noted that if the practice of sanctuary was a new experience for the United States churches, then how much more difficult
would the experience of the refugee be, in a foreign country, among
foreign people, with a foreign language and culture.

The symposium and consultation also allowed members of the
various sanctuary churches and communities to meet one another
and compare experiences. At the national consultation, time was set
aside for presentations by sanctuary workers from southern California, Arizona and Texas to explain their work to the non-border
churches. These sanctuary workers pleaded for patience and assistance from sanctuary participants in the non-border areas who
seemed preoccupied with receiving more refugees through the "Underground Railroad" without understanding the difficulties and
dangers involved. The workers from the Texas Rio Grande Valley
were especially eloquent in their plea, explaining the local custom
of a "quiet refuge" for all refugees, notwithstanding public declarations of sanctuary. In Texas, sanctuary—protection of refugees—
has long been provided by churches quietly and without publicity.
These sanctuary workers also revealed that there had been several
other incidents of government interference with sanctuary work be-

sides the publicized trials of Stacey Merkt and Jack Elder (see Chapter Three). Specifically, they told accounts of three churches being raided by the INS since 1983, of refugees being arrested in churches, of other sanctuary workers being detained or questioned by immigration authorities, and of cars being confiscated pending investigations of smuggling activities. Such incidents have not been widely publicized because the churches and workers involved did not want to attract more government attention to their efforts. Finally, the sanctuary workers from the Rio Grande Valley pointed out that most of the refugees they worked with were not candidates for sanctuary and that they did not make any distinctions between refugees in need. Only those refugees ready to speak out publicly and risk exposure and arrest are appropriate for sanctuary. The experience of the Tucson sanctuary workers is similar:

> Few of the refugees aided in Tucson go into public sanctuary. Most wish to hide, finding a niche in a refugee settlement center such as Los Angeles. Many who would otherwise wish to serve are too traumatized. Only a few are ready, in order to serve as a voice for their people, to endure the isolation and culture stress of life in public sanctuary.[42]

Thus, in order for sanctuary workers in border areas to facilitate the sanctuary work of the non-border areas, they must take on the additional responsibility of screening refugees as candidates for public sanctuary. The clear message was that the movement had to become more integrated nationally, with the non-border churches providing more concrete assistance to the border areas in order to facilitate the development of the entire movement. (The issues of organizational structure will be explored more fully in the next section.)

The Arizona and Texas prosecutions have also compelled changes in the sanctuary work along the border. Even before the Arizona indictments were announced, Jim Corbett had observed that "Tucson's foreground role in sanctuary evangelism has run its course; we must concentrate on our border work while others clear the way for further extensions of sanctuary."[43] After the indictments, it became evident that, at the very least, new sanctuary workers must take up the work of those indicted. The defendants now have new, albeit reluctant, roles as public spokespersons. Because they must prepare for their upcoming trials and respond to the resulting publicity, they cannot continue to engage in their sanctuary work as if nothing has happened. The experience of Stacey Merkt and Jack Elder in Texas is an example. Regardless of the outcome of their appeals, Merkt and Elder as individuals will find it almost impossible to continue their work. Indeed, the judge who sentenced them in March 1985 prohibited them from continuing to work at Casa Romero. They have become too visible and too vulnerable to increasingly severe treatment by the courts. They have become the reluctant first martyrs and spokespersons for the entire sanctuary movement.

The non-border areas must also continue to refine and develop their conceptions and practices of providing sanctuary. Many churches and congregations struggled over a long period of time to reach the point of a public declaration of sanctuary. However, if no refugees are immediately available to enter such sanctuaries, then the declaration seems to lose its meaning and become hollow. A "live body," a human face, is essential to the public character of public sanctuary. Yet it is clear that refugees are not commodities subject to the laws of supply and demand. The churches that have declared public sanctuary but are without refugees must therefore adapt their ministry to develop new or alternative methods of protecting and assisting the Central American refugees.

Jim Corbett notes that the sanctuary ministry has already expanded: sending church members as international observers in Central American refugee camps, establishing sister congregation relationships with churches in El Salvador, and sending workers to border areas. Rev. Fife has also eloquently described the development of the concept of sanctuary:

> I think we've all grown in understanding that sanctuary is what God created this world to be. Reverend Marta Benavides (of El Salvador) first told me what we really need to do is work with them to make Central America a sanctuary for Central Americans. Nuclear freeze people have come to me and said what we really need to do is make this earth a sanctuary from nuclear armaments.
>
> I think sanctuary is beginning to capture people's spirits and imaginations. It is the way the church community can really

be a covenant community and a way we can understand ourselves and our faith and our role in this world. I'm looking for
the whole community gathered to put our souls to work in discovering just what the symbol can mean and how it can explode
in our consciousness and lead us into all kinds of creative pilgrimages.[44]

After two long days of discussion and debate, a consensus
emerged at the national consultation in Tucson that the sanctuary
movement should remain a diversified grassroots movement and
should resist any pressures toward uniformity or excessive organization. Specifically, the national consultation of sanctuary churches
agreed to coordinate its fundraising through a separate body, the
National Sanctuary Defense Fund,[44a] and to establish a national
communication network involving regional representatives to facilitate the future coordination of national phone trees, mailing lists,
newsletters, legislative lobbying, and relationships with the media.
In the spirit of grassroots responsibility and accountability, each region would meet and select its own representatives and then gather
regional proposals at a national meeting in the spring of 1985. Thus,
the actual decision-making and implementation would remain
largely at the regional and local levels. The national body would be
a facilitator for the sanctuary movement rather than its control center. However, this consensus does not reflect the growing tensions
within the national sanctuary movement.

Tensions in Solidarity

The indictment of sixteen sanctuary workers in Arizona and
the week of meetings in Tucson, Arizona during January 1985 high-
lighted the tensions and diversity of the sanctuary movement. Increased media attention and the practical difficulties of articulating
and supporting a viable legal defense for those facing criminal prosecution have forced a closer examination of these tensions. The two
primary perspectives on the nature and the future of the sanctuary
movement have become characterized as a division between "Chicago" (the Chicago Religious Task Force on Central America or
CRTF) and "Tucson" (the Tucson Ecumenical Council Task Force
on Central America).[45] While this shorthand reference became part

of the vocabulary used at the national consultation in Tucson, such a characterization is misleading since the distinctive viewpoints represent tensions within the sanctuary movement as a whole rather than among regional factions. Jim Corbett acknowledges that the "contrasting styles, perspectives, and functions of the Tucson refugee support groups and the Chicago Religious Task Force complemented and reinforced each other," [46] and has publicly urged:

> Whatever the cause of the CRTF's recent actions, the sanctuary movement's problems are not in Chicago, and it would be both disastrously mistaken and inexcusably ungrateful if the CRTF were now to be treated as a scapegoat. Any move to exclude, censure, or censor the CRTF would be wholly inappropriate. [47]

One specific cause of the tension between Corbett (and the Tucson Ecumenical Council Task Force) and the Chicago Religious Task Force was the CRTF's refusal in the fall of 1984 to make its mailing list available to Corbett. Thus, in December 1984, before the January indictments were announced and before the national symposium and consultation, Corbett wrote a lengthy "accounting" of his role in the development of the sanctuary movement and his perspectives on the tensions within it. He wrote: "I bear the primary responsibility for the sanctuary network's growing pains,"[48] and then announced in his open letter his decision to withdraw from an active role in shaping the future of the movement:

> The rift that has developed with the CRTF does require that I cease to be involved in most organizing and speaking activities connected with the sanctuary movement and that I strip away all functions that involve any exercise of organizational power. I have given up my position on the TEC Task Force executive board. I'm willing to serve as a border consultant for network development, but I intend to avoid any role as a spokesperson or delegate for organizations connected with sanctuary. If anyone should wish to rally around me for organizational maneuvering or a counterattack, I simply won't be there. After giving the sanctuary network this personal accounting, I intend to avoid any active role in lobbying for the kind of network organization I consider to be desirable. Instead, I hope to stay in Arizona and, as far as sanctuary is concerned, to become a better

member of the Pima Meeting [of Quakers] and the refugee support group. The sanctuary movement will grow beyond this
transitional rift much more readily if I cease to have a prominent
part in network organization.[49]

Finding Corbett's accounting "disheartening and demoraliz-
ing," the Chicago Religious Task Force went to great lengths to engage in a dialogue over the disagreements by publishing statements
from Corbett, from the TEC Task Force on Central America, from
refugees in sanctuary, and from other sanctuary communities in a
special edition of their newsletter "Basta!" first made available at the
Tucson symposium and consultation. While acknowledging "an
ever escalating split," the CRTF pledged its commitment to "open
discussion of these differences in order to advance our analysis,
deepen our faith, enhance our effectiveness and strengthen our
movement."[50]

One of the key tensions within the movement is its self-identity
as either a political or a religious movement. Some maintain that the
two elements cannot be separated:

> For us, to love is to create a movement capable of stopping U.S.
> intervention in Central America, a movement not simply of pro-
> test or witness but of resistance. This effort is profoundly reli-
> gious and inevitably political.[51]

Others view the sanctuary movement as a religious response to
the needs of the refugees, without any overt political or foreign policy objectives:

> Our sanctuary covenant community in Tucson formed in the
> midst of shared risk, sacrifice, and tragedy; our meeting the ref-
> ugees brought us together into embryonic base communities,
> and then our subsequent experience was closer to combat than
> to the process of congregational conscience-wrestling that usu-
> ally preceded the decision for sanctuary. On the border, the dec-
> laration evolved from protective community with the refugees.
> Elsewhere, the decision for sanctuary usually comes first.[52]

However, those who believe that the sanctuary's political and
religious elements are inseparable fear that emphasizing only the re-

ligious aspect will reduce sanctuary to becoming only the latest model for the resettlement of refugees rather than seeking to remedy the problems which force the refugees to flee Central America. Such a view maintains that the movement should work toward solving these underlying problems so that Central Americans will not be forced to flee their countries in the first place instead of ignoring the underlying problems and focus only on resettling the refugees.

On the other hand, those who perceive the movement as essentially religious fear that the overpoliticization of the sanctuary movement might undermine its religious and humanitarian basis. According to this position, any claim that sanctuary activity is religiously motivated is weakened if the goal of sanctuary is portrayed as ending United States intervention in Central America. Such a question of religious or political character becomes especially critical during the criminal defense of sanctuary workers.

However, the two perspectives are not completely inconsistent or incompatible. For Jim Corbett, the two positions reflect two differing types of faith: a faith of "belief" which requires definitive doctrines and analysis, discerning how the present can be used to achieve the objectives of the future; and a faith of "trust," where future goals emerge out of the community and "concrete personal communion rather than being constructed according to the blueprint of a social or theological vanguard."[53] Corbett rejects the idea that there is a distinction between "apolitical humanitarian activities and political anti-intervention activities."[54] There is not an apolitical spiritual view opposing an unspiritual political view—rather both perspectives spring from faith. The difference arises from the differences between the faith experiences.

One of the ways in which these different perspectives conflict is over the question of national organizational structure. The dialogue between Tucson and Chicago exemplifies the two differing positions. Corbett articulates one perspective:

> . . . we need neither definitive creeds nor an executive superstructure, nor would our multidenominational composition permit it. Because our viability and strength as a network depend on base community initiative, no national body should be authorized in any way to speak, publish, organize actions, solicit funds, or establish policy for the network of sanctuary congregations.[55]

The Chicago Religious Task Force presents another view:

The sanctuary churches and synagogues are joined in a movement which needs goals and objectives as well as organization in
order to be effective in the exercise of their ministry and of support to the Central American people. The sanctuary movement
should be planned and deliberate, focused and organized.[56]

However, according to Jim Corbett responding on behalf of the
Tucson Ecumenical Council Task Force:

The sanctuary covenant community that has formed is a movement [defined by its political objectives while being distinguished by its religious identity] because we provide sanctuary
for the persecuted regardless of the political origins of their persecution or of their usefulness in promoting preconceived objectives. . . . It follows, then, that we cannot accept the
establishment of any over-all creed or set of objectives for the
sanctuary movement.[57]

The opposing view of the CRTF is:

The sanctuary movement has direction and purpose. It provides
refuge to some refugees, attempts to change U.S. immigration
policy and stop U.S. intervention in Central America. That
some sanctuary churches or synagogues do not accept this orientation does not nullify their objective participation in the realization of these goals of the movement. The movement is not
and should not be defined by the least common denominator.
To accept a direction for the sanctuary movement does not mean
that every religious sanctuary community must make a creedal
profession of faith in a political platform or legislative package.[58]

Furthermore, the CRTF asks what the purpose or value of
sanctuary could be if U.S. policies in Central America continue to
contribute to the conditions that create refugees.[59] They argue that
there seems to be little meaning in a sanctuary movement that only
seeks to assist refugees at the last stage of their pilgrimage, without
any concern for the causes of their persecution.

Another way that the issue of organization or national identity presents itself is the question of which communities can become sanctuaries. Jim Corbett has a clear theological view of sanctuary:

> There is no sanctuary movement apart from the covenant people whom the Christians among us customarily call "the Church." Churches and synagogues must decide whether they will adhere to the prophetic faith they proclaim, not whether they will become members of still another ecumenical organization. As Bishop Lona of Tehuantepec puts it with reference to Latin America's base communities, this is not a movement within the Church; rather, it is the Church on the move. . . . Functionally, providing sanctuary is the congregational analogue of the baptism of individual Christians: an initiating act of incorporation into the covenant people. [60]

The Chicago Religious Task Force disagrees:

> While it is courageous and prophetic for a congregation to offer its church, synagogue, or meeting place as sanctuary, we must not be so pretentious as to claim that only sanctuary churches are the true or authentic churches, that only sanctuary churches are initiated through an analogous baptism into the covenant people. Sanctuary churches are not the whole church on the move. Those congregations that declare themselves sanctuaries are in a movement within the church broadly understood. And indeed if these sanctuary communities become overwhelmingly numerous, they would merit being called a mass movement of communities within the broader church. But little is gained by discussing whether the churches becoming sanctuaries constitute a movement within the churches or the church on the move. [61]

Furthermore, the Chicago view of sanctuary includes communities and organizations without a religious character:

> In our efforts we must guard against arrogance and a new triumphalism. While in a certain theological sense it is true that there is no sanctuary apart from the covenant community (the church), it is also true that non-religious communities may offer

refuge and call themselves sanctuary. Since it is by their fruits that we shall know them [Matthew 7:16–20], we cannot claim to control the spirit of truth and love.[62] (citation added)

This attitude is echoed by Gil Dawes of the Faith United Methodist Church in Cedar Rapids, Iowa:

If the sanctuary movement goes down the path of separating within itself those of "religious" orientation from those of secular, or "intentional" motivation, it will have done the work of the oppressor for him. Those whose policies cause the oppressed to seek refuge in the first place must divide the opposition before they can conquer. If we think they will stop once they have destroyed secular resistance and honor the "religious" conscience of those who resist in "faith," then we will naively do their divisive work for them.[63]

There is concern that deemphasizing the overtly religious character of the sanctuary movement in order to include non-religious groups will change the direction of the movement as a whole. During its initial development, the sanctuary movement could distinguish itself from secular political activity because of its religious nature. To gain support and credibility, the sanctuary churches could point to the fact that their motivations were religious and not political. However, some in the sanctuary movement also recognized that the churches could be a powerful resource in the effort to change public opinion and United States government policies involving Central America. The sanctuary churches also recognized that they could not address such broader issues of government policy without the knowledge, skills and experience of the more traditional political organizations. The role of these political groups in the sanctuary movement has continued to develop. The increasing politicalization of the sanctuary movement, however, may create tension within the churches and communities that first declared sanctuary without such overt political perspectives and objectives.

The individual sanctuary church's understanding of the nature of the sanctuary ministry can evolve and change. One area where external resources have changed the self-understanding of the sanctuary movement involves the question of civil disobedience. When the first churches declared public sanctuary, their understanding of

the legal issues involved in offering sanctuary was generally unsophisticated and even simplistic. There was a willingness to break the
law if necessary in order to engage in the work of sanctuary. Since
that time, attorneys and others have been able to develop several
important legal theories and defenses for the work of the sanctuary
movement. As a result of this interaction between the churches and
secular supporters of sanctuary, most members of the sanctuary
movement now view their actions as not only moral but also as completely legal.

Thus Corbett has recently written:

> Individuals' and communities' refusal to collaborate with injus-
> tice often involves civil disobedience. Community action to do
> justice may also require civil disobedience. In these cases, civil
> disobedience serves to establish new liberties and to maintain
> established liberties. But when civil disobedience is used less
> discriminately, it may undermine established liberties. The dis-
> tinction between integral and contrived civil disobedience is es-
> pecially important for the sanctuary movement because our
> refusal to obey U.S. officials defends just laws. The legal de-
> fense of those who are persecuted for aiding refugees should be
> designed to maintain everyone's right to aid refugees rather than
> to intensify confrontation or to disrupt the judicial process; we
> would otherwise run the risk of reinforcing the Reagan admin-
> istration's efforts to destroy this country's ratified and legislated
> commitments to refugee rights.[64]

However, Chicago has a different perspective:

> Sanctuary by its very nature breaks the law and/or current im-
> plementation of law. All of us in the sanctuary movement have
> chosen to break the law, not as an end in itself, but to defend the
> powerless, the Central Americans in the U.S. and those still in
> their homelands.[65]

Corbett disagrees:

> Our refusing to collaborate with the government's violations of
> refugee rights is, therefore, incorrectly described as a challenge
> to unjust laws. Nor do we intend to violate any laws merely to
> heighten confrontation with an unjust government. Rather, we

seek to preserve and strengthen the refugee laws that the U.S. government has enacted, openly maintaining our legal right to aid refugees, regardless of threats and prosecution by government officials.[66]

The Chicago view points out that such a position is ultimately hypocritical because it is defiance of the law while publicly denying such defiance.[67] A public declaration of sanctuary inherently increases one's vulnerability to criminal prosecution. There are many alternatives for those who do not want to engage in any activity that could even be construed as unlawful. Private sanctuary offers protection for the refugees without making any public or political statements. All types of aid—donating money, food, clothing, and other necessities, sponsoring speaking engagements, raising bail funds, funding legal assistance for refugees, and the entire range of legislative lobbying, letter writing, and electoral campaigning—are certainly lawful and without any risk of criminal liabilities.

On the other hand, the rationale for public sanctuary can also be compelling. First, the refugees themselves have asked for the opportunity to speak out. As refugees, they have no voice or power in the United States. The refugees themselves view public sanctuary as one of the few ways that they, who have been fortunate enough to find temporary safety, can influence the United States public and government to bring about changes in their home countries that will allow them to return. Second, by a public declaration of sanctuary, the church or congregation declares its pride and lack of shame in its actions, emphasizing its collective belief that sanctuary is not only moral but lawful. Finally, a public declaration demands a different type of commitment by the sanctuary community—a willingness to publicly articulate its rationale for providing sanctuary and to join the refugees as public witnesses testifying to their faith and their convictions.

As the national sanctuary movement grows and develops, new themes, perspectives and tensions may emerge. For now, the creation of sanctuary for Central American refugees in United States churches has already inspired many new issues and topics for study, debate, prayer, reflection, and action.

CHAPTER TWO

United States Immigration Law Concerning Refugees

"Immigration law has long been a maverick, a wild card, in our public law. Probably no other area of American law has been so radically insulated and divergent from those fundamental norms of constitutional right, administrative procedure, and judicial role that animate the rest of our legal system. In a legal firmament transformed by revolutions in due process and equal protection doctrine and by a new conception of judicial role, immigration law remains the realm in which government authority is at the zenith, and individual entitlement is at the nadir."[1]

—Columbia University Professor of Law, Peter H. Schuck

Current United States Refugee Policies in Context

The current invocation of sanctuary by North American churches is a dramatic response to the refusal of the United States government to grant legal sanctuary, or asylum, under United States immigration laws, to refugees from El Salvador and Guatemala. Hundreds of thousands of refugees are fleeing civil wars in El Salvador and Guatemala, many of them coming to the United States for refuge. Rather than recognizing these refugees as deserving of asylum under United States immigration law, the Immigration and

Naturalization Service (INS) has carried out a deliberate policy of mass deportations of Salvadorans and Guatemalans. The INS was recently deporting Central Americans at a rate of about one thousand every month.[2] It has been well documented by international human rights organizations and by Central Americans themselves that many of these deportees are arrested, imprisoned, tortured, or even killed upon their return to Central America.[3] The reaction of the INS to such reports is that any deaths are only attributable to "random violence," and not to persecution.[4] The government's position ignores the fear of persecution by the deportees that has been tragically confirmed upon their return to their home countries.

These mass deportations raise serious questions about the United States government's compliance with its international obligations to refugees and its own domestic immigration laws. It is important to know and understand the evolution of current United States immigration law in order to recognize the underlying public policies that have created this policy of mass deportation. When most people begin to think about the history of immigration in the United States, thoughts turn to symbols of openness and humanitarianism such as the Statue of Liberty. There are probably rich images of a nation founded by immigrants and grateful memories of grandparents and parents who found refuge in this country. What is often unknown or overlooked is the darker side of United States immigration history: the involuntary importation of Africans as slaves, a series of racially-based exclusionary laws aimed at Asians, and *bracero* programs designed to exploit Mexican laborers. The common themes of these lesser-known aspects of our nation's immigrant history is that they were racially and economically motivated. In fact, it becomes evident that humanitarianism has seldom been the predominant public policy shaping United States immigration law. Much more powerful forces, such as economic needs for labor and foreign policy objectives, have been the primary influences. Thus, while the mass deportations of Central American refugees is a new policy, it is not necessarily inconsistent nor surprising in light of the history of United States immigration law.

Perhaps it will be surprising to some that the United States did not adopt any permanent, comprehensive policy concerning refugees until the Refugee Act of 1980.[5] Thus, it is necessary to review almost two hundred years of United States immigration laws and policies to understand the context of the current government position regarding today's refugees from Central America.

History[6]

Initially, it is important to remember that every United States citizen, with the exception of the Native American peoples, is either an immigrant or a direct descendant of an immigrant. Therefore, on one level, every United States resident entered the country with no greater "right" to entry than any other. The first years of this nation saw general openness in immigration policy. There were no formal national restrictions on immigration. The earliest federal immigration law was the Alien Act of 1798.[7] This legislation was also the first exclusionary legislation; it allowed the President to deport anyone he deemed dangerous to the peace and safety of the country. However, the general policy was still open and unrestricted borders, welcoming settlers to the newly-founded nation. Even the Constitutional provisions and subsequent Congressional legislation involving the slave trade were designed to create access to the country.

There was a minor exclusion law passed in 1875.[8] Then, the first racially restrictive immigration law was passed in the midst of the "Yellow Peril" and agitation from dissatisfied white laborers. The Chinese Exclusion Act of 1882[9] remained the law of the land until its final repeal in 1943. Another 1882 law also provided for a "head tax" of fifty cents per immigrant and barred the admission of "idiots, lunatics, convicts, and persons likely to become public charges."[10] These archaic exclusionary grounds reflect the language, policies, and prejudices of the turn of the century but are still found in the current immigration statute.[11]

Another policy underlying federal immigration law emerged from an 1888 law which authorized the deportation of contract workers (aliens obligated to work in order to pay for their passage to the United States) within one year after their entry.[12] This limited duration of stay enabled the immigrants to work but did not allow sufficient time to establish roots in the United States. The result was that the contract labor system became a program of one-year indentured labor, reliant upon the deportation power of the federal government for its economic profitability. The time within which those who entered the country illegally could be deported was also expanded from one year in 1891 to three years in 1903.[13] This expansion of the deportation power reflected the slow but certain shift of United States immigration policy from one of open welcome to an increasingly complicated system of selection and exclusion.

The first major codification of federal immigration legislation was the Immigration Act of 1917 passed by Congress over President Woodrow Wilson's veto. The Act imposed a literacy requirement for entry, codified all the prior exclusion grounds, created an "Asiatic Barred Zone" that continued to exclude Asians from entry, and allowed deportation within three to five years after entry.[14] Greater restrictions were being placed on who could enter the country and control over immigrants already in the country through the power of deportation was being expanded.

In 1921, Congress passed the First Quota Law,[15] which limited the annual immigration of persons of a given nationality to three percent of the number of such persons already in the United States in the year 1910. This was the first quantitative restriction on immigration and was originally intended only as a temporary measure. However, after 1917, qualitative (exclusion and deportation) and quantitative restrictions on immigration would become essential elements of national policy. The 1921 legislators were concerned about the seemingly unending wave of immigrants from Europe. However, by basing the percentage of members of each nationality group living in the United States in 1910, the quota system was designed to preserve a certain ethnic and racial composition of the nation. For example, under the 1921 system, Great Britain received forty-three percent of the total quota. Even the purported goal of family reunification did not take into account the relatives of the literally hundreds of thousands of the most recent immigrants, those that entered the country between 1910 and 1921. It is no coincidence that the majority of these most recent immigrants were from southern and eastern Europe, while most of the immigrants before that time came from northern and western Europe. Indeed, the shift in the countries of origin was dramatic: between 1881 and 1890, eighty percent of the European immigrants were from northern and western European countries, but between 1911 and 1920, seventy-seven percent of the European immigrants were from southern and eastern Europe.[16] The inherent ethnic bias of the national origins quota system would become a fundamental part of United States immigration policy.

The next major revision in the immigration law came in 1924. The Johnson-Reed Act[17] contained two features that would shape the country's immigration policies for the next decades: permanent overall numerical limits and national origins quotas. The numerical limits were a response to the continued migration of European immigrants: a total of twenty-three and a half million immigrants entered the country between 1881 and 1920.[18] However, continuing xenophobia and fluctuating economic conditions also played important roles in establishing this permanent structure for restricting immigration. These overall limits, in conjunction with the national origins quota system (first using the 1890 census and then the 1920 census as the base date[19]), the removal of any time limitation for the deportation of immigrants who entered the country without proper visas, and the continuing absolute exclusion of any Asian immigrants marked the entrenchment of an increasingly restrictive government attitude toward immigration, often drawn along racial and ethnic lines.

Other forces were also at work in shaping the immigration policy of the United States. In the late 1910's, the immigration laws were used to deport political activists, including many labor organizers who had become too effective in the eyes of big business interests. These efforts culminated in the notorious "Palmer Raids" under Attorney General A. Mitchell Palmer, when thousands of labor organizers were arrested and deported. In the southwest, Mexican workers who had worked in this country began to be deported in large numbers when labor organizing began in the early 1930's. When labor needs grew again in the 1940's, the federal government created the *bracero* program, which allowed the "importation" of Mexican agricultural workers into the southwest for each annual harvest. The workers were to return to Mexico immediately after each harvest season. While ostensibly justified by the shortage of United States workers able, or, perhaps more often, willing, to perform the menial labor, the *bracero* program also ensured that the agricultural businesses could pay the lowest possible wages and effectively precluded any unionization among the farmworkers. The Mexicans were forced to accept deplorable working and living conditions. The *bracero* program continued to provide cheap foreign labor until 1964.[20]

Immigration law and policy was responsive not only to racism and labor needs. National security soon became an explicit policy priority. In 1940, Congress enacted the Alien Registration Act,[21] the first federal legislation to require the registration and finger-printing of all aliens who were in the United States or were seeking to enter as immigrants. The new record-keeping system facilitated greater government control over immigrants. The 1940 Act also added "subversive persons" to the growing list of exclusion grounds.[22] The targeting of persons on the basis of political beliefs and activities continued throughout the 1950's McCarthy era. The Internal Security Act of 1950 provided for the exclusion and de-portation of non-citizens who were "politically dangerous" to the na-tional security and required all aliens to report their addresses to the INS every year.[23] Governmental authority to control immigration for explicitly political reasons had become part of the United States immigration policy.[24]

The next major recodification of the federal immigration law[25] occurred in 1952 with the Immigration and Nationality Act, com-monly known as the McCarran-Walter Act.[26] Again, Congress passed the legislation over a presidential veto, this time by President Harry S Truman. The bill maintained the overall limits on immi-gration, the national origins quota, and the numerous grounds for exclusion and deportation. The law provided that total annual im-migration should not exceed one-sixth of one percent of the number of inhabitants in the United States in 1920 and continued the special limits on immigrants from the "Asia-Pacific Triangle."

The next major change in the federal immigration law came in 1965.[27] These amendments to the Immigration and Nationality Act finally abandoned the national origins quota system and the re-maining exclusions of Asians. However, the amendments imposed new limitations by hemisphere, subjecting potential immigrants born in the western hemisphere to a total numerical quota of 120,000 annual admissions. The eastern hemisphere was allowed 170,000 annual admissions. Nationality still played a role in these limitations because each country in the eastern hemisphere was limited to 20,000 annual admissions. The 1965 amendments also created a preference system for the admission of immigrants to the United States that had the dual goal of family reunification and the filling of labor shortages in the United States. Thus, the persistent policies of preserving the racial/ethnic composition of the country and of importing foreign labor continued.[28]

Finally, the 1965 amendments to the 1952 Immigration and Nationality Act established, as part of its preference system, the first permanent provision for the continuing admission of refugees into the United States. Refugee admissions prior to 1965 had only been permitted on an *ad hoc* basis. The seventh preference enabled persons fleeing Communist-dominated or Middle Eastern countries because of persecution or fear of persecution on account of race, religion or political opinion to be admitted to the United States as immigrants called conditional entrants.[29] This statutory recognition ended several decades of ad hoc policies and legislation relating to the admission of refugees.

United States Refugee Policies

Early Legislation[30]

The United States was not confronted with the issue of mass refugee admissions of resettlement until after the Second World War. Prior to that time, there was no provision for the recognition of refugee status in United States law. Thus, any person who might now be recognized under either international or domestic concepts of refugee status had to seek entry into the United States through the ordinary methods of admission discussed in the preceding section.

After the end of the Second World War, when Europe was filled with persons displaced from their homes, the United States and the international community as a whole began to examine the question of refugees. The next section will review the international standards and definitions that have been developed for refugee recognition and resettlement. This section examines early United States immigration law and policy, which still did not recognize the distinct needs of refugees. Any admission of refugees was made only on an ad hoc basis, under extraordinary conditions.

The first statute relating to refugees was enacted as part of the 1950 Internal Security Act.[31] Ironically, the same legislation that expanded the power of the United States government to expel political dissidents from the country also authorized the Attorney General to withhold, or refrain from executing, the deportation of any persons who would be subjected to physical persecution in their own country. This withholding of deportation became the first governmental recognition that certain persons, namely refugees, required distinct treatment under United States immigration law. This also became the first statutory definition of refugees under United States law: those subject to physical persecution in their country of nationality. However, this statute did not actually admit such persons into the United States; only their deportation was withheld indefinitely.

The section regarding the withholding of deportation for persons subject to physical persecution was incorporated into the 1952 Immigration and Nationality Act.[32] However, the power to withhold deportation was explicitly made a discretionary one vested in the Attorney General. In practice, this discretion was rarely exercised and then only for those fleeing Communist countries.[33] Thus, this discretion was used only as a part of a broader Cold War foreign policy rather than because of humanitarian considerations. In 1965, amendments to the Immigration and Nationality Act changed the standard for eligibility for withholding of deportation from physical persecution to persecution on account of race, religion or political opinion.[34] However, the power to withhold deportation still remained discretionary and was still not widely exercised.[35]

The first Congressional enactment regarding the admission of refugees in the United States was a direct response to the millions of war refugees created after World War II. The Displaced Persons Act of 1948[36] admitted a select group of persons who had fled Nazi or Soviet persecution as a result of events which had occurred during the war. Three-fourths of the 409,696 immigrants admitted under the 1948 Act were from Poland, Germany, Latvia, the U.S.S.R. and Yugoslavia. Some ninety percent of these refugees were resettled by church and other social agencies, who were responsible for securing housing and employment for the new immigrants. Thus, the churches of the United States have been directly involved with refugees since the first Congressional enactment admitting them

into this country. The 1948 refugees were counted in the annual
quota admissions for each nationality but the INS charged or "mort-
gaged" future years' quotas to accommodate all those eligible for admission under the Act.[37] The 1948 Act also provided immigrant
visas for the Czechoslovakians who fled the 1948 Communist take-
over of their country. In 1953, five hundred war orphans were also
admitted as refugees.[38]

In the midst of its Cold War foreign policy, Congress enacted
the Refugee Relief Act of 1953, which provided emergency admissions to victims of racial, religious or political persecution fleeing a
Communist or Communist-dominated country, or a country in the
Middle East, as well as victims of natural calamities.[39] These admissions were to be made outside the quota system and were limited
to 214,000 persons. The refugees required a United States citizen
to be a sponsor, who would guarantee employment and housing.
Under the 1953 Act 189,021 refugees actually entered the country.[40]
While Congress was responding to the humanitarian needs of the
world's refugees, the criteria selected for refugee admissions was in-
fluenced by foreign policy objectives, namely, fighting Commu-
nism. Significantly, the 1965 amendments to the Immigration and
Nationality Act that would create the seventh preference simply
adopted the limited ideological and geographical definition of a refugee that had been established in 1953. The influence of foreign policy considerations would continue to determine United States
refugee policies, even to the present day.

In 1958 Congress admitted earthquake and flood victims from
Portugal and Dutch nationals displaced from Indonesia as non-
quota immigrants.[41] These 22,213 admissions continued the ad hoc
policy of refugee admissions. Such a policy was only reactive, responding to a specific natural disaster or political upheaval rather
than anticipating a continuing need for regular refugee admissions.

In that same year, Congress also moved to regularize the status
of 31,915 Hungarians who had been paroled into the country by the
Attorney General in 1956.[42] The parole authority was a limited discretionary power given to the Attorney General to temporarily admit certain individual immigrants into the United States. However,
in the absence of any consistent legislative action on refugees, this
power was exercised more and more to admit entire groups of persons as refugees. These Hungarian parolees could adjust their im-

migration status to become lawful permanent residents after two years of residence in the United States. This was the first Congressional action involving refugees *after* they had been admitted into the country. Without any permanent or continuing refugee policy, refugees admitted into the United States could not adjust their immigration status but remained in a legal limbo, with few rights or privileges. They were left with only a temporary status and an uncertain future.

In 1960, Congress passed the Fair Share Refugee Act, which admitted refugees on the contingency that other countries admit their "fair share" of the world's remaining refugees.[43] The United States only assumed responsibility for resettling up to one-quarter of the total number of World War II refugees remaining in the United States refugee camps. These refugees were admitted under the Attorney General's parole power. Thus, Congress chose to utilize the executive branch's discretionary power rather than enact a more general refugee admissions policy. The refugees-parolees who were admitted could adjust their status to lawful permanent residents after two years. About twenty thousand refugees were admitted under this Act.[44] While Congress was increasing its humanitarian commitment to admit and resettle the world's refugees, it was not ready to accept refugees on a continuing basis. Refugee admission was still viewed as a temporary international problem rather than part of national immigration policy.

Congress acted again in 1962, with the passage of the Migration and Refugee Assistance Act.[45] This legislation reflected the growing need to resolve the issues involving refugee resettlement as well as refugee admissions. As refugees continued to enter the country, it became evident that there was no mechanism existing within the immigration law to either regularize their legal status or to provide for their well-being once they had been admitted to this country. Thus, the Act consolidated federal refugee assistance programs into one omnibus package. The Act also made permanent the Attorney General's parole power to admit certain refugees still remaining in the United Nations refugee camps.[46] However, the adjustment of immigration status for refugees still required special legislation. Cuban parolees were allowed to adjust their status under legislation passed in 1966 and 1976.[47] Finally, the 1978 amendment to the Immigration and Nationality Act regularized the procedure for the adjustment of status of all parolees admitted to the United States before September 30, 1980.[48]

While United States refugee law was being passed in an ad hoc manner, the international community was active in defining the rights of refugees and establishing some degree of international responsibility for their security and protection. Since the 1980 Refugee Act was enacted with these international obligations in mind, the next section will review some of the international agreements relating to refugees.

International Obligations

The United Nations Convention and Protocol.[49] The earliest international agreements on the movement of persons between sovereign states involved the rights of extradition. These agreements allowed a nation to request the return of one of its citizens when that national became a fugitive in another country. Within these early instruments, there were provisions for asylum, or the right of the country harboring a fugitive to refuse to return him or her to his or her own country.[50] Asylum was considered a matter between nations rather the individual right of the fugitive. However, with the mass exodus of persons fleeing persecution after the First World War, the League of Nations began to examine the problems of refugees, statelessness and asylum in greater depth. The problem of political refugees, fleeing persecution in their own country, presented a different case than that of criminal fugitives seeking to escape extradition. The League of Nations established an office of a High Commissioner for Refugees in 1921 to oversee the League's efforts to address these new issues.[51] Then, in 1933, a multilateral Convention Relating to the International Status of Refugees first established the principle of *nonrefoulement*.[52] *Refouler* is a French word meaning expel or return. Signatories to the 1933 Convention agreed to refrain from forcibly returning individuals to their country of origin if they were likely to be persecuted there. This became the first international definition of refugee status: those likely to be persecuted if returned to their country of origin. In 1948, the United Nations created a new international refugee agency, the International Refugee Organization.[53] The Constitution of the International Refugee Organization would become an important foundation for future international law regarding refugees.

Then, in 1950, the United Nations convened the United Nations Conference of Plenipotentiaries on the Status of Refugees and Stateless Persons and transferred the functions of the International Refugee Organization to an expanded Office of the United Nations High Commissioner on Refugees (UNHCR).[54] The Conference established the most important international instrument regarding refugees, the 1951 Convention Relating to the Status of Refugees.[55] Under article 1 (A) (2), a refugee was defined as a person who

> as a result of events occurring before 1 January 1951 and owing to a well-founded fear of being persecuted for reasons of race, religion, nationality, membership of a particular social group or political opinion, is outside the country of his nationality and is unable or, owing to such fear, is unwilling to avail himself of the protection of that country; or who, not having a nationality and being outside the country of his former habitual residence as a result of such events, is unable or unwilling to return to it.

This broad definition of a refugee was based on the definition in the Constitution of the International Refugee Organization but was expanded to include "membership in a particular social group" as an additional ground of persecution.[56] The definition also included stateless persons but excluded from the protections of the Convention economic migrants[57] and victims of natural disasters. The U.N. definition also excluded persons displaced by military or civil unrest who did not have the requisite well-founded fear of persecution.[58] The 1951 Convention also specifically excluded those refugees who were firmly resettled in either their country of origin or in a third country, and those under the protection of the UNHCR in United Nations-sponsored refugee camps.[59]

The critical principle of *nonrefoulement* is found in both Article 32 and Article 33 of the Convention. Article 32 provides protection for refugees lawfully in the country of asylum:

> Article 32(1). The Contracting States shall not expel a refugee lawfully in their territory save on grounds of national security or public order.

Thus the protection for a refugee lawfully in the country of asylum is absolute except for the limited national security exception. This exception is elaborated upon in the remaining sections of Article 32:

Article 32(2). The expulsion of such a refugee shall be only in pursuance of a decision reached in accordance with due process of law. Except where compelling reasons of national security otherwise require, the refugee shall be allowed to submit evidence to clear himself, and to appeal to and be represented for the purpose before competent authority or a person or persons specifically designated by the competent authority.

Article 32(3). The Contracting States shall also allow such a refugee a reasonable period within which to seek legal admission into another country. The Contracting States reserve the right to apply during that period such internal measures as they may deem necessary.

Article 33 provides *nonrefoulement* protection to any refugee, regardless of their legal status in the country of asylum. The section tracks the Article 1 definition of a refugee:

Article 33. No Contracting State shall expel or return ("refouler") a refugee in any manner whatsoever to the frontiers of territories where his life or freedom would be threatened on account of his race, religion, nationality, membership of a particular social group or political opinion.

Thus, even if the refugee is not lawfully in the country of asylum, he or she is still entitled to the *nonrefoulement* protection of Article 33. The only exceptions are outlined in the Convention itself:

Article 33(2). The benefit of the present provision may not, however, be claimed by a refugee whom there are reasonable grounds for regarding as a danger to the security of the country in which he is, or who, having been convicted by a final judgment of a particularly serious crime, constitutes a danger to the community of that country.

Thus, although the precise phrasing of the two *nonrefoulement* provisions in the Convention are distinct, the protection afforded to refugees is generally the same, regardless of their legal status in the country of asylum. The distinction in the exceptions does not affect the substantive protection against *refoulement*. Finally, it is important to note that Article 33 is the only major substantive article in the 1951 Convention to which no reservations of any kind by the signatory states are allowed. Thus, a party to the Convention is obligated to comply with the principle of *nonrefoulement* unconditionally.[60]

The 1951 Convention had several significant shortcomings. First, while the principle of *nonrefoulement* was clearly established, the Convention does not create any individual right to asylum for the refugees. In other words, the Convention only obligates the signatory states not to deport refugees already in their country; there is no corresponding obligation to affirmatively admit refugees. The United Nations continued to attempt to resolve this difficult question and the General Assembly eventually adopted a unanimous Declaration on Territorial Asylum in 1967.[61] The Declaration sets forth a right to asylum as defined by the Universal Declaration of Human Rights (see next section), limited only for "overriding reasons of national security or in order to safeguard the population, as in the case of a mass influx of people."[62] However, the Declaration is not a legally binding international instrument.[63] An attempt to establish such an instrument at a 1977 United Nations Conference on Territorial Asylum in Geneva failed to result in any acceptable agreement.[64]

Part of the difficulty in establishing an individual right to asylum is that international law has generally been viewed as the law of nations, without any individual rights or obligations. As international law scholars continue to debate the character of international law rights and obligations, it is fairly clear that no sovereign state now yields its rights to control who enters its territory to any individual refugee's claim to asylum. Indeed, it is clear that the 1951 United Nations Convention Relating to the Status of Refugees does not create any duty on the part of the contracting states to affirmatively admit any refugees.[65]

Another problem presented by the United Nations Convention is its lack of any viable enforcement mechanism. There is no international body that can impose the requirements of the Convention or force signatory states to comply with their treaty obligations.[66] Each state is left free to determine the manner in which it will implement the terms of the Convention.[67] Although the Convention does include extensive provisions regarding the rights and privileges of a recognized refugee while in the country of asylum, the Convention only provides refugees temporary territorial asylum, where the refugee may lawfully remain indefinitely in the country of asylum but has no guarantees as to the future.[68]

A final shortcoming of the 1951 United Nations Convention is that it is extremely limited in scope. The Convention only applies to persons who had become refugees as a result of events occurring prior to January 1, 1951. Furthermore, signatory states also had the option of restricting the definition of a refugee to events which had occurred in Europe alone.[69] The 1967 United Nations Protocol Relating to the Status of Refugees corrected these limitations by incorporating all the substantive provisions of the 1951 Convention while eliminating the geographic and temporal limitations on the definition of refugee.[70] Significantly, the non-reservation clause relating to the principle of *nonrefoulement* remains a part of the Protocol.[71] Thus, the Protocol finally established the first internationally accepted definition of refugee that is both universal and non-discriminatory. Implicit in the adoption of the Protocol is the recognition that the issues of refugee admissions and resettlement are not merely temporary or crisis issues but ongoing world problems that must be continually addressed by the entire international community.

Nonrefoulement in Other International Instruments.[72] There are other international instruments that provide important protections for refugees. There are many interesting questions regarding the nature of international law and its application in the courts of the United States that have been capably examined elsewhere.[73] The *nonrefoulement* sections of the international instruments reviewed in this section are not examined with an eye toward preparing a specific legal argument for consideration by United States courts but rather to establish the extensive international consensus and commitment to the principle of *nonrefoulement* in particular and the protection of refugees in general. Any specific applications of the international law obligations of the United States will be considered in the next section.

First, the Universal Declaration of Human Rights affirms the right of any person to leave any country, including one's own country, and to return to one's own country.[74] The Declaration also establishes a limited right to seek asylum:

> Article 14(1). Everyone has the right to seek and to enjoy in other countries asylum from persecution.

> Article 14(2). This right may not be invoked in the case of prosecutions genuinely arising from nonpolitical crimes or from acts contrary to the purposes and principles of the United Nations.

The Declaration does not enumerate the grounds of persecution nor limit the right to asylum to those recognized as refugees. It does contain an exception to the right for the extradition of common criminals and for persons who otherwise have violated international law. However, the Declaration does not impose any duty to accept asylum seekers or to grant asylum.

Article 13 of the 1966 International Covenant on Civil and Political Rights contains the provision of the *nonrefoulement* of refugees:

> An alien lawfully in the territory of a State Party to the present Convention may be expelled therefrom only in pursuance of a decision reached in accordance with law and shall . . . be allowed to submit the reasons against his expulsion and to have his case reviewed by . . . the competent authority. . . .[75]

Similarly, Article 22(8) of the 1969 American Convention on Human Rights provides for *nonrefoulement*:

> In no case may an alien be deported or returned to a country, regardless of whether or not it is his country of origin, if in that country his right to life or personal freedom is in danger of being violated because of his race, nationality, religion, social status, or political opinion.[76]

Like the International Covenant on Civil and Political Rights, there are no exceptions to the *nonrefoulement* principle. This regional agreement of the Organization of American States is also the only

international instrument that expressly provides individuals the
right to be *granted* asylum:

> Every person has the right to seek and be granted asylum in a
> foreign territory, in accordance with the legislation of the state
> and international conventions, in the event he is being pursued
> for political offenses or related common crimes.[77]

Thus, while the right to a grant of asylum is provided, it is placed
back in the context of the law of extradition. Asylum seekers seem
to be entitled to asylum only when facing extradition from their
country of origin rather than deportation by the country of asylum.

A final important source of *nonrefoulement* protections are the
1949 Geneva Conventions relating to victims of war[78] and the 1977
Protocol Additional to the Geneva Conventions.[79] These international instruments establish the core of the international law relating
to armed conflicts known as international humanitarian law.[80] This
humanitarian law provides *nonrefoulement* protection to persons
fleeing their countries because of a civil war. Such *nonrefoulement*
protection would be available whether or not the alien is eligible for
refugee status. The *UNHCR Handbook on Procedures and Criteria for
Determining Refugee Status* explains:

> Persons compelled to leave their country of origin as a result of
> international or national armed conflicts are not normally con-
> sidered refugees under the 1951 Convention or the 1967 Proto-
> col. They do, however, have the protection provided for in other
> international instruments, e.g., the Geneva Conventions of 1949
> on the Protection of War Victims and the 1977 Protocol Addi-
> tional to the Geneva Conventions 1949. . . .[81]

Thus, the *nonrefoulement* protection of the 1949 Geneva Conventions is broader than that of the 1951 Convention and 1967 Protocol Relating to the Status of Refugees. Article 44 of the 1949
Convention (IV) provides a different definition of refugee: "Refugees are persons who do not enjoy the protection of any government."[82] The *nonrefoulement* principle is found in Article 45:

> Refugees may not be forcibly repatriated until after the cessation
> of hostilities.

Refugees may not be sent to any State that has not satisfactorily
demonstrated a willingness or ability to comply with humanitarian norms.

Article 147 of the 1949 Convention (IV) expressly defines deportations that violate such provisions as "grave breaches" of the
1949 Conventions. Article 85.5 of the 1977 Protocol Additional I to
the Conventions regards any grave breaches of the Convention as
war crimes. Thus, international humanitarian law creates additional
international obligations not to deport refugees in violation of the
principle of *nonrefoulement*.[83]

Application of International Law to
United States Refugee Policy: The 1980 Refugee Act

Under Article VI, clause 2, of the United States Constitution,
"all Treaties made, or which shall be made, under the authority of
the United States, shall be the Supreme Law of the Land." Thus,
all of the international instruments involving the status and rights of
refugees to which the United States is a signatory party become a
binding part of the United States law.[84] To date, the United States
has only ratified or acceded to the 1967 Protocol Relating to the Status of Refugees and the 1949 Geneva Conventions relating to victims
of war. The United States was also a member of the United Nations
General Assemblies which passed the Universal Declaration of Human Rights and the Declaration on Territorial Asylum.

Some commentators have criticized the delay and reluctance of
the United States government to ratify other international instruments relating to human rights.[85] In any case, the accession of the
United States to the 1967 Protocol remains the most important commitment to the international law protections for refugees. However,
the INS and the federal courts refused to acknowledge that the
accession of the United States to the Protocol changed any of the
law relating to refugees.[86] Such a conclusion was primarily supported by statements in the legislative history attempting to downplay the impact of the Protocol on United States immigration law
in order to gain Congressional support for accession. However, a
more careful analysis of the Protocol and the 1951 Convention
which was incorporated into the Protocol would reveal sharp conflicts and inconsistencies with pre-1980 United States law.

As early as 1970, the United States Congress recognized that accession to the Protocol indeed had changed United States obligations to refugees and that legislative reform of the immigration law was necessary.[87] There were several areas which especially merited legislative action. First, the United States needed to change its definition of refugee under the seventh preference category to the United Nations Convention definition. Second, the discretionary withholding of deportation section was inconsistent with the mandatory *nonrefoulement* principle of the Convention. Finally, there was no statutory mechanism in the United States immigration statute for refugees already physically present in the United States to seek asylum in the United States.

It is interesting to note that under the Carter Administration, witnesses from the Department of State, the Department of Justice and the INS all testified before Congress about the need for a broad definition of refugee in United States law. Indeed, the executive branch argued that such a definition should include economic migrants[88] and special relief for illegal entrants.[89] Such proposals would have provided a domestic definition of refugee that would have been broader than the Convention definition.

Witnesses in the Congressional hearings, especially during the crucial 1977–1978 session, often stressed the stated governmental policy of humanitarianism toward refugees.[90] However, the witnesses also acknowledged that this stated policy of humanitarianism often conflicted with and ultimately had to yield to national foreign policy objectives. The government had to avoid the awkward position of supporting a political ally on the one hand while providing asylum to nationals of that country because of government persecution on the other hand.[91] Thus, one key compromise involved the exclusion of "displaced persons" from the domestic refugee definition. The 1979 bill passed by the Senate had included "any person who has been displaced by military or civil disturbance or uprooted because of arbitrary detention or the threat of persecution, and who is unable to return to his usual place of abode" as a refugee.[92] However, the House rejected this definition and limited the class of refugees to those fleeing persecution.[93]

The Refugee Act of 1980[94] was the result of all these Congressional efforts to reform United States refugee law and policy.[95] First, the Act adopted the Convention definition of a refugee in a new section 101(a) (42) of the Immigration and Nationality Act, now codified at 8 U.S.C. § 1101(a) (42):

> The term "refugee" means (A) any person who is outside any country of such person's nationality or, in the case of a person having no nationality, is outside any country in which such person last habitually resided, and who is unable or unwilling to return to, and is unable or unwilling to avail himself or herself of the protection of, that country because of persecution or a well-founded fear of persecution on account of race, religion, nationality, membership in a particular social group, or political opinion, or (B) in such circumstances as the President after appropriate consultation (as defined in section 207(e) of this Act) may specify, any person who is within the country of such person's nationality or, in the case of a person having no nationality within the country in which such person is habitually residing, and who is persecuted or has a well-founded fear of persecution on account of race, religion, nationality, membership in a particular social group, or political opinion. The term "refugee" does not include any person who ordered, incited, assisted, or otherwise participated in the persecution of any person on account of race, religion, nationality, membership in a particular social group, or political opinion.

In adopting the international definition of a refugee,[96] Congress expressly intended to bring the United States domestic law into full compliance with its international obligations to refugees.[97] Accordingly, the 1980 Refugee Act eliminated the seventh preference/conditional entrant classification and established a two-tiered system for the admission of refugees.[98] Refugees outside their countries of nationality would apply for immigrant visas at United States consulates abroad just as any other immigrants. The consular officials would make the determination of whether the applicant qualified for refugee status under the new statutory standard.[99] The two tiers consisted of an annual or regular flow[100] (established at fifty thousand visas for the years 1980, 1981 and 1982 and to be determined by the President after consultation with Congress in the following years[101]) and the emergency admissions of refugees in accordance with the President's discretionary powers.[102] This two-tiered approach finally recognized the reality of refugee admissions, namely the need for both a continuous admissions policy as well as the ability to respond to crisis situations on an ad hoc basis. All these refugee admissions would not be counted in the total numerical limitations on immigration, but that total ceiling would be lowered to 270,000 to offset the increased number of visas generally available for entry into the United States.[103] Thus, the refugee admission policy of the United States was placed outside the ordinary preference/quota system of immigrant admissions but at the same time was recognized as part of permanent immigration law and policy.

Since the discretion of the President to admit refugees was now regulated by statute—both in defining who were refugees in § 1101(a) (42) (B) and in admitting refugees under the § 207 emergency flow section—the need for a flexible parole power was eliminated. Thus, the 1980 Refugee Act also expressly limited parole power to individual cases.[104] The executive branch could no longer parole groups of refugees into the United States. The Attorney General could only parole individuals where there were "compelling reasons in the public interest with respect to that particular alien" to parole the person into the United States rather than admit that person as a refugee.[105]

The 1980 Act also made a significant change in the withholding of deportation section. The new section 243(h) now reads:

> The Attorney General shall not deport or return any alien (other than an alien described in section 241(a) (19)) to a country if the Attorney General determines that such alien's life or freedom would be threatened in such country on account of race, religion, nationality, membership in a particular social group, or political opinion. . . .[106]

Thus, with only the exceptions relating to Nazi war criminals, those who persecuted others, those convicted of serious crimes and those who are dangerous to the national security, the United States law now follows the mandatory and unconditional international principle of *nonrefoulement*.[107] The nature of this new withholding of deportation section and its relationship to the right to asylum in the United States became the focus of the recent United States Supreme Court decision, *Immigration and Naturalization Service v. Stevic*.[108] The issues in that case will be treated more extensively in the following section.

Finally, the 1980 Refugee Act created an explicit statutory mechanism for granting asylum, or refugee status, to persons already physically present in the United States.[109] Thus, under United States law, "refugees" are those refugees outside the United States who are admitted as non-quota immigrants under § 207 while "asylees" are those persons already physically present in the United States who are recognized as refugees and given asylum under § 208.

Some of the pressure for an asylum procedure in the statute arose out of an incident in November 1970 that became known as the Kudirka Affair.[110] Simas Kudirka was a Lithuanian sailor who jumped from his Soviet fishing trawler onto an American Coast Guard ship while both vessels were in the territorial waters of the United States off the coast of Massachusetts. Kudirka requested asylum in the United States but the Coast Guard returned him to his ship without any consideration of his plea for asylum. Kudirka was physically assaulted upon his return to his vessel. As a response to this embarrassing incident, the Department of State announced that requests for asylum would now be considered whether made abroad or in the United States.[111] In 1974 the INS promulgated new regulations that formally allowed aliens physically present in the United States to apply to the INS for asylum, a status without any basis in the immigration statute.[112] The 1980 Act codified this administrative practice by creating a statutory basis for asylum for those persons physically present in the United States, regardless of their immigration status.[113] The decision whether to grant asylum is within the discretion of the Attorney General.[114] However the Attorney General is required to use the new statutory definition of a refugee in this determination of whether the applicant is eligible for asylum.[115]

It is important to emphasize that it was the explicit intent of Congress to bring United States domestic law into conformity with its international obligations toward refugees, and, specifically, to implement the United Nations Protocol Relating to the Status of Refugees which was acceded to in 1968.[116] While Congress is always free to supersede any United States treaties by passing subsequent inconsistent legislation,[117] Congress did not do so in 1980 regarding the Protocol. Thus, when government officials seek to implement and courts seek to review the 1980 Refugee Act, they should refer directly to this legislative intent. Courts particularly are bound by the rule of interpretation that requires them to construe United States law as consistent, if at all possible, with United States treaties.[118] The next section examines whether the practice of the United States government has conformed with the principles and policies reflected in the 1980 Refugee Act.

Asylum Under the 1980 Refugee Act

Procedures. Given the revised statutory framework for the admission and recognition of refugees into the United States, it seems incongruous that Salvadorans and Guatemalans are routinely denied asylum by the United States government. Although it is difficult to verify often-conflicting statistics, it is readily apparent that the rights to asylum created by the 1980 Refugee Act are almost universally unavailable to refugees from El Salvador and Guatemala. For example, in fiscal year 1984, only 328 Salvadoran applicants received asylum, out of 13,373 cases adjudicated (2.45% approval rate). Only three Guatemalan applicants, out of 761 cases adjudicated (0.39%), received asylum. These approval rates may be compared to an approval rate of approximately 20% for all asylum applicants and rates of 12.3% for applicants from Nicaragua, 32.7% from Poland, 40.9% from Afganistan, and 60.9% from Iran.[119] The disparity in the approval rates raises questions of equal treatment. While the asylum applicants from Nicaragua, Poland, Afganistan and Iran have had their meritorious claims to asylum recognized, applicants from El Salvador and Guatemala, who seem no less deserving of asylum, have had their claims denied. A closer examination of the procedures and practices involving asylum applications will reveal the significant shortcomings of current United States asylum law and may reveal why some have concluded that there is a need for refuge outside these procedures—in the sanctuary churches.

This examination will focus on the asylum and withholding of deportation sections in the statute since the sanctuary movement is primarily concerned with those Central Americans already physically present in the United States, instead of those applying for admission as refugees outside the United States. If no deportation or exclusion proceedings have been commenced against an alien, that alien may apply for asylum to the District Director of the INS district office closest to his or her place of residence in the United States.[120] The asylum applicant completes an application, INS Form I-589, and submits any supporting affidavits and documentation.[121] The applicant will then be interviewed by an INS officer, who forwards the application to the District Director.[122] The District Director is required to request an advisory opinion on the application from the Bureau of Human Rights and Humanitarian Affairs (BHRHA) in the Department of State.[123] After receiving this advisory opinion, the District Director then renders a written decision either approving or denying the asylum application.[124] No appeal lies from the discretion of the District Director,[125] but the application for asylum can then be renewed in any subsequent deportation or exclusion proceeding instituted against the applicant.[126] If the asylum application is approved, the asylee may adjust his or her immigration status to that of a lawful permanent resident after one year of residence in the United States.[127]

On the other hand, an alien subject to exclusion or deportation may apply to the presiding officer of the proceeding, the Immigration Judge, for the withholding of deportation and/or asylum.[128] The applicant submits Form I-589 for asylum. An application for asylum is also automatically considered as a request for withholding of deportation.[129] The burden of proof is upon the alien to establish the claim to asylum, and there will be an evidentiary hearing before the Immigration Judge on the merits of the claim.[130] An advisory opinion from the Bureau of Human Rights and Humanitarian Affairs is requested before the commencement of the hearing. However, if a prior advisory opinion had been received during a prior application for asylum before a District Director, then the Immigration Judge will request another opinion only if the judge finds that circumstances have changed so substantially that a second opinion would materially aid in the adjudication of the asylum claim.[131] Both the applicant and the INS may present oral and documentary evidence. The Immigration Judge then renders a written decision. If the asylum application is granted, the applicant receives asylum for one year and is eligible for adjustment of status at the end of that year.[131A] If the Immigration Judge denies the asylum application, the exclusion or deportation proceeding is reinstituted[132] and the denial of asylum becomes a part of the final order that may be appealed to the Board of Immigration Appeals (BIA),[133] and then judicially reviewed by a United States Circuit Court of Appeals.[134]

Access. There are many complex legal issues involving the asylum application process that cannot be explored here.[135] However, there are several issues which are highly relevant to the near-blanket denial of asylum to Salvadorans and Guatemalans.

First, recent litigation has focused on the access of potential asylees from Central America to the asylum application process.[136] Salvadorans and Guatemalans cannot receive asylum in the United States unless they specifically apply for status as an asylee. Several court decisions have criticized the INS for its practices of mass deportation and denial of due process to potential asylum seekers from Central America.

In a class action lawsuit filed by four Salvadorans and one Guatemalan against the local INS district office, the United States District Court for the Southern District of Texas granted a preliminary injunction requiring, among other things, that the INS affirmatively notify potential asylees detained by the INS of their right to apply for asylum.[137] In the 1982 decision *Nunez v. Boldin*, the district court first acknowledged the Fifth Amendment due process rights of the potential asylees:

> It is not necessary to discuss in depth the conditions existing in El Salvador and Guatemala. The daily news reports from those countries sufficiently detail the foundation for the fears many refugees have. Certainly the interests here are life and liberty.[138]

Given these protected interests, the district court then applied the traditional balancing test[139] to determine whether the INS procedures met the requirements of due process of law. The court first noted the current situation:

> The majority of detainees are completely uneducated as to INS procedures. They do not speak the English language, nor can they read the English language asylum application required for consideration. The detention center is not located in an area where detainees can easily find legal representation, nor are they entitled to appointed counsel under the law.[140]

In its findings of fact, the district court had also observed that the detention facility at Los Fresnos, Texas was located in a remote area; that access to the facility for attorneys and other legal assistants had been restricted; that the facility contained no law library and prohibited the personal possession by the detainees of any self-help legal materials as well as paper and pencils; that personal papers, including items containing the names, addresses, and telephone numbers of relatives, friends and attorneys, were read or confiscated by the detention center personnel; and that attorneys representing detainees were not notified of proceedings in their clients' cases.[141] The court also noted the INS practice of actively encouraging detainees to waive their right to a formal deportation hearing and their right to apply for asylum and instead leave the country under "voluntary departure" agreements.[142] Such agreements required an admission by the alien of being in the United States illegally and a willingness to leave within a short, specified period of time. While the alien who agrees to such voluntary deportation is freed from detention and may find it easier to lawfully re-enter the country at a later date (since no order of deportation is entered on the immigration record), the alien also waives significant rights. The district court briefly reviewed the Refugee Act of 1980 and concluded:

> What is obvious to the Court at this point is that the United States has, by treaty, statute, and regulations, manifested its intention of hearing the pleas of aliens who come to this country claiming a fear of being persecuted in their homelands. The intention is not necessarily stated as granting the privilege of asylum to all who come to this country but of hearing those pleas.[143]

Thus, the district court found that notice of the right to apply for asylum must be given by the INS before the alien is required to depart, either through the voluntary deportation agreement or through an order of deportation, and that such notice must be given so as to allow any alien wishing to apply for asylum the opportunity to do so meaningfully.[144] The district court ended its opinion with a stern warning:

> Providing refuge to those facing persecution in their homeland, however, goes to the very heart of the principles and moral precepts upon which this country and its Constitution were

founded. It is unavoidable that some burdens result from the protection of these principles. To let these same principles go unprotected would amount to nothing less than a sacrilege.[145]

Several months later, the United States District Court for the Central District of California considered another class action lawsuit by Salvadorans against the Attorney General and the INS. The district court granted a nationwide preliminary injunction requiring the INS to advise Salvadorans of their right to apply for asylum and of their right to a deportation hearing before requesting their voluntary departure.[146] In *Orantes-Hernandez v. Smith*, the district court first took judicial notice of the "voluminous evidence of the violent and dangerous conditions which permeate daily life in El Salvador," including the unexplained disappearances, random violence, arbitrary arrest and imprisonment, and retaliatory torture.[147] Despite the fact that many of the Salvadorans are eligible to apply for asylum and that all are entitled to a deportation hearing,

> [. . . t] he record before the Court indicates that the widespread acceptance of voluntary departure is due in large part to the coercive effect of the practices and procedures employed by the INS and the unfamiliarity of most Salvadorans with their rights under the immigration laws.[148]

Specifically, the district court credited the testimony of the detained Salvadorans that INS agents used "subtle persuasion to outright threats and misrepresentations" in order to obtain their consent to voluntary deportation. Such INS practices included: (1) telling the Salvadorans that they would be deported whether or not they signed the voluntary departure agreement, or that signing the form was mandatory, or that refusal to sign the form would result in a long period of detention; (2) telling the Salvadorans that any application for asylum would be denied, or that such an application would result in prolonged detention, or that the information contained in the application would be forwarded to the governmental authorities in El Salvador; (3) denying access to legal counsel, even when specifically requested by the detainees; (4) confiscating every piece of paper carried by the detainees, including the names and phone numbers of friends or relatives in the United States.[149] Furthermore, the district court found that the entire voluntary deportation processing procedure was often completed so quickly—"in a matter of hours"—that it was often physically impossible for attorneys to locate their clients or to intervene on their behalf.[150] The district court concluded:

> The record in this case indicates that the mistreatment of Salvadorans is not limited to any particular geographic area or to the conduct of a few INS agents. The experience of the plaintiffs and the proposed class members took place in a wide variety of locations, including California, Arizona, Texas, Oklahoma, and Massachusetts. . . . The sheer volume of evidence before the Court and the similarity of the experiences therein belie the contention by defendants that plaintiffs' claims center on isolated incidents of misconduct. Based on this record, the Court concludes that INS agents routinely give incomplete, misleading, and even false advice to Salvadorans regarding their legal rights.[151]

The district court then went on to examine the conditions in INS detention facilities, specifically those in the Central and Southern District of California, and found that the detained Salvadorans were poorly treated and continually denied access to legal information. Such abuses included the prohibition of receiving or possessing written materials, limited visiting hours, severe shortages of telephones for the use of the detainees, denial of access to paralegals to the facilities and the indiscriminate use of solitary confinement as punishment for minor infractions.[152]

After considering the numerous legal issues involving the provisional certification of the plaintiff class for the class action lawsuit,[153] the district court then found that the INS pattern and practice of coercing Salvadorans to sign voluntary departure agreements denied them their constitutional and statutory rights to a deportation hearing and to apply for asylum in the United States.[154] Citing *Nunez*, the district court concluded that the INS must provide affirmative notice of these rights to the detained Salvadorans:

> The creation of new procedures, the reaffirmation of a policy of welcoming "persons subject to persecution in their homeland," and the renewed adherence to the United Nations Protocol all

become meaningless if those intended to benefit by the asylum provisions are never informed of its existence.[155]

The district court found that "principles of due process and fundamental fairness require the INS to advise class members of their rights before requesting them to voluntarily depart" because the signing of the voluntary departure agreement is "tantamount to a waiver of the right to apply for asylum as well as the right to a deportation hearing."[156] In view of the coercive circumstances in which consent to voluntary departure was generally obtained, the district court found that such waivers were invalid and ordered the notice of rights as the appropriate remedy.[157] The district court declared:

> The Court believes and Congress has stated that those aliens with claims of persecution in their homeland should at least be heard and that those with valid claims should receive protection. In so mandating Congress has reaffirmed "one of the oldest themes in America's history—welcoming homeless refugees to our shores." [citation omitted] A decision that would effectively exclude Salvadorans from the asylum process would make a mockery of this tradition and indeed of this country's beginnings.[158]

These two district court decisions have far-reaching implications that have been extensively discussed and debated by legal scholars.[159] What is critical for this analysis is that these courts have concluded that the INS has not been a passive or neutral government agency relative to potential asylees from Central America. The decisions in these cases imply that the INS has engaged in a policy of coercion and abuse of governmental authority to deny Salvadorans and Guatemalans access to the asylum process.

Standard of Proof. In *Immigration and Naturalization Service v. Stevic*,[160] the United States Supreme Court examined the standard of proof required for the withholding of deportation under §243(h) of the Immigration and Nationality Act. This was the first case involving asylum law to reach the United States Supreme Court after the enactment of the 1980 Refugee Act. The Supreme Court reviewed a decision by the Court of Appeals for the Second Circuit[161] which had held that the Refugee Act of 1980 had lowered the standard of proof required for an application for withholding of deportation under § 243(h) from a "clear probability of persecution" standard to a "well-founded fear of persecution" standard. Several Courts of Appeal had considered the question of the proper standard of proof for both the withholding of deportation under § 243(h) and the granting of asylum under § 208 and had reached sharply conflicting conclusions.[162]

The United States Supreme Court recognized that different standards of proof had been used by the Board of Immigration Appeals (BIA) and the courts under the withholding section.[163] However, the Supreme Court found that, at least prior to the 1968 United States accession to the United Nations Protocol Relating to the Status of Refugees, an applicant for the withholding of deportation was required to demonstrate a "clear probability of persecution" or a "likelihood of persecution."[164] The Court then turned to the legislative history of the 1968 accession to the Protocol and concluded that the Protocol did not create new obligations for the United States nor require any statutory changes in United States immigration law.[165] While acknowledging that the BIA and reviewing courts had used a wide variety of formulations of the proper standard of proof under the withholding of deportation section after the 1968 accession, the Supreme Court brushed aside these differences by noting that several lower courts had reconciled the differences by ruling that the standards would eventually "converge."[166] Thus, the only question before the United States Supreme Court was whether the 1980 Refugee Act had changed any of these judicial interpretations of the withholding of deportation section.

Initially, the Court acknowledged three changes in the text of § 243(h) after the passage of the 1980 Refugee Act:

> The amendment (1) substituted mandatory language for what was previously a grant of discretionary authority to the Attorney General to withhold deportation after making the required finding; (2) substituted a requirement that the Attorney General determine that the "alien's life or freedom would be threatened" for the previous requirement that the alien "would be subject to persecution" and (3) broadened the relevant causes of persecu-

tion from reasons "of race, religion or political opinion" to encompass "nationality" and "membership in a particular social group" as well.[167]

However, in a long footnote, the Supreme Court held that these textual changes still did not change the standard of proof required for § 243(h) relief.[168] The Supreme Court concluded that although § 243(h) itself did not expressly provide for any standard of proof, the clear probability of persecution standard instead of a well-founded fear of persecution standard should continue to be used.[169] Thus, the Supreme Court made a distinction between an application for the withholding of deportation on the one hand and an application for asylum under § 208 on the other.[170] The Court held that different standards of proof are to be used under the two sections: the standard of proof required for the mandatory withholding of deportation is higher—a clear probability of persecution—than the standard of proof required for the discretionary grant of asylum—a well-founded fear of persecution.[171] The regulations state that an application for asylum under § 208 will also automatically be considered an application for the withholding of deportation.[172] What the Supreme Court decision in *Stevic* has held is that an application for withholding of deportation is *not* also considered an application for asylum under § 208.[173] The withholding or deportation provision is made a statutory last resort, requiring a high standard of proof for its protection.

The *Stevic* decision now leaves the task of the application of the two standards of proof for asylum and the withholding of deportation to the lower courts. In *Stevic*, the United States Supreme Court refused to elaborate upon the meaning of the clear probability of persecution standard beyond noting that it requires "evidence establishing that it is more likely than not that the alien would be subject to persecution on one of the specified grounds."[174] However, in an earlier footnote, the Supreme Court had pointed out that the key word in the standard was "probability," meaning "likelihood."[175] In the same footnote, the Supreme Court stated that the word "clear" "appears to have been surplusage" and held that the clear probability standard of proof was lower than one requiring "clear and convincing" proof.[176]

On the other hand, the Court did not provide any guidance

about the meaning of the well-founded fear of persecution standard of proof:

> We do not decide the meaning of the phrase "well-founded fear of persecution" which is applicable by terms of the Act and regulations to requests for discretionary asylum. That issue is not presented by this case.[177]

However, the Supreme Court did reject the proposition that the two standards were identical:

> For purposes of our analysis, we may assume, as the Court of Appeals [in *Stevic*] concluded, that the well-founded-fear standard is more generous than the clear-probability-of-persecution standard. . . .[178]

The United Nations High Commissioner on Refugees' *Handbook on Procedure and Criteria for Determining Refugee Status (UNHCR Handbook)*[182] emphasizes the importance of both the subjective and objective elements of the well-founded fear of persecution standard.[183] This *UNHCR Handbook*, based upon the UNHCR's twenty-five years of experience, has been recognized by the BIA[184] and the federal courts[185] as an important source for the interpretation of the Protocol and the incorporated Convention.[186]

The subjective element of a well-founded fear of persecution requires an evaluation of the applicant's own testimony,[187] personality,[188] opinions and feelings,[189] and personal and family background.[190] The applicant must subjectively fear persecution. The cumulative effect of several experiences that in and of themselves do not amount to persecution may create a well-founded fear of persecution.[191]

The objective element is essentially an evaluation of the alien's credibility;[192] the fear must be objectively well-founded. Such an evaluation should consider the personal experiences of the applicant as well as the testimony of friends, relatives or other members of the persecuted class.[193] Furthermore, the laws of the country of origin, particularly the manner in which they are applied, are also relevant evidence.[194] Finally, evidence of the general conditions in the country of origin can be relevant to the credibility of the applicant.[195]

The interpretation of the well-founded fear standard as set forth in the *UNHCR Handbook* also contains several caveats about the entire asylum application process. The *UNHCR Handbook* recognizes that most applicants flee their home countries without all the documents or evidence necessary to prove their asylum claims.[196] Thus, the absence of corroborative documentary evidence should not automatically defeat an application for asylum. Furthermore, the alien should be given the benefit of the doubt in the credibility evaluation.[197] Even testimonial inconsistencies or false statements should not completely undermine an application.[198] A person could have been afraid of and may still distrust government authorities, and only offer a minimum of information and cooperation.[199] The applicant may also fear reprisals against relatives and friends remaining in the country of origin. Thus, the *UNHCR Handbook* places a responsibility on the investigating officer to clarify and resolve any inconsistencies or insufficiencies of evidence through personal interviews with the asylum applicant[200] and the officer's own research of the case.[201] Finally, the examining officer should decide the case solely on the criteria outlined and the evidence presented, without any personal or political considerations.[202]

Unfortunately, the standards set forth in the *UNHCR Handbook* have still not been expressly adopted by Congress, the courts, or the INS. However, if the *UNHCR Handbook* interpretation of the well-founded fear of persecution standard is applied to the situations of asylum applicants from El Salvador and Guatemala, it becomes evident that the United States government now applies a stricter standard of proof to such applicants. The UNHCR conducted a fact-finding mission in 1981 to specifically monitor the INS processing of Salvadoran asylum applicants. The mission found much of the same conditions as detailed by the federal district courts in *Nunez v. Boldin* and *Orantes-Hernandez v. Smith* and recommended that the UNHCR

> . . . should continue to express its concern to the U.S. Government that its apparent failure to grant asylum to any significant numbers of Salvadorans, coupled with the continuing large-scale forcible and voluntary return to El Salvador, would appear to represent a negation of its responsibilities assumed upon its adherence to the Protocol.[203]

The report noted that only one Salvadoran had been granted asylum in fiscal year 1981. Thus, the UNHCR mission concluded:

> It is, therefore, fair to conclude that there is a systematic practice designed to forcibly return Salvadorans, irrespective of the merits of their asylum claims. [204]

Several months later, the UNHCR wrote a letter to the Department of State expressing its concern about the near-blanket denials of asylum to Salvadorans and specifically advising that, in its opinion, persons fleeing El Salvador were prima facie bona fide refugees, in the absence of clear indications to the contrary. [205] This UNHCR opinion was received and supported by a Congressional resolution on December 29, 1981. [206]

The principal response of the Department of State and the INS to these charges vis-à-vis Salvadoran asylum applications is that the asylum process requires individual, case-by-case determinations. [207] However, this contention, while true, is inconsistent with the past and current practices of the United States government in using its parole power to admit Cubans and Haitians as "entrants" in 1981 and the more recent classwide grant of extended voluntary departure status to nationals of Lebanon, Nicaragua, Ethiopia, Uganda and Iran. [208] These practices demonstrate that the INS and the United States executive branch are capable of making classwide determinations regarding asylum and refugee matters.

There are many reasons why asylum applications from Salvadorans and Guatemalans are routinely denied by the INS. Ostensibly, the Department of State and the INS continue to maintain that the applicants do not meet the definition of a refugee under the 1980 Refugee Act. Indeed, there is almost a unanimity among government officials that most, if not all, persons fleeing those countries are only economic migrants and therefore ineligible for asylum. [209]

There are several major flaws in the United States government's reasoning. First, it treats all Salvadorans and Guatemalans as a class. The same officials claimed that such classwide determinations were impossible when rejecting the UNHCR recommendations that Salvadorans were, as a class, bona fide refugees. Second, while it cannot be denied that some of the asylum appli-

cants do not have valid claims, it is clear that professors, labor leaders, medical professionals and others do not flee to the United States
simply in search of their career advancement. Such professionals
would not leave their families and social status in search of uncertain
economic opportunity. Finally, perhaps most insidious is the implication that the testimonies of the asylum applicants themselves
about their experiences with harrasment, arrest, torture, imprisonment and murder are, at the least, not credible, and, at the worst,
fabricated or imagined. Nevertheless, the United States government continues to scoff at the validity of these asylum claims.

A more plausible explanation for the near-blanket denials of
asylum applications for Guatemalans and Salvadorans is the inevitably political nature of the current asylum application process.[211]
The 1980 Refugee Act itself does not require any role by the Department of State; the BHRHA advisory opinions are merely a creation of INS regulations.[212] However, the District Directors and
Immigration Judges continue to rely heavily on these advisory opinions and follow the State Department's recommendation in nearly
every case.[213] Even the federal courts have recognized that these advisory opinions cannot be free of political and foreign policy biases:

> Such letters from the State Department do not carry the guar-
> antees of reliability which the law demands of admissible evi-
> dence. A frank, but official discussion of the political
> shortcomings of a friendly nation is not always compatible with
> the high duty to maintain advantageous diplomatic relations
> with nations throughout the world. The traditional foundation
> required of expert testimony is lacking; nor can official position
> be said to supply an acceptable substitute. No hearing officer or
> court has the means to know the diplomatic necessities of the
> moment, in the light of which the statements must be
> weighed.[214]

While the State Department might be the federal agency best
qualified to assess the current political conditions in any country
around the world, such assessments cannot be a substitute for the
objective, non-partisan evaluation required to adjudicate an application for asylum under the Convention definition.[215] As long as the
United States has foreign policy interests in El Salvador and Gua-

temala and continues to support those governments with extensive military and economic aid, it is unrealistic to expect that the State Department will be completely objective in its advisory opinions regarding asylum applications from Guatemalans and Salvadorans. It would be inconsistent for the State Department to acknowledge that these governments are persecuting their own citizens.

Some have suggested that greater judicial scrutiny could correct this politicalization of the asylum process. However, the courts have been extremely reluctant to depart from the long-established policy of judicial deference on matters of immigration law.[216] For example, the United States District Court for the Southern District of Florida, a jurisdiction that has had its dockets filled with immigration cases, has astutely noted in a case arising out of the "Freedom Flotilla":

> At root, the controversy here reflects a basic contradiction between, on the one hand, America's tradition of providing sanctuary for the homeless, the outcast and particularly the political refugee and, on the other, our immigration laws. That tension finds expression in the discomfiting question of who, and how many, can come to this country and in what circumstances. Resolution of that tension through promulgation and enforcement of a coherent immigration policy is a matter within the province of the Legislative and Executive Branches of government. This Court has neither the willingness nor the competence to interject itself into the arena of immigration policy, except insofar as such policy runs afoul of constitutional and statutory safeguards, as is the case here.[217]

Since there is no constitutional or statutory right to asylum,[218] courts will most likely continue to be extremely deferential to the determinations of the State Department and the INS.

On the other hand, Congress is in a position to debate the complex questions involved in United States refugee law and policy. The 98th Congress adjourned in October 1984 without resolving a stalemate over the controversial Simpson-Mazzoli bills (S. 529 and H.R. 1510) pending before the Conference Committee.[219] One little-publicized part of the proposed legislation was the restriction of the rights of asylum applicants.[220] However, many legal scholars continue to look to Congress as the most appropriate forum for reforms that will better implement both the letter and the spirit of the 1968 United Nations Protocol and the 1980 Refugee Act.

Whatever one concludes are the real reasons for the near-blanket denial of asylum applications from Salvadorans and Guatemalans, there are serious questions about whether current United States governmental policies and practices offer any real protection to these Central American refugees.

CHAPTER THREE

The Confrontation Between Church and State

"I burn, seethe and boil that the religion of my choice has placed its imprimatur on a crusade to destroy my country, advocating a breakdown of our laws."[1]

—INS District Director Richard M. Casillas, San Antonio, Texas, May 1984

Federal Prosecution of Sanctuary Workers

Churches and individuals engaged in sanctuary activity on behalf of Central American refugees are potentially subject to criminal prosecution under United States law. Those within the sanctuary movement are acutely aware of the legal consequences of their actions.[2] (The next chapter will examine the precise nature of those criminal charges and some of the possible defenses that potential defendants could raise against those prosecutions.) Churchpeople remain quite public about their actions; many have openly admitted to breaking the law.[3]

For many months, neither the Department of Justice nor the INS sought to prosecute the sanctuary churches. The federal government maintained its policy of not pursuing undocumented aliens in homes and churches.[4] Beginning in the spring of 1984, several individuals associated with the sanctuary movement in Texas and Arizona were arrested in isolated incidents and charged with the unlawful transportation of undocumented aliens. However, the government did not seek a direct confrontation with the sanctuary movement. That confrontation erupted in January 1985 with the announcement of criminal indictments against sixteen sanctuary workers in Arizona, after a ten-month undercover investigation of the sanctuary movement. The confrontation between the church and state in the court cases to be described in this chapter is one of the most dramatic elements of the sanctuary movement.

United States v. Stacey Lynn Merkt[7]

In the pre-dawn hours of February 17, 1984, Stacey Lynn Merkt, then 29, from Pinole, California, Sister Diane M. Muhlenkamp, 36, a nun from the order of the Poor Handmaidens of Jesus Christ in Fort Wayne, Indiana, and *Dallas Times-Herald* reporter Jack Edward Fischer, 30, were arrested by Border Patrol Agents Albert Montez and Manuel Rubio, Jr., while driving on Highway 649 near McAllen, Texas. The persons arrested were driving from Casa Oscar Romero, a religious "safe house" for refugees, in the town of San Benito in the Rio Grande Valley to San Antonio, Texas. The house is funded mainly by the Roman Catholic Diocese of Brownsville, Texas. There were also three Salvadorans in the car driven by Muhlenkamp: Mauricio Valle, 23, Brenda Elizabeth Sanchez-Galan, 19, and her two-year-old daughter Bessie Guadelupe. The Salvadorans were going to San Antonio to visit Lutheran pastor Daniel Long, whom Valle had met when Long had visited El Salvador. The refugees hoped to eventually make their way to the Old Cambridge Baptist Community in Cambridge, Massachusetts, where they had been offered sanctuary. The charge against Merkt, Muhlenkamp and Fischer was the unlawful transportation of undocumented aliens. (The next chapter will examine this charge in detail.)

Both Sanchez-Galan and Valle had fled El Salvador in December 1983. Their stories are typical of the flight of refugees from Central America. Brenda Sanchez-Galan was a student and a health worker in El Salvador. While she was a student at a Catholic high school in San Salvador, she was once caught in the middle of an ambush by government soldiers. Street fighting in the neighborhood had been especially severe that day and so the students had been sent home early. While waiting for her bus, Brenda took cover in a nearby garage when she heard gunfire erupt. The government tank pulled up to the garage and indiscriminately opened fire. Dozens were killed. Brenda was drenched in blood as she lay under a pile of bodies but she miraculously escaped injury.

In February 1981, Brenda's closest friend, who was only eighteen years old and a newlywed, was dragged from her home at night by members of the government-sponsored death squads. Three days later, her body was found, decapitated and cut in half. This woman was also three months pregnant; her fetus was also brutally severed in half. Three months later, the husband of this murdered friend was also kidnapped and brutally killed. His body was also found cut into many pieces.

In the midst of such personal violence, Brenda was employed by her local Lutheran church as a medical assistant. She was one of the first health workers trained to go to the "Faith and Hope" refugee camp. She worked with the wounded from late 1981 until November 1983, only taking a temporary leave from May to October 1982 to give birth to and care for her daughter Bessie. During this time, Brenda was often followed by members of the security forces and questioned about her work. As a church worker and a medical assistant, she was suspected of being a guerrilla sympathizer. In April 1983, her pastor and the doctor with whom she worked were imprisoned and tortured by the army. They were finally released in October 1983.

Finally, in November 1983, the violence around Brenda grew to an intolerable level. Several co-workers were dragged from their homes at night by the National Police and were "disappeared," a euphemism for kidnapping and unverified murder. Another close friend and neighbor, twenty-one years old and three months pregnant, was dragged from her house at midnight by members of the death squads. This friend was taken to the military barracks in Ilopagno, where she was first gang-raped and then shot to death. She was shot from the rear while forced to bend over; the bullet tore away her face as it exited. In December 1983, Brenda took Bessie and fled for their lives.

Mauricio Valle's story is similar. He was confirmed as a Lutheran in July 1983 and was active in the local Lutheran church in San Salvador. He was a driver for the church and often served as a guide for Christian visitors to the Salvadoran church. Mauricio came from a family committed to helping the victims of the civil war. His father was accused of being a guerrilla sympathizer and his name was placed on a death list after he had treated a wounded man. The subsequent anxiety and stress led to a fatal heart attack. Mauricio's sister was a nursing assistant. Her name also appeared on a death list after she nursed the wounded. She was driven to commit suicide.

Like Brenda, Mauricio was often followed and questioned about his church involvement and his work with the wounded and refugees. Once, when mistaken for someone else, he was arrested off a bus, blindfolded and asked whether he would be rather shot or decapitated. He was only released when the official in charge realized that Mauricio was not the man they wanted. He also endured repeated incidents of torture and murder among his friends and co-workers. When looking for one missing friend, Mauricio found him in a hole, decapitated. He, too, decided to leave El Salvador in December 1983.

Brenda and Mauricio had found their way to Casa Romero where they were helped by Stacey Merkt, who worked there. Sr. Diane Muhlenkamp had come to Casa Romero as part of the Global Ministries Program to study the problems of the refugees. The newspaper reporter was working on a story. Criminal charges were not brought against the reporter, Jack Fischer. However, Merkt and Muhlenkamp were charged and indicted with four counts of transporting undocumented aliens, conspiracy to transport undocumented aliens and aiding and abetting the transportation of undocumented aliens. Both were freed on $10,000 personal recognizance bonds.

Muhlenkamp opted for a pre-trial diversion program in exchange for her agreement to testify for the prosecution against Merkt. However, she was not actually called to testify in Merkt's trial. The charges against Muhlenkamp will remain pending until 1985 and then will be dropped and the record of her arrest expunged if she does not commit any other "unlawful" act in the meantime.

Stacey Merkt plead not guilty to all the charges and faced a jury trial in the federal district court in Brownsville, Texas with Judge Filemon Vela presiding. The jury heard the reluctant testimonies of Valle and Sanchez-Galan,[8] as well as the testimonies of local immigration attorneys and Roman Catholic Bishop John J. Fitzpatrick. Although Judge Vela permitted the defense to introduce evidence during the trial that the INS District Director in Harlingen (the INS district in which the arrests took place) had never granted asylum to any Salvadoran applicant and that he summarily arrested and detained such applicants, the judge refused to allow the jury to consider any defense theories related to this evidence. Indeed, Judge Vela specifically instructed the jury to find that Merkt still violated the law even if she sought to help the refugees apply for asylum elsewhere, such as San Antonio, the location of the next nearest INS district office. After three and a half days of deliberation, the all-Hispanic jury found Merkt guilty on three felony counts. In June, Merkt was sentenced to two years' probation and a ninety-day suspended sentence. The case is now on appeal before the Fifth Circuit Court of Appeals. Meanwhile, the Salvadorans are now free on $4,000 bonds, awaiting the conclusion of the deportation proceedings initiated against them.

United States v. Philip M. Conger[9]

On March 17, 1983, at around 11 P.M., Border Patrol agents arrested Philip M. Conger, 26 (the Project Director of the Tucson Ecumenical Council's Task Force on Central America and an associate member of the Southside Presbyterian Church) and Katherine Flaherty (also from the Task Force) for transporting four Salvadorans on Highway 82 outside Nogales, Arizona. One of the refugees in the car was a former student activist at the University of San Salvador, Oscar Andraoe-Alfaro; another was a catechist, Maria Camero-Colocho, who had worked with the four United States churchwomen who were murdered in El Salvador in 1980. The other two Salvadorans were Maria's two teenaged sisters. The three had fled El Salvador after their father was killed and their mother raped in their house by members of the government armed forces.

The arrests of Conger and Flaherty raised many questions for the sanctuary movement. The 1976 Ford station wagon that they were driving was registered to the Southside Presbyterian Church and therefore could have subjected the church to the first criminal prosecution for sanctuary activity. The arresting officers also seized many documents containing comprehensive information about the national sanctuary movement during the arrest and subsequent search of the car. However, Conger and Flaherty were both released after several hours of detention without being charged with any crimes.

It was not until May 15, the day after Stacey Merkt was convicted by the jury in Texas, that Conger, the son of Methodist missionaries who had worked in Latin America, was charged and indicted on four counts of transporting undocumented aliens. Charges were not brought against Flaherty, a former Peace Corps volunteer in El Salvador, nor against any church. Conger pled not guilty to all the charges. After a considerable delay in prosecution and several pre-trial hearings, United States District Court Judge Alfredo Marquez ruled on July 20, 1984, that the Border Patrol did not have a reasonable suspicion to stop the car that Conger had been driving and ordered the charges to be dropped.[10] Meanwhile, the four Salvadorans remain free on bond pending their deportation proceedings.

United States v. John ("Jack") Elder[11]

On April 13, 1984, federal marshals entered Casa Romero to arrest its director, Jack Elder, for transporting three Salvadorans, Valentin Cruz, Epifanio Canales and Transito Fuentes, to a bus station in Harlingen a full month earlier on March 12. Elder was charged and indicted by a federal grand jury on three counts of transporting undocumented aliens after the Salvadorans had identified him after their own arrests by the INS. This was the first time that the federal statute had been invoked to arrest anyone *after* the allegedly unlawful transportation had been completed. Furthermore, it was the first time that anyone had been arrested for unlawful transportation over such a short distance (Harlingen is only about six miles from San Benito).

Elder was asked to surrender voluntarily but he remained at Casa Romero, forcing the federal authorities to bring the Salvadorans with them for a one-person show-up identification of Elder and of the car used in the allegedly unlawful transportation.[12] The arrest also marked the first time that governmental authorities intruded upon a sanctuary's property to make an arrest. Elder, a former weekend volunteer at Casa Romero who left a high school teaching job to become its director, pleaded not guilty to all the charges.

In December, the venue for the trial was changed from Brownsville to Corpus Christi. Pre-trial hearings continued in January 1985. During a five-day pre-trial hearing on the defense's motion to dismiss based on Elder's First Amendment right to the free exercise of religion (see Chapter Four for legal analysis), United States District Court Judge Hayden Head, Jr. heard extensive testimony from various participants in the sanctuary movement. Judge Head found that Elder, a former Peace Corps worker in Costa Rica, did have a religious motivation for his actions. The judge specifically ruled:

> There is arguably a basis in Catholicism to demonstrate the activity charged in the indictment could fall within the religious beliefs of a seriously committed and practicing Catholic. This court rules they can.

A total of fifteen witnesses were ready to testify on Elder's behalf but the judge made his ruling after hearing only ten of them, finding that the evidence of religious motivation was sufficient. However, the prosecution was able to convince the judge that there was an overriding government interest in the enforcement of the immigration statute (apparently based on testimony by government witnesses that undocumented migrants hurt the United States economy) and the judge accordingly denied the motion to dismiss. The judge then also denied the other four defense motions to dismiss (including motions based on the rights of refugees to remain in the United States).

The trial proceeded on January 22, 1985, before a seven-man, five-woman jury. After less than two hours of deliberation following a two-day trial, the jury found Elder not guilty of the charges of unlawful transportation of undocumented aliens. Jurors told the press that the government had failed to prove that Elder was furthering the Salvadorans' violation of the immigration laws by giving them the short ride to the bus station.[13] (See, requirements for the crime of unlawful transportation of undocumented aliens in Chapter Four.)

United States v. Jack Elder and Stacey Merkt[14]

On December 4, 1984, a federal grand jury brought new indictments against Jack Elder and Stacey Merkt. Elder was still awaiting trial and Merkt was free on probation while awaiting the disposition of her appeal. Merkt was charged with two counts of transporting and one count of conspiracy (18 U.S.C. § 371). Elder was charged with one count of conspiracy, two counts of transporting, two counts of bringing into and landing in the U.S. undocumented persons, and one additional count of conspiracy with unknown persons to bring into and land in the U.S. undocumented persons. The indictment alleged that Elder and Merkt had helped two Salvadorans into the United States and transported them from Casa Romero to a bus depot in McAllen, Texas.

Merkt was arrested on December 6 for violating the conditions of her probation. Elder and Merkt were arraigned on December 10. Bail for Merkt was set at $25,000 cash and for Elder at $2,500 cash. The Roman Catholic bishop of Brownsville, whose diocese funds Casa Romero, personally secured the money for their release.

In February 1985, the case went to trial before United States District Court Judge Filomen Vela. Judge Vela first moved the venue of the trial from Brownsville to Houston because he found that an impartial jury could not be impaneled in Brownsville after all the pre-trial publicity about the sanctuary movement. However, in an unusual decision, the judge decided to go to Houston himself to preside over the trial rather than letting the judges in the Houston district preside over the trial on February 20 and 21.[15]

The main witness called by the prosecution was Salvadoran Jose Andrea Mendez-Valle, who testified that Merkt and Elder had helped him and four other aliens (three of them being juvenile cousins of Mendez-Valle) across the United States-Mexico border. However, Mendez-Valle also admitted that border agents had told him that they would help him to visit relatives in Washington, D.C. and that they would not deport him if he cooperated with their investigation. Another prosecution witness, a ticket agent at the McAllen bus station, testified but failed to identify Merkt as the person who had purchased bus tickets for the Salvadorans.

The defense presented testimony from the other adult Salvadoran, Maria Caetena Rosales Cruz, who could not identify either

Elder or Merkt as the persons who helped them. The defense also presented extensive testimony from several witnesses (including airline agents and Merkt's probation officer) that Merkt was in Long Island, New York attending a wedding on November 21, 1984, the date the prosecution alleged that she drove the Salvadorans from Casa Romero to McAllen. The defense was not allowed to present any evidence about United States refugee law or about the religious motivations of the defendants.

A jury of ten men and two women, after four hours of deliberation, found Merkt not guilty of the unlawful transportation counts but guilty of the conspiracy count. The jury also found Elder guilty on all six counts against him. On March 26, Judge Vela revoked Merkt's earlier probation and on March 27, sentenced Merkt to serve the 90-day sentence for the earlier conviction, to run concurrently with an order to serve 179 days of an 18-month sentence for the conspiracy conviction. The judge also ordered Merkt to disassociate herself from Casa Romero and not to speak publicly about the sanctuary movement pending any appeals. However, she remains free until her appeals are heard. On March 27, Elder refused the same conditions offered to him for a two-year probation term and was therefore sentenced to six one-year prison terms, to run concurrently. However, Judge Vela was persuaded by defense attorneys to reconsider the sentence, and on March 28 Vela reduced the sentence to 150 days in a halfway house. Elder began serving his sentence in April.

United States v. Aguilar, Clark, Conger, Corbett, Emery, Espinosa, Fife, Flaherty, Hutchison, LeWin, MacDonald, Martel-Benavidez, Nicgorski, Priester, Quinones and Waddell[16]

On January 14, 1985, the U.S. Attorney in Phoenix, Arizona announced a 71-count indictment against sixteen sanctuary workers from Arizona and Mexico. The first count charges the sixteen with conspiracy to bring "illegal aliens" into the United States and to harbor, conceal and transport them to places throughout the United States. The remaining seventy counts charge one or more of the sixteen indictees with specific acts punishable under 8 U.S.C. § 1324(a).

The indictees are:

Rev. John M. Fife, pastor of Southside United Presbyterian Church in Tucson, which was one of the first churches to publicly declare sanctuary in March 1982;

James A. Corbett, the retired Quaker rancher who largely initiated the sanctuary movement and the underground railroad;

Philip M. Conger (who has recently married and changed his last name to Willis-Conger), director of the Tucson Ecumenical Council Task Force on Central America, who was arrested and indicted on an unlawful transportation charge in the spring of 1984 but had the charges dismissed on a legal technicality, as previously stated;

Katherina M. Flaherty, also of the Task Force, who was arrested with Conger in 1984 but never had charges brought against her;

Sr. Darlene Nicgorsky, a School Sister of St. Francis and a former missionary in Guatemala who also worked with refugees in Mexico and was hired by the Chicago Religious Task Force on Central America to help prepare refugees arriving in Arizona for entry into sanctuary sites across the United States;

Peggy Hutchison, who works with Methodist Metropolitan Ministries in Tucson;

Fr. Antonio Clark, a Roman Catholic priest at Sacred Heart Church in Nogales, Arizona;

Sr. Mary Waddell, a Sister of Charity of the Blessed Virgin Mary in Phoenix;

Sr. Ana Priester, from the same religious order;

Cecilia del Carmen Juarez de Emery, a Salvadoran living in Phoenix;

Mary Kay Espinosa, a secretary for the Association of Educational Reform at Sacred Heart Church;

Wendy LeWin, a volunteer church worker from Phoenix;

Nena McDonald, a college student, nurse and mother of two from Lubbock, Texas, who had worked as a volunteer for the TEC Task Force during the summer of 1984;

Fr. Ramon Dagoberto Quinones, a Roman Catholic priest from Nogales, Sonora, Mexico, and pastor of the Sanctuary of Our Lady of Guadalupe and St. Martin church;

Maria del Socorro Pardo de Aguilar, also from Nogales, Sonora, Mexico;

Bertha Martel-Benavidez, a Salvadoran working in a laundry in Phoenix.

The indictment also names 49 refugees as "illegal alien unindicted co-conspirators" and 25 other sanctuary workers as "unindicted co-conspirators." While it is unlikely that these persons will be indicted later, many of the refugees have been arrested and placed into deportation proceedings. The "unindicted co-conspirators" have been subpoenaed to testify against the defendants under a grant of immunity, whereby they would have no right to refuse to testify or otherwise invoke the constitutional protections of the Fifth Amendment.

The U.S. Attorney has also filed a motion *in limine* along with the indictment, seeking to prohibit any testimony or evidence (1) that the aliens involved were refugees, (2) that the defendants' conduct was justified as a result of their religious beliefs, or any other good motives and beliefs which might negate the requisite criminal intent, (3) regarding any "alleged episodes, stories or tales of civil strife, war or terrorism that may have occurred or are occurring in Central American countries" which contributed to the presence of the aliens in the United States or the defendants' beliefs about them, (4) regarding the number of aliens from Central America who have applied for and have been granted or denied asylum under the Refugee Act of 1980, and the comparison of such statistics with asylum policies for aliens from "either Communist-dominated governments or countries undergoing a Socialist or Communist revolution," and (5) involving any reference to the Department of State, Central Intelligence Agency, Department of Defense, or any other federal agencies or international organizations associated with those departments. The purported rationale of the government's motion is that the case only involves the smuggling of undocumented aliens and should not include what the prosecution regards as extraneous issues.[17]

While the indictment alleges that the conspiracy began "about late 1981 or early 1982," the specific facts charged concern the time period between April 30, 1984 and January 7, 1985. During that time, two informant infiltrators, Jesus Cruz and Salomon Delgado (who also used the aliases "Solomon Graham" and "Jose Morales"), posed as sanctuary workers and gained the trust of the nationwide network of churches and church workers. However, they were collecting evidence through body wiretaps while they participated in the planning, discussion, and implementation of sanctuary activity. Supervised by two INS agents, Cruz and Delgado recorded over one hundred hours of conversations, and meetings, which has been transcribed into 40,000 pages of transcript evidence. Cruz and Delgado had been specifically recruited by the INS in Phoenix to infiltrate the sanctuary movement. They had admitted to participation in an 1980 alien smuggling operation for a Florida ranch but had become government witnesses in exchange for immunity from prosecution. Since that time, they had both worked on and off as informants for the INS.[18]

Over the weekend of January 14, over 60 refugees were arrested all across the United States (including Tucson and Phoenix, Arizona; Seattle, Washington; Philadelphia, Pennsylvania; Rochester, New York; and Germantown, Wisconsin) as the indictments were announced in Phoenix. It was initially unclear whether some of these refugees were arrested on INS warrants or on criminal warrants charging them as material witnesses/unindicted co-conspirators. However, all were released on bond or on their own recognizance. In several cases, the INS used the same ploy—calling a sanctuary church, asking for the current addresses of refugees on the pretense of wanting to deliver Christmas presents to them—as the method of discovering the exact location of the refugees in order to arrest them. Furthermore, the personal residences of several sanctuary workers indicted were broken into and thoroughly searched, and evidence was seized.

Thirteen of the sixteen indictees (two others, Fr. Ramon Dagoberto Quinones and Maria del Socorro Pardo de Aguilar, were Mexican citizens, over whom the United States District Court had no personal jurisdiction, and one requested a delay to obtain an attorney) were arraigned in the United States District Courts in Phoenix and Tucson on January 26. Some eight hundred to a thousand people marched through downtown Phoenix in support of the sanctuary workers while another thirteen hundred persons crowded into Temple Emanu-El in Tucson for the opening day of the Inter-American Symposium on sanctuary. All thirteen of the indictees pleaded not guilty to all charges. After the arraignments, eight of the defendants released a statement declaring their intent "to continue to engage in sanctuary ministry," despite their agreement not to violate any laws as a condition of their release without bond.

Meanwhile, the two Mexican nationals, Maria del Socorro Pardo de Aguilar and Fr. Ramon Dagoberto Quinones, presented themselves for indictment in Phoenix on February 21. Although they had not been properly served subpoenas through the Mexican government, they wish to stand trial with the United States citizens. The two Salvadoran women from Phoenix, Cecilia del Carmen Juarez de Emery and Berta Martel-Benavidez, have pleaded guilty to reduced misdemeanor charges and have been dropped from the case. Defense spokespersons speculate that these women were included in the indictment so that the trial could be held in Phoenix rather than Tucson, where all the other defendants reside. The defense will request a change of venue to Tucson for the trial. Finally, charges have been dismissed against Sisters Anna Priester and Mary Waddell. The government's reasoning was that Sr. Anna was too ill to stand trial and that Sr. Mary had to care for her. The two nuns have rejected the government's pretense of compassion, pointing out that Sr. Anna's Hodgkin's disease is in control and that Sr. Mary has a full-time job and is not needed to care for Sr. Anna. Both sisters declared that if the government wanted to show its compassion, it could show it to the refugees and the entire group of sanctuary workers. United States District Court Judge Earl H. Carroll has scheduled oral argument on the prosecution's motion *in limine* for May 21 and postponed the date of the trial to July 9, 1985.[19]

The Future

The announcement of the extensive undercover investigation and subsequent indictments in Arizona marked a turnaround in the government's response to the sanctuary movement. For months, the INS had remained skeptical about the seriousness of the sanctuary movement. The government's earlier position was well-summarized by Bill Joyce, Assistant General Counsel for the INS:

> We're not about to send investigators into a church and start dragging people out in front of the TV cameras. We'll just wait them out, wait until they leave the church. This is just a political thing that the churches are dreaming up to get publicity—a

game to pressure the government to allow Salvadorans to stay here. If we thought it was a significant problem, then maybe we'd take a look at it. But there are plenty of illegal aliens out there.[20]

Northern California District Director of the INS, David Il-chert, had echoed Joyce's sentiments:

I don't know whether they are seeking a direct confrontation with immigration or if these good religious people are seeking an avenue of publicity to espouse a foreign policy that is different to what the present administration has. . . . We are not seeking a confrontation with church groups. The major thrust of the INS enforcement is directed toward illegal aliens holding well-paying jobs that go to U.S. citizens or lawful residents. We go to work sites, not into neighborhoods, into homes or churches. The fact that some minister may call us up and say that some alien is living in his church, sleeping in his pew, would be a low priority for us.[21]

Bill Johnston from the Tucson INS office also pointed out:

It's not really cost effective to go after one alien in the back of a church or the back of a car on the way to Seattle. And it means nothing that the driver wears a Roman Catholic collar.[22]

On the other hand, government officials had always been quick to point out that there is no immunity for churches against prosecution. Washington, D.C. INS spokesperson Verne Jervis had warned:

It's illegal . . . there is nothing in the law that provides for sanctury in a church. But the law does prohibit harboring illegal aliens, and the churches know it. Most say quite publicly that they are violating the law.[23]

District Director Ilchert stated:

Some churches have supported ecclesiastical sanctuary, but there is no such legal entity. . . . We don't want a confrontation with churches. But if my officers have a proper warrant, they would have a legal right to go onto church property.[24]

In early 1984, INS Spokesperson Duke Austin had threatened: "We will have to put them [the sanctuary churches] on notice that this is civil disobedience and that sometime in the future they will be held accountable."[25] However, at the same time Austin had continued to downplay the importance of the movement: "When you put it into perspective, the sanctuary movement is really not that big and is receiving an unjustified amount of attention."[26] However, at least one INS official also acknowledged the highly volatile nature of the potential confrontation between government and the sanctuary churches. Leon Ring, chief of the Border Patrol in Tucson, admitted the political nature of the earlier policy of non-enforcement:

> This underground railroad—or the various church groups— wanted publicity. They were baiting us to overreact. Therefore, we have deliberately been very low-key. Certain arrests could have taken place if we wanted to, but we felt that the government would end up looking ridiculous, especially as far as going into church property—anything where the ethics involved would be questioned.[27]

Another INS official has acknowledged that the legal issues involving church sanctuary have not yet been finally decided. Beverly McFarland, spokesperson for the Miami, Florida INS district office, has said: "There is nothing under United States Immigration and Naturalization Service regulations that provides for sanctuary, but the issue has never been determined in court."[28]

Meanwhile, the "look the other way" attitude of the INS had two important consequences: it created a de facto[29] sanctuary or asylum for the Central American refugees and it provided temporary immunity to the churches from prosecution for harboring the refugees. The government policy of non-enforcement had in fact created a twentieth century sanctuary privilege in America.

CHAPTER FOUR

Legal Implications for Sanctuaries and Sanctuary Workers

"There must be a distinction between acts performed with the purpose of supporting or promoting an alien's illegal conduct, and acts which are incidental to or merely permit an individual to maintain his existence, albeit his existence occurs in this country and he is not duly admitted here."[1]

—United States District Court, District of Kansas, May 1984

Sanctuary Under United States Law

The legal privilege of sanctuary has never been directly considered by the American courts. The only known reference to the privilege was made by Justice William Douglas in the 1967 United States Supreme Court case, *Warden, Maryland Penitentiary v. Hayden:*[2]

> The right of privacy protected by the Fourth Amendment relates in part of course to the precincts of the home or office. But it does not make them sanctuaries where the law can never reach. There are such places in the world. A mosque in Fez, Morocco, that I have visited, is by custom a sanctuary where any refugee may hide, safe from police intrusion. We have no sanctuaries here.[3]

The Fourth Amendment provides the closest legal parallel to the privilege of sanctuary. In the same case, the United States Supreme Court recognized an historical and legislative intent by the authors of the Fourth Amendment to "preserve a zone of privacy which no government official may enter": namely, a person's home.[4] However, this protection had its roots in the English common law concept that "a man's home is his castle"[5] rather than in any privilege claimed by the churches. Furthermore, this sanctuary of the home is never absolute; it may be easily invaded with a proper search warrant. Justice Douglas wrote in *Osborn v. United States:*[6]

> A home is still a sanctuary, however the owner may use it. . . .
> This does not mean he can make his sanctuary invasion-proof
> against government agents. The Constitution has provided a
> way whereby the home can lawfully be invaded, and that is with
> a search warrant.[7]

Thus, the United States legal system has not recognized any historical privilege of sanctuary.[8]

Many in the sanctuary movement and in the media have referred to Canon 1179 of the Code of Canon Law of the Roman Catholic Church as a basis for a sanctuary privilege. This Canon from the 1917 Code reads:

> A church enjoys the right of asylum, so that guilty persons who
> take refuge in it must not be taken from it, except in the case of
> necessity, without the consent of the ordinary, or at least of the
> rector of the church.[9]

However, this particular Canon was not included in the 1983 revision of the Code of Canon Law.[10] Thus, although it still may be invoked by Roman Catholic churches as part of its traditional or customary Canon Law, its force even within the church has been significantly diminished. Furthermore, the Canon has never been applied or invoked in the United States. Since there is no concordat between the Vatican and the United States government detailing which of the Canons of the church shall be binding in this country, the Code of Canon Law of the Roman Catholic Church will not be incorporated into the jurisprudence of any court of the United

States.[11] Despite the recent upgrading of diplomatic relations between the Vatican and the United States, no such concordat is likely to be agreed upon in the future. Finally, any provision of Canon Law that directly contradicted a "secular" federal statute would probably not supersede the Congressional enactment. (See section on First Amendment Free Exercise of Religion later in this chapter.) Thus, Canon 1179 remains an antiquated remnant of the medieval sanctuary privilege, with diminished authority even within its own denominational jurisprudence. Any force it adds to the current sanctuary movement's legal arguments are derived only from its moral force rather than from any concrete legal principle or precedent.

Unlawful Harboring and Transportation of Undocumented Aliens

Thus, the courts have not yet determined whether a legal privilege of sanctuary exists under United States law.[12] The recent prosecution of sanctuary workers in Texas and Arizona have focused on the unlawful transporting rather than the unlawful sheltering of undocumented aliens. Both crimes are defined in the same federal statute and this analysis will consider them together, with emphasis on the harboring provisions which are the most directly relevant to any legal liability for the provision of sanctuary.

The harboring or transporting of an undocumented alien (one not duly admitted by an immigration officer or not lawfully entitled to enter or reside within the United States) is a federal felony punishable by a $2,000 fine and/or five years imprisonment. The liability and penalty can be imposed for *each* alien unlawfully harbored or transported. Section 274(a) of the 1952 Immigration and Nationality Act, now codified as 8 U.S.C. § 1324(a), provides:

> Any person, including the owner, operator, pilot, master, commanding officer, agent, or consignee of any means of transportation who—
>
> 1) brings into or lands in the United States, by any means of transportation or otherwise, or attempts, by himself or

through another, to bring into or land in the United States, by any means of transportation or otherwise;

2) knowing that he is in the United States in violation of law, and knowing or having reasonable grounds to believe that his last entry into the United States occurred less than three years prior thereto, transports, or moves, or attempts to transport or move, within the United States by means of transportation or otherwise, in furtherance of such violation of law;

3) willfully or knowingly conceals, harbors, or shields from detection, or attempts to conceal, harbor, or shield from detection, in any place, including any building or any means of transportation; or

4) willfully or knowingly encourages or induces, or attempts to encourage or induce, either directly or indirectly, the entry into the United States of—

any alien, including an alien crewman, not duly admitted by an immigration officer or not lawfully entitled to enter or reside within the United States under the terms of this chapter or any other law relating to the immigration or expulsion of aliens, shall be found guilty of a felony, and upon conviction thereof shall be punished by a fine not exceeding $2,000 or by imprisonment for a term not exceeding five years, or both, for each alien in respect to whom any violation of this subsection occurs: Provided, however, that for the purposes of this section, employment (including the usual and normal practices incident to employment) shall not be deemed to constitute harboring.

The specific provision regarding the harboring, concealing and shielding of undocumented aliens, § 1324(a) (3), appears misplaced in a statute that seems targeted primarily at the smuggling of aliens into the country. The statute's legislative history reveals part of the reason for this disjointed structure.

Section 1324(a) (3) was enacted in 1952 in response to the holding of the United States Supreme Court in *United States v. Evans*.[13] In *Evans*, the Supreme Court held that there was no penalty for concealing or harboring aliens not entitled to enter or reside in the

United States under § 8 of the Immigration Act of 1917[14] and affirmed the dismissal of the indictments for concealing and harboring five named aliens. The Supreme Court noted that the 1917 amendment to the original 1907 Act[15] had added the prohibition against concealing or harboring aliens but that the penalty for a violation of the amended prohibitions had been left "undefined and too vague for reasonable assurance of its meaning."[16] Specifically, the Court found that the penalty provisions of § 8 applied unambiguously only to landing, bringing in, or attempting to land and or bring in aliens and not to concealing, harboring, or attempting to conceal or harbor the aliens.[17] Finally, the unanimous Court invited Congressional response:

> This is a task [of construction] outside the bounds of judicial interpretation. It is better for Congress, and more in accord with its function, to revise the statute than for us to guess as to the revision it would make. That task it can do with precision. We could only do no more than make speculation law.[18]

Such Congressional response came four years later with the passage of § 274 of the 1952 Immigration and Nationality Act, which amended the section into its present form.[19] However, the ambiguity of whether harboring or concealing aliens was a separate offense, without some relation to the process of smuggling aliens, still remained.

The first appellate court to consider the meaning of the old 1917 statute was the Sixth Circuit Court of Appeals. In *Susnjar v. United States*,[20] the court held:

> One of the principal objects of the immigration statutes is to exclude from the country all aliens who have unlawfully succeeded in effecting an entry. [Citation.]
>
> When taken in connection with the purposes of the act, we conceive the natural meaning of the word "harbor" to be to clandestinely shelter, succor, and protect improperly admitted aliens, and that the word "conceal" should be taken in the simple sense of shielding from observation and preventing discovery of such alien persons.[21]

The Court affirmed the convictions for concealing and harboring aliens in homes in Detroit and Cleveland (and transporting them between the two cities). In 1940, the Second Circuit relied on the *Susnjar* definitions in *United States v. Smith*,[22] holding that "harbor" meant "sheltered from the immigration authorities and shielded from observation to prevent their discovery as aliens."[23] Thus, the defendants' convictions for maintaining alien women from Canada in a house of prostitution were affirmed. It was no defense that the prostitutes did have some limited contact with the public, that is, with their customers. The defendant still maintained sufficient secrecy to be liable under the statute. In another 1940 case, *United States v. Mack*, involving a Canadian prostitute in the same Court of Appeals, Judge Learned Hand held that the word "harbor" often connotes "surreptitious concealment."[24] However, since the statute also required the defendant's knowledge of the alienage of the person harbored and there was insufficient evidence of such knowledge, the conviction for unlawful harboring was reversed.

These three Court of Appeals decisions were the only precedents existing before the 1952 amendment to the statute.[25] It is clear that the statute, as interpreted by these initial decisions, was directed at conduct quite different from that of sanctuary churches today. Two cases involved houses of prostitution near the Canadian border, where the immigration law violations seemed to be one way for the federal authorities to control international prostitution. The third case did involve the inland transportation of aliens, but only as part of a larger smuggling operation.[26] Thus, the motives of all the defendants were purely commercial. In contrast, there is no profit motive involved in the sanctuary movement. Instead, the sanctuary workers aid the refugees because of their humanitarian, religious and political beliefs.

It was not until 1975 that an appellate court considered the meaning of the statute in light of the 1952 amendment. In *United States v. Lopez*,[27] the defendant was the owner of several single-family homes in New York and lodged undocumented aliens for $15 a week. Lopez also provided assistance obtaining employment for the aliens, transported them to and from their jobs, arranged sham marriages with United States citizens, and prepared their applications for United States citizenship.

The Second Circuit Court of Appeals repudiated its earlier decisions in *Smith* and *Mack* and held that the word "harbor" was "intended to encompass conduct tending substantially to facilitate an alien's remaining in the United States illegally, provided, of course, the person charged has knowledge of the alien's unlawful status."[28] Thus, the Court rejected any requirement of secrecy or surreptitious conduct and broadened the meaning of "harbor" to a dictionary definition of "to give shelter or refuge."[29]

In its enthusiasm to sweep all of the defendant's activities within the prohibition of the statute, the court greatly expanded the scope of criminal liability under § 1324(a). First, the court noted that the United States Supreme Court in *United States v. Evans* had raised the possibility that "harbor" might reasonably be construed to encompass the sheltering of aliens unrelated to the smuggling of aliens to the United States. The Second Circuit lamented the absence of a clear Congressional definition of the word "harbor"[30] but then judicially adopted a standard of criminal liability that included activities unrelated to smuggling. This interpretation of the statute departed from prior decisions that viewed the statute only in the context of smuggling or other illegal activity such as international prostitution. While the defendant in *Lopez* was obviously engaged in a complex, profit-making enterprise, many of his activities, such as providing transportation or assisting applications,[31] were innocuous. It is unclear whether the *Lopez* court intended to create criminal liability for each of these acts standing alone or only as part of the elaborate business of this particular defendant. However, if each of the activities of the defendant Lopez could be prosecuted separately as a violation of § 1324(a), then it has conceivably become a federal felony not only to transport and shelter an undocumented alien, but also to simply give one a ride to work.

Second, the broad "substantial facilitation" definition articulated by the Second Circuit places great importance on the *mens rea* or mental element of the crime. Every crime requires both a *mens rea* and an *actus reus*, or conduct.[31a] Since the *actus reus* of substantial facilitation can be committed by numerous persons and institutions—bus drivers, hotels, even hospitals—it becomes critical that such persons are distinguished and not held liable under the statute. Thus, the prosecution in a § 1324(a) case must carefully establish the requisite knowledge of the alien's unlawful status and criminal willfulness in order to establish criminal liability.

Two other Courts of Appeals have followed the *Lopez* "substantial facilitation" definition.[32] In *United States v. Acosta de Evans*,[33] the Ninth Circuit specifically questioned the continued validity of the *Susnjar* definition of "harbor" and instead construed "harbor" to mean "afford shelter to."[34] In a footnote, the Court also expressly recognized that harboring did not necessarily involve smuggling since § 1324(a) (3) was "aimed at preventing aliens from remaining in the United States as well as preventing aliens from entering."[35] In another footnote, the Court drew a distinction between the phrases "harbor," "conceal," and "shield from detection" but did not elaborate on their differences.[36] This was the first judicial indication that separate meanings would be assigned to the different terms in the statute, possibly resulting in independent offenses under each distinct term.

The defendant in *Acosta de Evans* was acquitted of harboring four aliens who alleged that they were in the defendant's apartment by chance when the Border Patrol agents arrived and were only there *en passant*. Thus, the requirement of knowledge of specific intent was still critical to criminal liability. However, the defendant's conviction for harboring a relative who the defendant knew was illegally in the country and had been living at the apartment for two months was affirmed. This was the first conviction upheld by an appellate court for assisting a friend or a relative in a non-business relationship. The class of new criminals was being steadily broadened.

In the 1977 case, *United States v. Cantu*,[37] the Fifth Circuit adopted verbatim the *Lopez* substantial facilitation definition of "harbor."[38] The Court affirmed the conviction of an employer who had assisted his undocumented alien employees in their attempt to escape from INS agents in the employer's restaurant. The defendant employer had demanded a warrant from the agents, had solicited rides from restaurant patrons for the aliens, and had helped the aliens change clothes and leave through the restaurant's rear door.[39] Thus, the Court applied the *Lopez* definition in yet another distinct fact situation, unrelated to either smuggling or sheltering activities.

In *Cantu*, the Fifth Circuit also tried to provide some further definitions of the statutory terms, concluding that "shield from detection" did not mean to hide but that "conceal" did.[40] Furthermore, the Court rejected any arguments that the terms were vague or overbroad.[41] The Court also held that the words "in any place" were meant to be "broadly inclusive, not restrictive."[42]

In 1981, the Fifth Circuit continued to follow the *Lopez* definition in *United States v. Varkonki*[43] and affirmed the conviction of the defendant. This was another case where an employer sought to protect his undocumented alien employees from INS agents. Here the scrap metal yard proprietor twice physically assaulted an INS agent trying to enter the premises and also gave verbal warnings to his employees regarding the presence of the INS. The defendant then repeatedly insisted to the agents that the employees were documented while attempting to persuade the employees not to surrender to arrest.[44]

The Fifth Circuit again applied the *Lopez* definition to an employment situation in *United States v. Rubio-Gonzales*.[45] However, in this case, the defendant was an employee. When stopped and questioned by plainclothes INS agents, the defendant produced documentation identifying himself as a lawful resident alien. The INS agents followed the defendant, however, and observed him "gesturing and apparently pointing in the agents' direction."[46] The INS agents themselves were still too distant to hear the defendant but the aliens that the defendant was addressing later testified that he had said, in Spanish, either "immigration" or "immigration is here."[47] Based on this testimony and the fact that the warned aliens then dropped their tools and attempted to flee, the Fifth Circuit ruled that the defendant had substantially facilitated the warned aliens' remaining in the United States illegally.

The *Rubio-Gonzalez* decision raised many more questions about § 1324(a) (3) than it answered.[48] First, the Fifth Circuit cavalierly acknowledged that the evidence concerning the defendant's critical *mens rea* "was wholly circumstantial" and then concluded that it was "amply sufficient."[49] Given the extremely broad scope of punishable conduct under the *Lopez* substantial facilitation definition, this casual treatment of the *mens rea* requirement is profoundly disturbing. Indeed, the Court found that the requisite *mens rea* existed because (1) the defendant had made five illegal entries himself, at least two of which were similar to those of the warned aliens; (2) as an alien himself, he "had the opportunity to become aware" of the documentation required of aliens and the procedure for gaining legal-resident status; (3) in the several months that the warned aliens worked at the company, they had spoken with the defendant, who was their foreman, only in Spanish; (4) the two warned aliens and the defendant were all from the same state in Mexico; (5) the defendant's brother was also an undocumented alien working at the same site; (6) there were several other "illegal aliens" working at the same company.[50] In essence, the Fifth Circuit imputed the knowledge requirement to the defendant based on his own immigration history and the circumstances at his place of employment over which he had no personal control or responsibility. Indeed, the Court seemed to place the burden of proof on the criminal defendant to prove the *absence* of the requisite *mens rea* by rhetorically asking what other reason the defendant had for such "precipitous action" and noting that no other explanation of his conduct had been proffered by the defendant.[51] If the *mens rea* required for criminal felony liability can now be imputed from such facts as the defendant's place of birth or general knowledge of the United States immigration law, *and* if the defendant has the burden of proof to rebut such imputed knowledge, then the potential sweep of § 1324(a) (3) is almost limitless.

Furthermore, the only *actus reus* committed by the defendant was pointing in the direction of the INS agents and uttering a single phrase. While similar acts may have been punished under the statute in prior cases, the defendants in those cases also committed other affirmative acts such as delaying the INS agents and actively arranging escape in *Cantu*, or physically assaulting the INS agents in *Varkonki*. Here, the defendant cooperated completely with the INS agents and did not deter their investigation in any way. However, the Court rejected the argument that "shield from detection" implies any requirement that a physical barrier, trick or artifice be involved.[52] The Court's decision has thus made a simple warning—consisting of a single gesture and the utterance of a single phrase—a federal felony. One commentator wonders whether a casual glance in the presence of INS officials will be the next factual basis of criminal liability under such an expansive interpretation of § 1324(a) (3).[53]

Despite its extremely broad interpretation of the statute, the Fifth Circuit Court in *Rubio-Gonzalez* continued to struggle with the similarities and differences between the terms "harbor," "conceal," and "shield from detection." The Court first stated:

> Section 1324(a) (3) by its express terms may be violated in any one of several ways by harboring, *or* by concealing, *or* by shielding from detection *or* by attempting to do any of these. . . . It matters not whether the particular conduct and state of mind at issue be labeled "harboring" or "concealing" or "shielding from detection," for each are [sic] equally violative of subparagraph (3). [emphasis in original][54]

However, in a long footnote, the Court stopped short of rejecting any distinctions between the words:

> We do not construe section 1324(a) (3) as constituting harboring, concealing and shielding from detection as distinct offenses, each separate and distinct from the other. Rather, we view it as proscribing a single offense which may be committed in different ways. . . . Our decisions have referred to subparagraph (3) as a unitary whole. . . . We do not suggest the words "harbor," "conceal," and "shield from detection" are synonymous. . . .[55]

Specifically, the Court noted, as did the Ninth Circuit in *Acosta de Evans*,[56] that the employment proviso at the end of § 1324(a) applies only to harboring. Thus, the Fifth Circuit could only be equivocal in its attempt to provide a definitive interpretation of subparagraph (3):

> We feel the failure to extend the employment proviso to "conceal" and "shield from detection" reflects merely a prudential limitation on the reach of the provision, coupled with the recognition that "harbor" is perhaps a somewhat broader concept than "conceal" or "shield from detection," rather than an indication that Congress intended to provide for three distinct and separate offenses in subparagraph (3).[57]

Such semantic hairsplitting is more than an academic exercise in statutory interpretation. The increase in the number of appellate cases construing the statute since 1972 reflects an attempt by the

federal courts to pinpoint its meaning. However, the current definition adopted by the Second, Ninth and Fifth Circuits is extremely
broad and has the potential of making criminal many acts that were
never originally contemplated by Congress. Although the Court in
Rubio-Gonzalez went the farthest in expanding the scope of the statute, it was also the most confused in its statutory interpretation. The
Court could not resolve whether the statute was creating a single
offense or whether each term constituted a separate offense. While
acknowledging differences in meaning between the statutory terms,
the Court never adequately defined or distinguished each of the
terms. Notably, the United States Supreme Court has denied review in several of these cases, i.e. *Lopez*, *Acosta de Evans* and *Cantu*,
perhaps allowing the lower appellate courts to continue to work out
the precise meaning of the statute. However, the current substantial
facilitation definition presents many difficulties and dangers.

Defenses

Sanctuary Activity Outside the Statute. Several arguments
might be raised as defenses to the criminal prosecution of sanctuary
churches and workers for the unlawful harboring and transporting
of Central American refugees. First, the churches might argue that
certain behavior involving the sheltering and assisting of undocumented aliens is not prohibited by the statute. A starting point for
such an argument can be derived from the observation of the Fifth
Circuit Court of Appeals in *Rubio-Gonzalez:*

> The full reach of section 1324(a) (3) in every imaginable situation
> is not before us. We need not determine in this case whether one
> can conceive of willful or knowing conduct tending to substan-
> tially facilitate an alien's remaining in the United States illegally
> that nevertheless might not be within a fair reading of the words
> knowingly or willfully harboring, concealing or shielding from
> detection an illegal alien or attempting to do so.[58]

As a penal statute, § 1324(a) is to be construed in favor of the
defendant.[59] Thus, any doubts as to whether a sanctuary worker's
conduct is proscribed by the statute should be resolved in favor of
the sanctuary worker. Furthermore, courts should strive to construe
any statute in accordance with the intent of Congress in enacting the

legislation.[60] When § 1324(a) was enacted, Congress could not have foreseen that churches would become involved in a sanctuary movement and that these churches would be prosecuted under this statute. In the absence of a clear legislative intent to punish the activity of the sanctuary churches, any doubts should be resolved in favor of the potential defendants.

One possible interpretation of the statute that would exclude the activity of the sanctuary churches is that § 1324(a) intended to punish only activity motivated by commercial advantage or private profit. Although proposed legislation is always a dubious guide to statutory interpretation, it is noteworthy that such a clarifying amendment to § 1324(a) was part of the final House of Representatives version of the Simpson-Mazzoli bills considered by the 98th Congress.[61] In the Congressional debate, Representative Miller (D.-Calif.) urged support for the clarifying amendment because he argued that the law should not make criminal the good faith efforts of those helping aliens applying for asylum.[62] One should not overlook the fact that the sanctuary churches have entirely different motivations than persons previously prosecuted under § 1324(a).[63] None of the churches are profiting monetarily from their sanctuary activities.

On the other hand, the expansiveness of the *Lopez* substantial facilitation definition would not permit such a restrictive reading of the statute. The courts using that definition have displayed an eagerness to sweep almost any related activity into the prohibition of the statute. Thus, the churches may then have to argue that the substantial facilitation definition itself is too broad and therefore impermissible.[64]

Lawful Refugees Are Not "Illegal Aliens." Another legal argument that might be raised on behalf of a sanctuary church worker is that no crime has been committed because the aliens assisted are lawfully entitled to remain in the United States. Such an argument would have two components. First, it would negate the specific intent required for the crime. Part of the knowledge required for conviction under § 1324(a) is the knowledge that the alien assisted is not duly admitted by an immigration officer or not lawfully entitled to enter or reside within the United States. At least one court has expressly recognized that a defendant's reasonable belief that the aliens were not aliens at all or that they had been legally admitted to the

United States is a defense to a criminal prosecution under §
1324(a).[65] Given the lengthy and often uncertain process of granting
asylum status to refugees from Central America, the sanctuary
workers could raise their reasonable belief that the aliens are entitled
to asylum as a defense to the charge under § 1324(a). This argument
would become problematic where the aliens had not yet applied for
asylum. However, an argument still might be made that the aliens'
status was uncertain pending such an application.

Second, the government has the burden of proving that the
aliens involved are not lawfuly entitled to enter or reside in the
United States under the terms of *any* law relating to immigration.[66]
In all the relevant cases, this critical fact regarding the immigration
status of the involved alien was either admitted by the defendant or
assumed, without any challenge from the defendant, by the court.
No such admission would be made by churches and sanctuary
workers prosecuted under the statute. Quite to the contrary, they
would argue that the aliens they were assisting have a right to remain
in the United States under both international and domestic law. (See
Chapter Two.) The strategic advantage of such an argument from
a defendant's point of view is that it shifts the focus of the inquiry
away from the conduct of the defendant and onto the status of the
alien. Such an argument would also put the government on the de-
fensive and would allow a judicial review of the government's refugee policies relating to Central Americans. The INS would be
required to justify its near-blanket denials of asylum to Salvadoran
and Guatemalan refugees, in contravention of the 1980 Refugee Act
and the United Nations Protocol.

The argument that the assisted refugees do have a legal basis
for remaining in the United States can be bolstered by a case arising
out of the "Freedom Flotilla" of Cuban refugees into the United
States in 1980. In an unusual *en banc* decision by all the judges of the
United States District Court for the Southern District of Florida,
United States v. Anaya,[67] the district court held that § 1324(a) only
applied to "surreptitious, fraudulent or evasive entry into this country by aliens."[68] Thus, "open, non-fraudulent presentation of aliens
to immigration officials" did not come under the prohibition of the
statute against aiding the unlawful entry of the Cubans.[69] The indictments against those that had transported the Cuban refugees
were accordingly dismissed.[70] The district court concluded:

The imposition of criminal penalties on those who merely aid aliens in lawfully seeking to apply to this country for political asylum would make a mockery of the often-quoted words of invitation inscribed on the Statue of Liberty.[71]

On appeal, the Court of Appeals for the Eleventh Circuit upheld the dismissal of the indictments.[72] However, the Court in *United States v. Zayas-Morales* based its decision on the government's failure to prove the requisite general criminal intent on the part of the defendants rather than on the technical "non-entry" of the Cuban refugees.[73] The Eleventh Circuit placed great weight on the section of the stipulated facts concerning the intent of all the defendants to present the aliens to the proper immigration authorities to facilitate their application for asylum. Such intent "to submit the aliens to proper authorities in full compliance with the law" necessarily negated the presence of the required criminal intent.[74]

While it is highly speculative to extend the rationale of this unusual case to the sanctuary situation, several parallels can be drawn. First, the churches could argue that Central American refugees today are in a comparable situation with the Cubans in *Anaya/Zayas-Morales*. Persons from both groups have prima facie claims to refugee status in the United States. The only difference is that the United States government ultimately chose to *ex post facto* grant the Cubans a special "entrant" status while continuing to deny asylum status to the Central Americans.

Second, the sanctuary churches could argue that they also lack the criminal intent required by the statute because they are also only seeking to assist the Central Americans to gain asylum in the United States. The churches might argue that it is only the government's failure to comply with its international and domestic law obligations that forces the aliens to resort to alternative methods of securing safe refuge.

While not based on the *Anaya/Zayas-Morales* case, a similar defense was raised in the Stacey Merkt trial and will be a critical argument in the appeal of her case. The defense for Stacey Merkt focuses on the 1983 Fifth Circuit decision, *United States v. Pereira-Pineda*,[75] construing the unlawful transportation section of the statute.[76] The *Pereira-Pineda* court affirmed the convictions of the defendant on five counts of unlawful transportation. The defendant had argued that the Salvadorans that he was transporting were automatically entitled to seek political asylum and therefore had a legal right to remain in the United States until they had fully ascertained and explored their right to apply for asylum. The court rejected this argument:

> The mere possibility that El Salvadorans may file asylum applications at some point in the future, and thus be allowed to remain at liberty under bond or parole while their right to asylum is determined, does not make them—from the moment they enter this country—entitled to "reside" here for the purposes of § 1324(a) (2).[77]

However, the *Pereira-Pineda* decision leaves several avenues of argument open for sanctuary workers prosecuted for unlawful transportation. First, the court acknowledged that a contrary decision had been reached by the First Circuit in *United States v. Kavazanjian*.[78] The First Circuit held that an elaborate profit-making scheme to aid Christians of Iraqui citizenship enter the United States from Greece in order to then apply for asylum in the United States[79] did not constitute a crime under § 1324(a) (4).[80] The court first discussed whether a technical entry had occurred when the aliens were given parole status after they filed their applications for asylum.[81] The court ruled that although the aliens and the defendants may have made fraudulent misrepresentations regarding their entry, the aliens were "nonetheless lawfully entitled to seek asylum and to reside in this country if successful in obtaining parole."[82] Thus, the First Circuit recognized that a defendant is entitled to raise the ultimate status of the involved alien, even if not determined until a later date, as a defense to the criminal charge under § 1324(a). If this argument were applied to a transporting or harboring situation involving sanctuary workers, then the refugee status of the aliens, even if not determined until some later date, may be properly raised as a defense to the criminal prosecution.

However, the Fifth Circuit in *Pereira-Pineda* declined to follow the First Circuit's reasoning in *Kavazanjian*.[83] Instead, the Fifth Circuit looked to its own precedent in a 1983 case, *United States v. Hanna*.[84] In *Hanna*, the defendant was the captain of a vessel which had transported one hundred and forty-eight Haitians from Haiti to

Miami, Florida. Upon his arrival in Miami, he contacted the police and informed them that he had picked up his passengers from a stranded cay in the Bahamas.[85] In *Hanna*, the Fifth Circuit had distinguished the situation of the defendant before it from the defendant in *Kavazanjian* and held that the possibility of parole for the involved aliens should not be a defense to a § 1324(a) charge.[86]

Thus, there is still no clear consensus among the appellate courts on the question of whether the status of the involved alien, determined to be lawful at a later date, will provide a defense for one prosecuted under § 1324(a). This unresolved issue is further complicated by the fact that both the *Kavazanjian* and *Hanna* decisions were decided before the new asylum and withholding of deportation sections were created by the 1980 Refugee Act. These sections make explicit the right to apply for asylum, where the aliens in the earlier cases could only hope for discretionary parole status.

Furthermore, in *Pereira-Pineda*, the defendant made two fatal stipulations: first, that he knew that the aliens were not duly admitted by an immigration officer and did not otherwise possess documents permitting entry,[87] and, second, that he had no intention of aiding the aliens in any efforts to apply for asylum.[88] The defendant seemed to argue that simply because the aliens were *theoretically* eligible to apply for asylum, they therefore had an *absolute* right to reside in the United States.[89] Such a position is untenable since it would force the courts to grant all aliens with any theoretical claim to asylum the right to remain lawfully in the United States.

On the other hand, absent such stipulations, the trial court judge in *Pereira-Pineda* expressly recognized a defense to a charge under the statute for those seeking to assist aliens actually applying for asylum:

> . . . if a person is bringing people into this country for the idea of rescuing them from oppression, for the purpose of driving them to the nearest immigration officer to turn themselves in for asylum, I think that is a defense.[90]

Such a defense would also be consistent with the Eleventh Circuit's decision in *Zayas-Morales*. The sanctuary workers might then be able to present evidence of their knowledge of the specific facts that would provide a basis for the asylum claims of the aliens they were assisting. They may also be able to present evidence of their knowledge of the near-blanket denials of those applications for asylum by the INS and the need to transport the asylum applicants away from the border. This futility argument is crucial because the 1980 Act does not specify where or when to file for asylum. A convincing argument could be advanced that the conduct of the sanctuary workers which is prosecuted as the unlawful harboring or transporting of the Central Americans is actually necessary assistance to enable the refugees to apply for asylum at their intended destination in the United States, or at an INS office where there might be a more receptive hearing of their asylum claims. (See Humanitarian Transportation defense, explained later in this chapter.)

All the courts that have considered the question have agreed that the burden of proof is upon the government to prove that the alien or aliens involved are not lawfully entitled to enter or remain in the United States under the terms of any law relating to immigration.[91] Such laws clearly include those relating to refugee status or asylum in the United States. The only disagreement focuses on when such a lawful status is to be considered and recognized. One could argue that the status of a refugee is not dependent upon a formal determination by the INS. Indeed, the *UNHCR Handbook* sets forth this interpretation of refugee status:

> A person is a refugee within the meaning of the 1951 Convention as soon as he fulfills the criteria contained in the definition. This would necessarily occur *prior* to the time at which his refugee status is formally determined. *Recognition of his refugee status does not therefore make him a refugee but declares him to be one.* He does not become a refugee because of recognition, but is recognized because he is a refugee (emphasis added).[92]

In other words, the status of a refugee is a conclusion of law based solely on a set of facts that need not and cannot be changed by any governmental discretion, or worse, misapplication of law. The role of the government vis-à-vis refugees is therefore only declarative and not constitutive.[93] The government's only role is to confer legal rights, benefits and privileges upon those it recognizes as refugees. However, in the case of a criminal prosecution against a sanctuary worker for unlawfully harboring or transporting an alien, the alien involved is not seeking any legal rights or privileges. The legal status of the alien is only relevant in establishing one essential element of the crime charged against another person. If there is any reasonable doubt about the involved alien's legal status, then the prosecution will have failed to prove the criminal charge.

Equal Protection Under the Employment Proviso. The knowledge and motivations of the defendants in any prosecution for sanctuary activity also raises the possibility of a defense based on the employment proviso in § 1324(a).[94] This proviso, found at the end of § 1324(a), exempts "unwitting employers" from the prohibitions against harboring undocumented aliens.[95] The defendant still has the burden of showing that the employment in question is "usual and normal to the industry generally, not just the employer's own practice."[96] Thus, the proviso only exempts bona fide employment activities rather than any activity which the defendent believes to be employment.[97] Finally, the proviso only provides a defense to the criminal charge of "harboring" under the statute.[98]

An equal protection challenge to this section of the statute, namely why only employers and not other potential defendants are exempted from criminal liability, has been raised in three prior cases.[99] All three courts rejected the equal protection argument summarily, deferring to the legislative perogative to enact any statute Congress found necessary. For example, the Ninth Circuit noted in *Acosta de Evans:*

> There may be something unfair about the exemption of employment from harboring—many of the aliens enter this country in search of jobs; the statute allows those who exploit their labor to escape punishment while penalizing persons who, in some instances, may be acting in a neighborly and humane fashion—but it is the kind of unfairness which is for Congress, not the courts, to cure.[100]

However, the churches may be in a stronger position than the individual defendants in these cases to argue for equal protection. Those individual defendants had no comparable interest to the interests of the employers to harbor the aliens; they were simply seeking a way to avoid their convictions. In contrast, the churches do have substantial interests in the welfare and well-being of the harbored aliens.[101] One might argue that these interests of the sanctuary churches should be at least given the same protection as those of the employers.

Humanitarian Transportation Not in Furtherance of the Aliens' Violation of the Law. Another defense might be made under the unlawful transportation section of § 1324(a). The federal courts have ruled that the government must prove five elements to convict a defendant under § 1324(a) (2):

> . . . (1) defendant transported alien within the United States, (2) the alien was in the United States in violation of law, (3) this was known to the defendant, (4) defendant knew or had reasonable grounds to believe that the alien's last entry into the United States was within the last three years, and (5) defendant acted willfully in furtherance of the alien's violation of the law.[102]

The courts have effectively created a judicial employment proviso for this transportation section of the statute by holding that the incidental transportation of aliens during the course of employment fails to meet the fifth element of the offense. In *United States v. Moreno*,[103] the Ninth Circuit held:

> In the case at bar, Mr. Moreno was transporting the aliens as part of the ordinary and required course of his employment as foreman. As such, his transportation of the aliens was only incidentally connected to the furtherance of the violation of the law, if at all. It was too attenuated to come within the boundaries of § 1324(a) (2).[104]

The *Moreno* court ruled that "there must be a direct and substantial relationship" between the transportation and the furtherance of the alien's presence in the United States in order to make the transportation unlawful under the statute.[105] Thus, the transportation section of the statute seems to allow the development of a much broader exemption to the statute than one limited to employers. Indeed, the *Moreno* court implicitly recognized a humanitarian defense based on this fifth element of § 1324(a) (2):

> Based on purely humanitarian concern, the transportation of a
> *known* undocumented alien to a hospital following an injury or
> illness does not appear to come within the purview of §
> 1324(a) (2) (emphasis added).[106]

Thus, even if there is knowledge of the alien's undocumented
status, a humanitarian motive may still negate the requisite fifth element of the unlawful transportation offense. If one can raise the defense because of a humanitarian motive to care for the sick or
injured, the sanctuary churches could argue that their motives in
providing sanctuary for Central American refugee are no less worthy of judicial recognition. The *Moreno* decision seems to support
such an interpretation of the statute:

> A broader interpretation of the transportation section would
> render the qualification placed there by Congress a nullity. To
> do this would potentially have tragic consequences for many
> American citizens who come into daily contact with undocu-
> mented aliens and who, with no evil or criminal intent, inter-
> mingle with them socially or otherwise. It could only exacerbate
> the plight of these aliens and, without adding anything signifi-
> cant to solving the problem, create, in effect judicially, a new
> crime and a new class of criminals. All our freedom and dignity
> as people would be so reduced.[107]

Finally, a recent decision by the federal district court in Kansas
has extended the rationale of the *Moreno* decision and excluded the
incidental transportation of friends and co-workers from the prohibition of the statute:

> There must be a distinction between acts performed with the
> purpose of supporting or promoting an alien's illegal conduct,
> and acts which are incidental to or merely permit an individual
> to maintain his existence, albeit his existence occurs in this coun-
> try and he is not duly admitted here.[108]

In *United States v. Salinas-Calderon*, the district court acquitted
a defendant who had intended to give a ride from Colorado to Florida to six of his co-workers. The co-workers rode in the back com-
partment of the defendant's truck and had offered to share any

expenses of the trip. When the truck was stopped by a Kansas Highway Patrol Trooper, there was no evasive behavior and complete cooperation by the defendant and the aliens. The district court commented:

> Viewing this evidence, the Court cannot find beyond a reasonable doubt that the defendant acted in willful furtherance of the aliens' illegal presence in the United States. The Court notes that there was no concealment or harboring in this case. While concealment or harboring are [sic] not requisites of a transportation violation, these factors are indicative of whether the defendant acted willfully in furtherance of the aliens' illegality. The defendant clearly was not involved in a smuggling operation nor was he financially remunerated for his efforts. The defendant's passengers were friends, co-workers and companions—not cargo.[109]

A sanctuary worker prosecuted for unlawful transportation would have a much stronger argument than the defendant in *Salinas-Calderon* because any sanctuary activity would be intended only to facilitate the protection of Central American refugees without any pecuniary or other unlawful motives. Indeed, one motive of a sanctuary worker prosecuted for unlawful harboring or transportation—the practice of religious convictions—might be the basis of another affirmative defense.

First Amendment Free Exercise of Religion. The First Amendment safeguards the free exercise of one's chosen form of religion: "Congress shall make no law respecting an establishment of religion, or prohibiting the free exercise thereof . . . "[110] It is undisputed that the First Amendment guarantees the absolute freedom of belief.[111] However, there is no consensus as to the nature of the "free exercise" of religion—the freedom to act upon one's religious beliefs. Criminal prosecution for sanctuary activity would not restrict any freedom to believe but would present the question of whether one's conduct, based on religious beliefs, should be exempt from criminal prosecution and punishment. The sanctuary situation squarely raises the dilemma presented by the free exercise clause of the First Amendment: if the sanctuary worker may only think religious thoughts and believe religious beliefs but may never act upon those thoughts or beliefs, then the First Amendment protection can become illusory.

The freedom only to believe is somewhat meaningless because it is already an axiom of criminal law that one may not be punished for mere beliefs or thoughts.[112] On the other hand, if the First Amendment does provide an exemption or immunity from an otherwise valid and facially neutral penal statute, then the integrity of the criminal justice system might be eroded by a wide variety of claims to religious exemptions.

Unfortunately, the legislative history of the free exercise clause does not reveal any definitive interpretation.[113] Furthermore, the United States Supreme Court has been unable, or perhaps unwilling, to articulate a clear and consistent interpretation of the free exercise clause.[114]

The United States Supreme Court first considered the meaning of the free exercise clause in an 1878 case involving the criminal prosecution of a member of the Church of Jesus Christ of the Latter-Day Saints, commonly known as the Mormons, for the practice of polygamy.[115] In *Reynolds v. United States*, the Supreme Court premised its analysis upon a rigid dichotomy between belief and action, holding that the free exercise clause only protected the freedom of belief: "Congress was deprived of all legislative power over mere opinion but was left free to reach actions which were in violation of social duties or subversive of good order."[116] The Court's analysis was based upon a selective reading of the legislative history of the First Amendment, relying primarily on the writings of Thomas Jefferson regarding the disestablishment of a state religion in the state of Virginia.[117] The Supreme Court utilized a "slippery slope" argument to hold that there was no exemption under the First Amendment to the criminal prohibition against polygamy.[118] In finding that no individual is above the law of the land,[119] the Supreme Court essentially ignored the free exercise clause and did not consider the burden that the criminal statute would have on the practice of the Mormon faith. By limiting the protection of the First Amendment to belief alone and rejecting any religious exemption to any criminal law, the Court restricted the First Amendment to its narrowest possible interpretation.[120]

The restrictive interpretation established by the Supreme Court became the standard for free exercise claims for almost the next century.[121] However, in *Cantwell v. Connecticut*, the 1940 Supreme Court upheld a challenge by a member of the Jehovah's Witnesses to a state statute which prohibited door-to-door solicitations for books and pamphlets without a license from the secretary of the public welfare council.[122] The *Cantwell* court retreated from the rigid belief/action dichotomy established in *Reynolds:*

> Thus the [First] Amendment embraces two concepts—freedom to believe and freedom to act. The first is absolute but, in the nature of things, the second cannot be. Conduct remains subject to regulation for the protection of society. The freedom to act must have appropriate definition to preserve the enforcement of that protection. In every case the power to regulate must be so exercised as not, in attaining a permissible end, *unduly* to infringe the protected freedom.[123] (emphasis added)

The *Cantwell* court recognized that some conduct—that which is unduly infringed upon by the government's power to regulate— is protected by the free exercise clause.

The Supreme Court turned its attention to the nature of the burden on the free exercise of religion in *Braunfeld v. Brown.*[124] In this 1961 case, the Court upheld the constitutionality of a Pennsylvania Sunday closing law against the challenge of Orthodox Jews who were strict Sabbatarians. The plurality opinion reasoned that the statute only regulated a "secular activity," and only made the practice of the Sabbatarians' religious beliefs "more expensive."[125] The Court minimized the magnitude of the harm to the religious interests of the Orthodox Jews, labeling it a "financial sacrifice" rather than the infringement of religious belief.[126] In contrast, the state of Pennsylvania had a weighty interest in a uniform day of rest for all and there was no alternative means for the state to achieve its goals.[127] The Supreme Court concluded that legislation which imposes only an indirect burden on the exercise of religion did not violate the First Amendment.[128]

Another free exercise claim by a Sabbatarian was raised two years later, with an entirely different outcome. In *Sherbert v. Verner*, the Supreme Court held that the state of South Carolina could not deny unemployment compensation benefits to a Seventh-Day Adventist who was discharged from her job and who was unable to accept other work because of her refusal, in accordance with her religious beliefs, to work on Saturdays.[129] The Court concluded that

one's Sabbatarian beliefs justified an exemption to the statute's requirement that claimants accept suitable work before becoming eligible for benefits:

> . . . to condition the availability of benefits upon this appellant's
> willingness to violate a cardinal principle of her religious faith
> effectively penalizes the free exercise of her constitutional lib-
> erties.[130]

The Supreme Court first examined the burden on the free exercise claimant and held that even an indirect burden can trigger the
protection of the First Amendment.[131] Then the Court required the
state to show a "compelling" interest in the statute, borrowing the
language of free speech cases.[132] The Court required a showing of
"only the gravest abuses, endangering paramount interests," not
just rational or reasonable state interests.[133] Finally, the Court
looked for an alternate means to achieve the state interests without
burdening the free exercise of religion.[134]

In the case before it, the Supreme Court found that the burden
on the Sabbatarian was substantial and the state of South Carolina
had failed to prove a compelling interest in denying her the exemption to the statute.[135] This conclusion raises serious conflicts with
the *Braunfeld* decision.[136] First, the burden on the *Sherbert* Sabbatarian could be no more—and perhaps even less—direct than the
burden on the *Braunfeld* Sabbatarians. In *Braunfeld*, there was evidence that some of the Sabbatarians would be forced out of business;[137] here, there was only the loss of temporary unemployment
benefits for not more than twenty-two weeks.[138] Second, it is difficult to see the distinction between the state interests in the two
cases. The proferred state interest in *Braunfeld* was the uniformity
of a day of rest.[139] The interest in *Sherbert* was the uniformity of eligibility for unemployment compensation benefits.[140] The *Sherbert*
analysis represented a fundamental shift in the Supreme Court's
First Amendment rulings.[141] The Court was now willing to scruti-
nize the interests of the state as well as the burden on the religious
claimant and then deny an exemption only when the state demonstrated a compelling interest in doing so.

In its next major free exercise case, the United States Supreme
Court considered the claims of several Old Order Amish parents for

an exemption to the compulsory education law of Wisconsin. In *Wisconsin v. Yoder*, the Amish claimed that compulsory education of their children after age fourteen would violate their religious beliefs about strict separation from the secular world.[142]

The Court retreated from the *Sherbert* balancing test and only required state interests of the "highest order" and of "sufficient magnitude" in order to outweigh the religious claim.[143] While the Court made it clear that a balancing process would be required regardless of the importance of the state interest, it did not use the "compelling" state interest language of *Sherbert*. Thus, the balance was no longer weighted on the side of the religious claimant.[144] Indeed, the Supreme Court in *Yoder* made its first attempt to examine the nature, extent and validity of the burden on religion.[145] The Court concluded that a sliding scale analysis should be used: the greater the burden on the religious interest, the more important the state interests had to be to justify their infringement.[146] Under the *Yoder* decision, the burden on the free exercise of religion was no longer a threshold inquiry to trigger the *Sherbert* balancing test. The religious claimant had the additional burden of showing that the religious interest was substantial. One method of demonstrating such a burden was to show that the religious belief involved was central to the claimant's religion as a whole.[147]

Although the Court had carefully refrained from defining or limiting the scope of religion protected by the First Amendment,[148] its use of a centrality test required some examination of the content of the religious claim. In *Yoder*, the Court went to great lengths to describe the Amish religion to support its finding of centrality.[149] The Court noted that the Amish beliefs about the education of their high school age children had an objective centrality because such beliefs were shared by an organized group as a result of a religious tradition[150] which had a written origin in the Bible.[151]

The question of centrality also shifted the focus of the judicial inquiry from the individual claimant to the claimant's religion as a whole.[152] In *Yoder*, the Court noted that the Amish, as a community, were "productive and law-abiding members of society."[153] The Court's conclusion focused on the potential destruction of the entire Old Order Amish community as a whole rather than on the burden to the individual claimants' religious interests.

The centrality test had been used by several lower courts as the key to the free exercise clause.[154] For example, in *People v. Woody*, the California Supreme Court recognized a free exercise defense for Navajo Indians who had been convicted for the unauthorized possession of peyote.[155] The California Supreme Court set forth the *Sherbert* balancing test[156] but then proceeded to examine in depth the nature of peyote and its role in the religion practiced by the defendants as members of the Native American Church of California. The Court concluded:

> The record thus establishes that the application of the statutory prohibition of the use of peyote results in a virtual inhibition of the practice of defendants' religion. To forbid the use of peyote is to remove the theological heart of Peyotism.[157]

The California Supreme Court contrasted the case before it with the 1878 polygamy case before the United States Supreme Court:

> The test of constitutionality calls for an examination of the degree of abridgement of religious freedom involved in each case. Polygamy, although a basic tenet in the theology of Mormonism, is not essential to the practice of the religion; peyote, on the other hand, is the *sine qua non* of the defendants' faith. It is the sole means by which defendants are able to experience their religion; without peyote defendants cannot practice their faith.[158]

The California court found that the state interest in the rigorous enforcement of the narcotics laws and the detection of fraudulent claims of the asserted religious use of peyote were insufficiently compelling to outweigh the freedom of religion interests involved.[159]

However, in *Town v. State ex rel. Reno*, the Florida Supreme Court distinguished *Woody* and denied a free exercise exemption for the sacramental use of marijuana despite an undisputed finding of centrality.[160] The trial court had expressly found that the Ethiopian Zion Coptic Church was a religion protected by the First Amendment and that the sacramental use of marijuana was an "essential portion" of the church's religious observances.[161] Nevertheless, the Florida Supreme Court upheld the state interest in restricting the use of the "dangerous drug"[162] because the marijuana smoking was done throughout the day by members as well as non-members, including minors, the smoking was not restricted to the particular religious ceremonies, and the smoking took place in a residence where there might be a threat to public safety and welfare from participants under the influence of marijuana "constantly coming and going."[163]

In *Leary v. United States*,[164] the Fifth Circuit held that the personal use of marijuana as a means of practicing one's religion did not outweigh the compelling governmental interest in averting a substantial threat to public safety, peace and order.[165] The court noted that the use of marijuana by the defendant was not a formal requisite of the defendant's religion and was, at most, an aid "by which an individual can more easily meditate or commune with his god."[166] Furthermore, the court observed that, unlike the members of the Native American Church in *Woody*, the defendant sought unrestricted freedom to use the controlled substance rather than limiting its use to a sacramental context that composed the "cornerstone" of the religion.[167]

Finally, the centrality test has been used to uphold religious exemptions in several other cases[168] but has also been used to reject several claims by Native Americans for access to sacred sites.[169] Commentators remain divided as to the wisdom and utility of the test.[170]

In the next major United States Supreme Court case to consider the free exercise clause,[171] the Court upheld unemployment compensation benefits for a member of the Jehovah's Witnesses who lost his job when he refused, for religious reasons, to work in a job directly engaged in the production of weapons.[172] In *Thomas v. Review Board, Indiana Employment Security Division*, the Court relied on *Yoder* to hold that a statute neutral on its face could still be deemed unconstitutional in its application if it unduly burdened the free exercise of religion.[173] The Court also relied on *Sherbert* to hold that a state may not constitutionally force a person to choose between the freedom to practice one's religion and participation in an otherwise available state benefit program.[174] Although the Court found that the burden on the free exercise of religion in the *Thomas* case was only indirect, it was substantial enough to outweigh the government interest that was neither compelling nor the least restrictive means of achieving the statute's purpose.[175]

In *Thomas*, the Supreme Court retreated from its attempts in

Sherbert and *Yoder* to define the scope of religion protected by the First Amendment. The only inquiry the Court required was the determination of whether the alleged religious belief was sincerely held.[176] The Supreme Court commented:

> Courts should not undertake to dissect religious beliefs because the believer admits that he is "struggling" with his position or because his beliefs are not articulated with the clarity and precision that a more sophisticated person might employ. . . . Intrafaith differences . . . are not uncommon among followers of a particular creed, and the judicial process is singularly ill equipped to resolve such differences in relation to the Religion Clauses . . . the guarantee of free exercise is not limited to beliefs which are shared by all of the members of a religious sect. Particularly in this sensitive area, it is not within the judicial function and judicial competence to inquire whether the petitioner or his fellow worker more correctly perceived the commands of their common faith. Courts are not arbiters of scriptural interpretation.[177]

As long as the reviewing court is satisfied with the credibility of the claimant's motivation for acting, there cannot be any review of the veracity of the belief.[178] If the examination of religious belief is limited to the subjective motivation or sincerity of the religious claimant, then *Thomas* seems to contradict the requirement of the objective centrality of the belief.[179] The *Thomas* Court specifically held that the religious beliefs "need not be acceptable, logical, consistent or comprehensible to others to merit First Amendment protection."[180] As long as the belief is sincerely held, there would be no attempt to examine the nature of the burden on religion. The *Thomas* Court returned to the threshold analysis of the burden on religion but then expanded the scope of religious freedom by abandoning the requirement of centrality.[181]

The dissenting opinion in *Thomas* argued that the granting of the religious exemption would constitute an impermissible establishment of religion.[182] The relationship between the two religion clauses in the First Amendment has been the subject of much scholarly debate[183] but it is clear that there is an inherent conflict between the free exercise of religion clause and the establishment clause if either one is interpreted at the extreme.[184] In *Thomas*, the majority

opinion responded to the argument by holding that the accommodation of religion under the free exercise clause did not constitute
an establishment of religion.[185]

The next United States Supreme Court case to examine the
free exerise clause again involved a member of the Old Order
Amish. In *United States v. Lee*, the religious claimant had refused to
pay the employer contributions to support the federal social security
system.[186] The Court first declined to extend the religious exemption in the statute created for self-employed individuals to this
Amish employer of other Amish employees.[187] The Court then accepted the sincerity of the religious belief of the Amish that both the
payment and receipt of social security benefits are forbidden as
worldly entanglement.[188] However, the Court then articulated yet
another balancing test: "The state may justify a limitation on religious liberty by showing that it is essential to accomplish an overriding governmental interest."[189] The Court found that the
governmental interest in assuring the mandatory and continuous
participation in and contribution to the social security system is
"very high."[190]

The Court then focused on how the accommodation of the
Amish belief would burden the fulfillment of the governmental interest.[191] This inquiry into the burden on the governmental interest
seems to turn the least restrictive means test on its head; prior to *Lee*,
the inquiry had been about the burden on the religious interest, not
the governmental interest.[192] In *Lee*, the Court inflated the governmental interest and considered the effect of a widespread religious
exemption to the social security system rather than limiting its inquiry to the effect of a limited exemption for the Amish claimant
before the Court.[193] Fearful of "myriad exceptions flowing from a
wide variety of religious beliefs," the Court denied the exemption.[194]

Justice Stevens noted in his concurring opinion that the Court
had overstated the effect of the exemption sought by the Amish
claimant.[195] The Court had drawn an analogy between the claim be-
for it and a general religious exemption for the payment of all
taxes.[196] Despite the fact that only Justice Stevens wrote a separate
opinion, the nearly unanimous *Lee* decision left much uncertainty as
to the future resolution of issues under the free exercise clause.[197]

The uncertainty left by the *Lee* decision was not resolved in the most recent United States Supreme Court case to consider a free exercise claim. In *Bob Jones University v. United States*, the Court upheld the revocation of federal tax-exempt status to two religious schools that engaged in racial discrimination on the basis of a religious belief in the separation of the races.[198] The sincerity of the religious belief was not at issue in the case.[199] After a lengthy analysis, the Court concluded that the tax-exempt status under Section 501(c) (3) of the Internal Revenue Code could not be granted to a school that nullified its charitable purpose by its violation of the public policy against racial discrimination.[200]

The Court then turned to the issue of whether the revocation of the tax-exempt status would violate the free exercise rights of the religious schools. The Supreme Court first quoted the balancing test articulated in *Lee:* "The state may justify a limitation on religious liberty by showing that it is essential to accomplish an overriding governmental interest."[201] However, when the Court actually applied the test, it used the language of *Sherbert* to require a compelling rather than merely an overriding governmental interest:

> On occasion this Court has found certain governmental interests so compelling as to allow even regulations prohibiting religiously based conduct. . . . The government interest at stake here is compelling. . . . The government has a fundamental, overriding interest in eradicating racial discrimination in education. . . .[202]

By using the language of both the *Sherbert* and *Lee* tests, it is unclear whether the Court intended that the two formulations actually mean the same thing or whether the Court is now returning to the higher compelling state interest test. The court may also have actually found a compelling government interest—the public policy against racial discrimination in education—and therefore held that both tests were satisfied. The Court found that this governmental interest "substantially outweighs whatever burden denial of tax benefits places on petitioners' exercise of religious beliefs."[203] Furthermore, the free exercise interests of the religious schools could not be accommodated, since there were no less restrictive means to achieve the governmental interest.[204] Thus, the Court seemed to return to the use of the less restrictive means inquiry temporarily abandoned in *Lee*.[205] Finally, in a footnote, the Court rejected the argument that the denial of tax-exempt status to these religious schools would violate the establishment clause by giving preference to those religions whose tenets did not require racial separation.[206] Although the *Bob Jones University* decision was unanimous on the free exercise issue,[207] it still did not establish any coherent guidelines for the resolution of claims to religious exemptions under the free exercise clause.[208]

The belief that one's religion requires or motivates the provision of sanctuary to Central American refugees could be a basis for a free exercise claim to an exemption from the criminal statute prohibiting the unlawful transporting and harboring of undocumented aliens. This defense was the predominant subject of the first reported decision from a prosecution of a sanctuary worker for sanctuary activity. In the January 1985 Jack Elder case, United States District Court Judge Hayden Head denied Elder's motion to dismiss under the Free Exercise Clause.[209] (See Chapter Three.) Initially, the court recognized that the exercise of religious freedom can sometimes excuse criminal conduct.[210] The district court found that Elder had met his burden of proof of demonstrating that religious beliefs had motivated his conduct:

> [Elder] is a Roman Catholic who feels a charitable Christian commitment, founded in the Gospel, which motivates him to assist those who flee the violence in El Salvador. Elder presented the testimony of various Christian clergymen who confirmed that assistance to those in need remains a fundamental aspect of Christianity.[211]

Significantly, the court accepted the sincerity and centrality of Elder's religious beliefs even though the beliefs were largely derived from Elder's individual conscience as a layperson rather than the teachings or doctrines of the institutional church to which he belonged:

> Bishop John Fitzpatrick, Bishop of the Roman Catholic Diocese of Brownsville, testified that meeting human material needs represents an essential aspect of Christianity, and that each individual remains free to fulfill this obligation according to the directives of his or her own conscience. Although no law of the Roman Catholic Church specifically requires Roman Catholics to provide sanctuary or rides to Salvadorans, Bishop Fitzpatrick believes that providing such assistance constitutes an appropri-

ate expression of the Christian gospel. According to the testimony of various ministers, this conclusion also holds true in other denominations.[212]

The court specifically ruled that Elder could raise the free exercise claim even if other members of Elder's religion rejected his interpretation of their common religion:

> The Court understands that other members of the Roman Catholic faith may oppose Elder's activist response to the situation in Central America. The Court emphasizes that it is not an arbiter of canon law. The Court simply finds that Elder fulfilled his Christian obligations as he genuinely perceived them to be and that Elder presented substantial testimony to support his view of Christianity. This Court's conclusions are not intended to define the Christian gospel or Christian response to it. The Court need not correctly interpret Christian doctrine in order to hear the position of the Defendant.[213]

After finding the threshold religious interest, the court then examined the nature of the governmental interest involved. The court ruled that "the government meets its burden of demonstrating an overriding interest in protecting a congressionally-sanctioned immigration and naturalization system designed to maintain the integrity of this nation's borders."[214] Thus, the court used the "overriding government interest" test from *Lee* rather than the "compelling government interest" tests from the *Sherbert, Yoder, Thomas,* and *Bob Jones University* cases. Furthermore, the district court took an expansive view of the governmental interest, characterizing it as maintaining the "integrity" of the United States borders rather than the more narrow interest in denying Elder a religious exemption for sanctuary activity. The court concluded that the circumvention by individuals of the congressionally-prescribed procedure for the admission and entry of aliens into the United States, even if religiously motivated, would undermine the legitimate goals of immigration control.[215] However, Elder was not charged with facilitating the illegal entry or admission of undocumented aliens; he was only charged under 8 U.S.C. §1324(a) (2) with the unlawful transportation of undocumented aliens. Nevertheless, the court examined the governmental interest in controlling the entry and admission of *all* aliens rather than the more narrow governmental interest in preventing the unlawful *transportation* of *undocumented* aliens.

The district court also found that the federal government was utilizing the least burdensome method to accomplish its purpose in securing the nation's borders. Fearing that an exemption would permit religious individuals to formulate their own "personal immigration policies," the court ruled that any government accommodation of Elder's religious beliefs "would result in no immigration policy at all."[216] Accordingly, Elder's motion to dismiss was denied.[217]

Since Elder was acquitted at his January 1985 trial (see Chapter Three), the decision of the district court on his motion to dismiss will not be directly reviewed by any appellate court. No one can predict how other courts will choose to examine the First Amendment claims of other sanctuary workers who are criminally prosecuted for sanctuary activity. The absence of clear and coherent guidelines from the Supreme Court on the free exercise clause only adds to the unpredictability. However, it seems that few cases could present the question of a religious exemption to a criminal statute in a purer fashion. The provision of sanctuary, if motivated by sincere religious beliefs, is conduct that is otherwise valued and encouraged by society: sheltering the homeless, feeding the hungry, giving transportation to the needy.[218] While the provision of sanctuary is not and never has been the central teaching of any of the sanctuary churches, the history of sanctuary is also an indisputable part of their religious traditions. How the United States courts will ultimately determine the claim to the free exercise of religion as expressed by sanctuary activity remains one of the critical but unresolved legal questions raised by the sanctuary movement.[219]

CHAPTER FIVE

The Ancient Tradition of Sanctuary

"And the Lord said to Moses, 'Say to the people of Israel, when you cross the Jordan into the land of Canaan, then you shall select cities to be cities of refuge for you, that the manslayer who kills any person without intent may flee there.' "

—*Numbers 35:9–11*

While it is important to understand the legal issues concerning church sanctuary for Central American refugees, it is also critical to understand the rich religious and historical tradition of sanctuary. The history of sanctuary reflects many periods of growth, development and even abuse that may often seem irrelevant to the current manifestation of sanctuary. However, unless one understands the complex societal forces underlying the practice of the sanctuary privilege throughout history, one cannot appreciate its endurance as a concept. By examining the historical tradition of sanctuary, it becomes evident that the contemporary invocation of sanctuary is not simply a legal or a political phenomenon but rather the revival and continuation of an ancient tradition. To those in the sanctuary movement who understand this history, the provision of sanctuary for Central American refugees today is a profound identification with that ancient tradition.

Church sanctuary in the United States today traces its roots to the Judaeo-Christian heritage.[1] There are two historical types of sanctuary found in the Hebrew Scriptures or the Old Testament: communitarian sanctuary and altar sanctuary.

124

Old Testament Cities of Refuge

Communitarian sanctuary, or the asylum established by the Hebrew cities of refuge, is probably the best known form of historical sanctuary. The primary biblical text is Numbers 35:6–34. (See Appendix.) Moses was commanded to create six cities of refuge from the land given the Levitical tribe. A "manslayer who kills any person without intent" could flee to one of these cities. This manslayer could be one of the Israelites or a stranger or sojourner among the people of Israel. The avenger of blood, who was the next of kin of the person slain, was allowed to kill the accused "manslayer" only if the accused was caught before reaching a city of refuge. Thus, the asylum provision was incorporated into the ancient regulation of blood feud. The underlying Hebrew presumption was that any killing—even if accidental—could not be expiated by monetary compensation ("ransom"), but only by another death. The shedding of blood required the shedding of blood.[2] Thus, the avenger of blood (go-el) was not only an avenger but a redeemer because he restored the balance of blood and life. Accidental killing presented a problem for the Israelites because while blood had been shed, it would be too severe to demand the blood of the unintentional killer. Thus, the cities of refuge mitigated the harshness of the blood feud.

When the accused manslayer reached the city of refuge, he had to first prove through a trial by the "congregation," probably the elders of the city that acted as a court, that the killing had indeed been accidental. The fugitive would then be protected from the blood avenger as long as he remained within the city or its suburbs. If found outside the city by the avenger of blood, the fugitive could still be killed. Thus, this protection was tantamount to the commutation of capital punishment to life imprisonment. Finally, the fugitive could return home and the avenger of blood would lose the right of vengeance if the reigning high priest died.

The Numbers institution of the cities of refuge contains two seemingly unrelated themes: the establishment of Levitical cities and provisions regarding criminal law, specifically the law of intentional, unintentional, negligent and accidental homicide. However, there is an important reason why the problem of unintentional killing was placed in the context of the Levitical office of the high priest. The fugitive's life would be spared but the fugitive would not be free to leave one of the Levitical cities until the death of the high priest. The high priest's death, already symbolic of communal expiation (see Leviticus 16), would be the substitutionary death that would satisfy the requirement of expiation of killing by blood.[3] Thus, one of the earliest traditions of sanctuary depended upon a connection between the criminal law and the religious practices of the people. A religious figure, the Levitical high priest, stood at the center of the sanctuary privilege.

A parallel passage regarding the cities of refuge is found in Deuteronomy 19:1–13:

> When the Lord your God cuts off the nations whose land the Lord your God gives you, and you dispossess them and dwell in their cities and in their houses, you shall set apart three cities for you in the land which the Lord your God gives you to possess. You shall prepare the roads, and divide into three parts the area of the land which the Lord your God gives you as a possession, so that any manslayer can flee to them.
>
> This is the provision for the manslayer, who by fleeing there may save his life. If any one kills his neighbor unintentionally without having been at enmity with him in time past— as when a man goes into the forest with his neighbor to cut wood, and his hand swings the axe to cut down a tree, and the head slips from the handle and strikes his neighbor so that he dies—he may flee to one of these cities and save his life; lest the avenger of blood in hot anger pursue the manslayer and overtake him, because the way is long, and wound him mortally, though the man did not deserve to die, since he was not at enmity with his neighbor in time past. Therefore I command you, You shall set apart three cities. And if the Lord your God enlarges your border, as he has sworn to your fathers, and gives you all the land which he promised to give to your fathers—provided you are careful to keep all this commandment, which I command you this day, by loving the Lord your God and by walking ever in his ways—then you shall add three other cities to these three, lest innocent blood be shed in your land, which the Lord your God gives you for an inheritance, and so the guilty of bloodshed be upon you.
>
> But if any man hates his neighbor, and lies in wait for him, and attacks him, and wounds him mortally so that he dies, then the elders of his city shall send and fetch him from there and

hand him over to the avenger of blood, so that he may die. Your
eye shall not pity him, but you shall purge the guilt of innocent
blood from Israel so that it may be well with you.

There are several important differences between the two passages. In Deuteronomy, the cities of refuge are not specifically set
apart as Levitical cities. Futhermore, there is no provision for the
freedom of the fugitive after the death of the high priest. These distinctions have led several commentators to conclude that the Deuteronomy passage is the later one, when the cities of refuge had
become more institutionalized.[4] The Old Testament records that
the cities were in fact established by Moses (Deuteronomy 4:41–43)
and Joshua (Joshua 20:1–9).

There is much rabbinic tradition and law regarding the cities
of refuge.[5] The roads leading to the cities were to be clearly marked
and carefully maintained.[6] The Talmudic scholars also recon-
structed several procedures, including an escort to protect the
fugitive[7] and a curious requirement that the mothers of the high
priest furnish the fugitives with food and clothing, so that the fugitives might not pray for their son's death.[8] The fugitive was entitled to lead a normal life and earn his livelihood while in the city
of refuge.[9] However, certain trades which might result in interaction with the blood avenger, such as the manufacture of textiles,
ropes and glassware, were forbidden, as well as the sale of hunting
tools and arms.[10] A later tradition envisioned the expansion of the
asylum of the cities of refuge to all the Levitical cities. The only difference was that asylum had to be specifically requested and rent
had to be paid by the fugitive in these other Levitical cities not specifically set apart as cities of refuge.[10a] It is unknown how long the
cities of refuge operated, especially after the centralization of worship in Jerusalem under the united monarchy of King David and his
successors.[10b]

Old Testament Altar Sanctuary

There was another ancient cultural tradition of sanctuary that
was independent of the cities of refuge. Among desert Arabs, any
tent could serve as a sanctuary, providing temporary asylum for

some customary period of time (usually a few days). Furthermore, some tents or other places were set aside as perpetual sanctuaries according to tribal law.[11]

There are two examples in the Old Testament of altar sanctuary, or protection given to fugitives who fled to the local temple altar. While there is no direct Scriptural basis for such sanctuary protection, there is an implicit reference to the protection of the altar in early Mosaic law:

> Whoever strikes a man so that he dies shall be put to death. But if he did not lie in wait for him, but God let him fall into his hand, then I will appoint for you a place to which he may flee. But if a man willfully attacks another to kill him treacherously, you shall *take him from my altar*, that he may die (Exodus 21:12–14) (emphasis added).

Indeed, some commentators suggest that the asylum of the cities of refuge was probably necessitated by the abolition of local sanctuaries. When the Israelites first entered Canaan, they found numerous sanctuaries devoted to local deities. When such worship was replaced by the centralized worship of Jehovah, there had to be a replacement for the asylum protection of the local altars.[12] Other commentators have suggested that the cities of refuge did not completely replace the altar sanctuary protection, which was local and temporary, but simply expanded the sanctuary protection to a more permanent institution. Under this view, the local sanctuaries remained viable adjuncts to the cities of refuge.[13] It has also been noted that most of the six Levitical cities chosen as cities of refuge were already Hebrew shrines or places of historical or religious significance.[14] Thus, the Hebrews may have simply applied the Canaanite custom of altar sanctuary to their own sacred places. In any case, the biblical examples of altar sanctuary must be understood as predating the received biblical law.

The two Old Testament incidents involving altar sanctuary are found in the First Book of Kings and are both related to the ascendency of Solomon to the Israelite throne. When Adonijah attempted to usurp the throne, King David had Zadok the priest anoint Solomon as his successor. When Adonijah learned of this, he invoked the protection of altar sanctuary.

And Adonijah feared Solomon; and he arose, and went, and caught hold of the horns of the altar. And it was told Solomon, "Behold, Adonijah fears King Solomon; for, lo, he has laid hold of the horns of the altar, saying, 'Let King Solomon swear to me first that he will not slay his servant with the sword.' " And Solomon said, "If he proves to be a worthy man, not one of his hairs shall fall to the earth; but if wickedness is found in him, he shall die." So King Solomon sent, and they brought him down from the altar. And he came and did obeisance to King Solomon; and Solomon said to him, "Go to your house" (1 Kings 1:50–53).[15]

However, Solomon was not as merciful with Adonijah's co-conspirator Joab:

When the news came to Joab—for Joab had supported Adonijah although he had not supported Absalom—Joab fled to the tent of the Lord and caught hold of the horns of the altar. And when it was told King Solomon, "Joab has fled to the tent of the Lord, and behold, he is beside the altar," Solomon sent Benaiah the son of Johoiada, saying, "Go, strike him down" (1 Kings 2:28–29).

Benaiah carries out Solomon's order in verse 34. It is difficult to distinguish between the recognition of asylum for Adonijah but not for Joab. Some have speculated that Joab's crime was intentional and therefore inexcusable,[16] but there seems to be little difference from Adonihah's crime of treason. In any case, these passages evidence the existence of altar sanctuary in Old Testament times. However, the passages also indicate that altar sanctuary could be violated with impunity by a strong-willed ruler. Its moral force was dependent upon mercy, not justice.

Greek and Roman Sanctuaries

In contrast to the important theological elements of the sanctuary provisions of the Old Testament, the temple asylum of Greek and Roman culture was often secular. It is difficult to separate myth from actual practice in reviewing temple asylum in these early civilizations. For example, Romulus, the mythical founder of Rome, reputedly made the Palatine Hill an asylum for fugitives in order to increase the male population of Rome.[17] There are also abundant references to sanctuary and its violations in Greek historical literature, itself a mixture of myth and fact.[18]

It is clear that some privilege of sanctuary existed and was rooted in the sacredness of the temples. Being a divine privilege, the right of asylum could not be abolished without sacrilege.[19] However, it is also clear that the privilege was widely abused, eventually providing refuge for enterprising criminals rather than for the poor or oppressed fleeing from the harshness of the law.[20] Such abuses were aggravated by the extension of sanctuary protection to cemeteries (where there were tombs of Greek heroes), forests, and even entire cities.[21] Thus, the original purpose of sanctuary as a shelter for those who committed involuntary crimes continued to be eroded. Ultimately, Greek temple asylum became an institutional mitigation of punishment, purely secular in operation.[22]

Under the Roman Empire, sanctuary was limited and regulated. The first Roman emperors suppressed the Greek asylums by imposing the impossible requirement that the temples produce legal proofs of the right to exercise the privilege. When the privilege was invoked, it only provided temporary immunity from prosecution. The fugitive had to undergo a formal inquisition and submit what amounted to full legal defense before even being admitted into sanctuary. Even then, the fugitive lost the protection of the sanctuary at the time of actual trial.[23] Rome also witnessed the abuses of sanctuary as claims of asylum were made by those fleeing to statues and busts of the Caesars, pictures of the emperors, battle standards of the Roman legions and even the persons of vestal virgins.[24] Although abused in practice, the Roman Empire generally sought to limit the protection of the sanctuary privilege for the unfortunate and needy who would be unable to endure the often harsh and merciless application of the criminal law.[25]

Early Christian Sanctuaries

With the fall of Jerusalem in 70 A.D., the Jewish people were again forced into exile. At the same time, the early New Testament Christian church was struggling to survive. Since the first Christians were persecuted, there was no opportunity for any resurrection of the Levitical cities of refuge within the early Christian communities. However, Constantine's conversion in the early fourth century marked the beginning of the institutionalization and legitimization of the Christian church. Constantine himself did not expressly legislate a privilege of asylum for the emerging Christian churches, but the churches soon exercised a privilege of sanctuary much broader than either the Hebrew cities of refuge or the temple asylum in the Greek and Roman societies.[26]

The first explicit reference to the sanctuary privilege exercised by Christian churches is found in the Theodosian Code of 392. Since the Theodosian Code only explained and regulated sanctuary practices, it is presumed that such practices existed before the reign of Theodosius the Great but were simply never the subject of any legislation. Public debtors (those who embezzled money owed to the state) as well as Jews, heretics and apostates were excluded from the sanctuaries.[27] Thus, according to the earliest sanctuary legislation in the Christian era, eligibility for asylum depended on both the nature of the crime and the character of the accused. These criteria persisted and became critical in the later development and in the demise of the sanctuary privilege.

Another section of the Theodosian Code revealed the sophisticated nature of the privilege: fugitives could be fed and lodged only in the churchyards and the surrounding church precincts, not in the actual churches themselves.[28] This section reflected the tension between the sacredness of the actual church building—a sanctity which was the foundation for the legal privilege—and the inherent worldly or secular desecration personified by the fugitive criminal.[29] This juxtaposition of the sacred and the profane will continue to create tension during the historical expansion of the sanctuary concept.

The Theodosian legislation anticipated a later statute under Theodosius the Younger which recognized that the sanctuary protection extended from the church building proper to the surrounding churchyard and precincts.[30] This extension in the early fifth century included houses of the bishops and clergy, cloisters, and cemeteries. Pope Leo I confirmed the emperor's decrees and added that "the steward and the advocate" of the church (the precise nature of the these church offices is unknown) should act as an inquisitor and examine all persons seeking sanctuary.[31] The papal decree reflected a subtle but important change in the sanctuary privilege. By emphasizing the role of the inquisitor, the focus of the sanctuary shifted from the sacredness of the *place* to the sacredness of the *person* administering the sanctuary. As the sanctuary privilege continued to be refined, the personal intercessory role of the bishop developed in significance. The early extensions of the area of geographic protection to the houses of the bishops and clergy as well as to the churches per se also reflected this shift in focus.

However, most of the early Roman Christian legislation and church council pronouncements on sanctuary involved the flight of fugitive slaves from their masters.[32] An edict dated by one scholar at 432 (by Theodosius and Valentinian) provided for the return of the slave to the master after the clerics had secured the master's pardon for the slave's flight.[33] Presumably, such a pardon also guaranteed that the slave would not be punished upon returning to the master. However, returning the slave with a pardon from the master did not redress the predicament of a slave who had a well-founded complaint of ill-treatment. Thus, the Council of Orange allowed bishops to intervene between the fugitive slave and the master. If the slave's complaint was valid then the master was forced to sell the slave to the church or to another owner. The early church paid much money to redeem slaves in this way. If the slave was returned to the master, the master first had to take an oath that the pardon would be given. Violation of the slave master's oath carried a penalty of payment of slaves to the church.[34] The Council of Mayence in 813 seemed to assure the protection of the fugitive slave with this decree:

> Let no one dare to remove a wrongdoer who is a fugitive to a church, nor give him up from there to punishment or death, that the honor of the churches may be preserved; but let the rectors be diligent in securing his life and limb. Nevertheless he must lawfully compound for what he had wrongfully done.[35]

Thus, the early Christian sanctuaries were premised not so much on the territorial sanctity of the churches but on the personal sanctity of the bishops and clerics as intercessors.[36] These religious played active roles in securing pardons and humane treatment for the fugitive slaves who fled to them. The sanctuary protection became a path to salvation for the slaves if they were redeemed by the bishops. It is interesting that the Levitical cities of refuge were also intimately connected with a redemptive role of an individual, the high priest. However, unlike the assembly of elders of the Hebrew cities of refuge, the early Christian bishops in the Roman Empire operated not only as the fugitives' physical protectors, but as their intercessors and advocates as well. Finally, if the predominant use of these early Christian sanctuaries was by fugitive slaves, only the slaveowners, not the government, had an interest in the sanctuary-seeking slaves. Any confrontation over the sanctuary privilege was limited to the church and the slaveowners. The state's legal system had yet to become involved. The clash of church and state over the sanctuary privilege had yet to take place.

CHAPTER SIX

The Law of Sanctuary in England

"In England the institution of sanctuary had three distinct stages, first of growth, then of development, and lastly of decay. The Anglo-Saxon period was the one which saw its definite origin in England and its growth into a national institution; the centuries succeeding the Norman conquest saw its development throughout the length and breadth of the land and its greatest prosperity; but with prosperity came abuse, familiarity bred contempt, and the Tudor and Stuart periods witnessed, first an attempt at reform and limitation, when many of the existing sanctuaries were done away with, then, when the Reformation had done its work, the almost total abolition of sanctuary, abjuration, and all their attendant evils and abuses."

—Norman M. Trenholme,
"The Right of Sanctuary in England"[1]

The Anglo-Saxon Period

The preceding overview of the origins and different theories of the ancient privilege of sanctuary provides a background for its development in English law.[1a] The first reference to sanctuary is found in the earliest known Anglo-Saxon legal code, promulgated by King Ethelbert in 597. Ethelbert had been converted and baptized that same year by Augustine and his forty monks, who had landed as missionaries at Kent in south England. Ethelbert established a pen-

134

alty for violation of the church's peace (*frith* or *fryth*). This penalty was double the amount for a violation of the king's peace (*girth* or *gryth*). Our modern English word for peace includes two Teutonic words, *gryth* and *fryth*, that would parallel the two species of immunities eventually granted to the Christian churches.

The king's peace, or *gryth*, was a distinctly Anglo-Saxon legal concept and could only be granted by charter. This was a particular protection granted by the king and enforceable in the king's courts by fines payable to the king (*wites*). This specific protection was distinguished from the general concept of the king's peace, or *mund*, which was a privilege that every free man enjoyed. Such a privilege attached to the house of every free man and carried its own system of punishment. The more exalted a man's rank and the greater his authority, the more grievous the breach of this *mund*. Of course, the king's *mund* was the highest and the widest protection, and its breach the most serious.[2] On the other hand, the church's peace, or *fryth*, was a protection created by the power of the church and rested in any sacred place (the Germanic root of the word *fryth* refers to the sanctuaries of sacred woods).[3]

Under the ancient Saxon law of bloodfeud, any offender was subject to the revenge of the group or individual injured. Such a broad bloodfeud law can be contrasted with the more limited rights of the Hebrew avenger of blood. Under the ancient Teutonic tribal laws, most offenses involved a breach of the general peace, thereby making the offender an outlaw, at feud with the entire community. That peace could only be restored by coming to terms with the injured party. However, the victim had certain rights of vengeance. The system of *bot*, or amends, provided a limit to this law of feud and vengeance by fixing the amount of compensation required from the offender. (In later years, the payments also became punitive in nature, becoming more similar to fines than to compensation.)[4] The entire scheme of Anglo-Saxon *bot* payments is irregular and extremely complex. It is sufficient to understand that the sanctuary privilege existed as part of a more general law involving bloodfeud, the rights of one's peace and the intricate system of compensation.

Around 680, Ine, the king of Wessex, enacted a legal code to restrict and regulate, and ultimately, limit, the bloodfeud.[5] Note how Ine incorporated the privilege of sanctuary into the system of bloodfeud:

5. If anyone is liable to the death penalty, and he flees to a church, his life shall be spared and he shall pay such compensation as he is directed [to pay] by legal decision.

5.1 If anyone renders himself liable to the lash and flees to the church, he shall be immune from scourging.[6]

The second provision seems to recognize the intercessory role of the church as it had operated in the late Roman Empire. It is likely that this second provision also applied predominantly to fugitive slaves since slaves were the primary targets of punishment by scourging.[7] Indeed, an eighth century collection of laws for the clergy, the *Exerptiones Egberti*, contain the following decrees:

LXXVI. . . . those who flee to a church ought not to be taken out but after a promise of intercession has been given, let their lords persuade them [to return].

LXVII. If anyone shall for any reason injure someone who has fled to a church . . . he shall amend and shall also remain under hard penance for seven years; otherwise he must be excommunicated from the entire Catholic Church.[8]

The authority of the church was used as an intermediary between the fugitive and his master or lord. As in the late Roman Empire, the church had the power to determine the validity of any complaint of ill-treatment by a fugitive slave.[9] By the eighth century, the church was already utilizing its two most powerful sanctions—penance and excommunication—against those who violated the sanctuary protection. Ine's code also had a specific penalty for the breaking of the oath of pardon and good-treatment taken by masters upon receiving their fugitive slaves from the churches:

13. If anyone bears false witness in the presence of a bishop, or repudiates a pledge which he has given in his presence, he shall pay 120 shillings compensation.[10]

In the Anglo-Saxon era, superstitious beliefs further guaranteed the inviolability and the power of protection of the church grounds since it was commonly believed that locally-revered saints were the special guardians of the churches. Furthermore, the churches were also under the royal protection of the king and any breach of the king's peace would result in further fines.[11]

The first express statutory grant of asylum comes from Alfred the Great in 887:

> 2. If a man flees, for any manner of offense, to any monastery which is entitled to receive the king's food rent, or to any other free community which is endowed, for the space of three days he shall have asylum, unless he is willing to come to terms [with his enemy].

> 2.1. If, during that time, anyone injures him by a [mortal] blow, [by putting him in] fetters, or by wounding him, he shall pay composition for each of these offences in the regular way, both with *wergeld* and fine, and he shall pay 120 shillings to the community as compensation for violation of the sanctuary of the Church, and he [himself] shall not have the payment due him from the fugitive.[12]

In Alfred's grant, sanctuary lasting for three days is available to anyone accused of any crime. There are severe penalties for violating the sanctuary and injuring the fugitive in any way during the time of protection. Alfred's law also indicates that one purpose of the sanctuary was to facilitate composition settlements between feuding parties. Presumably, the protection of the sanctuary allowed more rational negotiation. Such settlements included the exchange of hostages (including freedom for the sanctuary seeker), pledges and reparations.[13] There were separate sanctions for violating the amends settlements of the feuds.[14] Thus, while the legal provisions regarding sanctuary grew increasingly complex, the privilege remained in the context of the bloodfeud laws. Sanctuary only facilitated negotiation and settlement; it had not yet become an alternative to the ordinary operation of the law.

Another later provision under Alfred's reign as King of Wessex provided for half-value composition settlements when one confessed to an unsolved or undiscovered crime.[15] Again, the purpose of the sanctuary was to facilitate some compensatory settlement and to limit the violence of bloodfeud rather than to release all guilt or responsibility. Such confessions were likely only when the threat of vengeance under bloodfeud was still imminent. Therefore, the provision of half-value payments was probably an incentive for the resolution of such outstanding cases. Another ninth century enactment by Alfred the Great broadened the sanctuary privilege:

> 5. Further, we grant to every church consecrated by a bishop this right of sanctuary: if a man, attacked by enemies, reaches it either on foot or horseback, he shall not be dragged out for seven days, if he can live despite hunger, and unless he [himself comes] out [and] fights. If, however, anyone does try to drag him out, he shall forfeit the amount due for violation of the king's guardianship and the fine for violating the sanctuary of the church— and a greater amount if he seizes more than one person in such a place.

> 5.1. If the community have so great a need of their church [that it cannot be used as an asylum] he [the fugitive] shall be kept in another building, and this shall not have more doors than the church.

> 5.2. The chief authority of the church shall see to it that during this time no food is given to him.

> 5.3. If he himself is willing to hand over his weapons to his enemies, they shall hold him in their power for thirty days; and they shall send formal notice of his position to this kinsman.[16]

This enactment expressly granted every church the privilege of sanctuary and imposed duties upon the church officials to provide lodging but prevent food from reaching the fugitive. These provisions helped to ensure the physical protection of the fugitive but also limited the duration of stay in the sanctuary. On the one hand, hunger pressured the fugitive toward settlement. On the other hand, the pursuers of the fugitive had to maintain a vigil around their hostage fugitive so that there would be no escape. Such waiting forced these pursuers to cool their emotions and also pressured them to reach more rational settlements. While the concept of sanctuary protection granted here is similar to the Greek and Roman idea of "a place from which a man is not to be dragged,"[17] it also has parallels to the Anglo-Saxon protection given to each man's home, from which is derived the expression and lingering belief that a "man's home is his castle."[18]

Alfred's sanctuary legislation also mitigated against the increasingly harsh legislation against theft.[19] When a thief fled to a sanctuary, the law would guarantee the commutation of the death sentence and the thief could ransom his life by paying a fine or by binding himself to slavery.[20]

King Athelstan (or Aethelstan), Alfred's grandson, also promulgated important legislation regarding sanctuary. First, Athelstan distinguished between the types of sanctuaries available:

> IV Aethelstan 6.1. And if he seeks the king, or the archbishop, or a holy church of God, he shall have respite for nine days; but let him seek [whomsoever or] whatsoever he may, unless he cannot be captured, he shall not be allowed to live longer, if the truth becomes known about him.

> IV Aethelstan 6.2. If he seeks a bishop or a nobleman, or abbot or *ealdorman* or a *thegn*, he shall have a respite for three days. But let him seek whatever he may, he may not be spared longer, if he is caught.[21]

It is important that the distinction between sanctuaries is still dependent on the status of the person present at the sanctuary rather than on the inherent sacredness of the place. King Aethelstan is also credited with granting St. John's of Beverly its first charter of liberties in 937, including the privilege of sanctuary. This great chartered sanctuary extended a league (over a mile) from the church door in every direction, with its boundaries marked by carved crosses. Fines for violating the sanctuary were also provided in the charter. These fines were based upon the territorial sacredness of the sanctuary rather than the sacredness of the church official. The entire sanctuary area was divided into six concentric zones and the fines increased with the proximity of the violation to the altar. A violation of the sanctuary in the sixth zone in the center, which included that altar, was *botless*, an offense so grave that no mere compensation could redeem it.[22] As the sanctuary privilege developed, it began to use both personal and territorial sacredness to justify its expansion.

Three Types of Sanctuary

It would be fruitful at this point to digress momentarily from the historical development of English sanctuary and note the distinctions between the three types of sanctuaries that existed in England. The first and most widely used type was the general sanctuary privilege available to every parish church and churchyard.[23] However, the second type of sanctuary, the chartered sanctuaries, derived their authority not from the general ecclesiastical law but from a royal grant, protected by the king's peace. Such sanctuaries were controlled by local church officials and often able to extend permanent immunity to fugitives. Charters were often granted because of the special sanctity of the shrines of notable saints, such as St. John of Beverly.[24] It was this type of sanctuary that led to abuses, especially in the city of London.[25] Since the privilege of sanctuary was determined by the charter, such privileges became a "mixture of law and custom, grant and prescription, forgery and usurpation."[26]

There was a third type of sanctuary that is often overlooked: the purely secular jurisdictions where the local lord had royal rights and the king's writ did not run.[27] It was the independence from the king's jurisdiction that gave these secular sanctuaries their privileges. They could provide sanctuary just as a foreign jurisdiction could provide asylum to fugitives. Such protection would be theoretically unlimited in time but controlled by the local lord. A sanctuary seeker merely had to cross the border and enter into one of these independent jurisdictions to claim sanctuary.[28] However, when the privilege of church sanctuary was abrogated in England beginning in the fifteenth century, many sanctuary seekers still continued to seek refuge with the central churches of the independent jurisdictions. Thus, even after the general abolition of sanctuary privilege by Henry VIII, some of the churches in these independent jurisdictions continued to exercise the sanctuary privilege, no doubt to the confusion of many historians throughout the centuries.[29]

The Late Anglo-Saxon and the Norman Periods

As the Saxon kings began to grant the privilege of chartered sanctuaries more freely,[30] the general sanctuary privileges of the churches also became more institutionalized and complex. For example, King Ethelred (or Aethelred) "the Unready" decreed in 1014 that violations of church sanctuary would be fined depending on the status of the church:

> 5. Not all churches are to be regarded as possessing the same status in civil law, though from the side of religion they all possess the same sanctity.

> 5.1. Amends for violation of the protection of a principal church, in cases in which the compensation can be paid, shall be made by the payment of the fine for the breach of the king's mund, i.e. 5 pounds in districts under English law, and in the case of a church of medium rank, by the payment of 120 shillings, i.e., by the fine due the king [for insubordination], and in the case of one still smaller [where, however, there is a graveyard], by the payment of 60 shillings, and in the case of a county chapel, by the payment of 30 shillings.[31]

This was the first English legislation where the distinction between sanctuary privileges seemed to depend only on the place of sanctuary rather than the person that place is associated with. Of course, the status or rank of the church depended on the rank of the cleric who presided there. However, this law referred only to the place and not to the person. The tension between person and place would continue as the institutions of church and state would begin to clash in English society. The churches and the clergy would claim that the sanctuary privilege was rooted in the sanctity of the place, irrevocable by the monarch. On the other hand, the king would claim that the privilege was merely a personal privilege granted to the clergy, revocable at the king's will.

Ethelred's 1014 law also demonstrated that, at least through the early eleventh century, the privilege of sanctuary was still part of the basic Saxon law of *bot* (damages) and *wite* (fines). As the injured party, the church collected the fines for any sanctuary violations.[32] However, as the criminal justice system in England evolved, the system of personal damages became less and less important. As the government gradually assumed greater responsibility for the fugitives as subjects of the criminal laws, the churches gradually lost their power to mediate or intercede on behalf of the sanctuary seekers.[33]

Outlawry was one specific institution of England criminal law that developed alongside the sanctuary privilege. The law of outlawry subjected all fugitives, including sanctuary seekers, to the emerging criminal law. The English government had begun to regulate not only the operation of the sanctuaries but also the fates of the sanctuary seekers. By the end of the Saxon period, this institution had developed into an elaborate procedure. If a fugitive could not be located by the local sheriffs, then he or she was declared an outlaw by the county court. The fugitive's goods and chattels were forfeited to the king and land escheated to the immediate lord. Outlaws—now without land or possessions—had several alternatives. They could flee to another country, subject themselves to capture in another jurisdiction (an outlaw could not be killed if held by another court), or enter the king's service (since such service protected one's chattels from seizure). There was also the romanticized alternative of becoming a "professional" outlaw, usually in a group or band, such as the legendary Robin Hood. This was often an attractive alternative because pardons could sometimes be purchased or obtained if one waited long enough. However, all outlaws were subject to immediate execution without trial if caught by any of the king's officers. Captured outlaws were simply brought before the court, read the charges or the indictment, and then taken out for execution.[34] In the twelfth and thirteenth centuries, many outlaws were simply killed when captured.[35] Outlawry would become even more important with the development of the sanctuary privilege and the abjuration of the realm.

The privilege of sanctuary continued to develop under Norman rule. While William the Conqueror did not specifically codify the privilege, it was his general practice to confirm and preserve any existing Anglo-Saxon legislation.[36] The collection of laws known as *Leis Williame* does preserve a form of the Ethelred/Canute progressive system of fines for removing a fugitive from sanctuary in violation of the privilege.[37] Finally, there is an abundance of legislation regarding sanctuary in the collection of laws entitled *Leges Edwardi Confessoris*, now dated as originating around 1130–1135. These laws guarantee the fugitive's safety within the church but require thieves to return stolen property or to make restitution to their victims.[38]

There is an interesting provision in *Leges Edwardi Confessoris* regarding those fugitives who sought sanctuary repeatedly:

> 5.3. If, however, he has done this repeatedly and happens to take refuge repeatedly in this way, after restoring what he has stolen, he shall abjure the province [*provinciam*] and shall not return. And if he should return, let no one dare to receive him, save by the leave of the justices of the lord king.[39]

This provision seems to establish an early form of the abjuration of the realm which would be so widespread in later centuries.[40]

The Plantagenet Period

The privilege of sanctuary reached its highest state of development and most widespread use during the reign of the Plantagenet kings. First, the early Plantagenets established many great abbeys and priories throughout England and often endowed these churches with chartered sanctuary privileges.[41] On the other hand, the Plantagenet period was also the time that the English monarch sought to subject the independent lords to the royal jurisdiction. Such consolidation of power would also restrict the sanctuary privileges of these areas. However, Henry II's bid for consolidation was severely weakened after his confrontation with Thomas à Becket, the Archbishop of Canterbury. The assassination of Becket in his own cathedral in 1170 is often characterized as the most famous violation of sanctuary. The outcry against the monarch after Becket's murder insured that general ecclesiastical liberties would be preserved.[42]

It would be difficult to catalogue and discuss all the relevant sanctuary legislation during this historical period. However, it is important to note the growing detail surrounding the privilege.[43] The first reference to sanctuary in the Statutes of the Realm appear in Edward II's reign, in the 1315–1316 session:

> They that abjure the Realm so long as they be in the Common Way, shall be in the King's Peace, nor ought to be disturbed of any Man; and when they be in the Church, their keepers ought not to abide in the Church yard, except Necessity or Peril of Escape do require so. And so long as they be in the Church, they

shall not be compelled to flee away, but they shall have their
Necessaries for their Living, and may go forth to empty their
Belly. And the King's Pleasure is that Thieves and Appellors
whensoever they will, may confess their Offences unto Priests,
but let the Confessor beware that they do not erroneously in-
form such Appellors.[44]

The provision of greater freedom of movement for the fugitives
evidences greater concern for them. The sanctuary seekers were allowed to be fed and to leave the church building. It is also clear that
by the fourteenth century, the use of sanctuary privilege had become inseparable with the practice of the abjuration of the realm.

Abjuration of the Realm

Abjuration of the realm was tantamount to permanent exile for
the sanctuary seeker. The sanctuary seeker would be protected in
the sanctuary for a limited time and then would be required to leave
England permanently. Rather than being forced to pay compensation to satisfy the Anglo-Saxon law of bloodfeud, the sanctuary
seeker now had to submit to the operation of the criminal law. Limiting private revenge was no longer the primary purpose of the sanctuaries. Instead, sanctuaries had become part of the criminal law,
facilitating the imposition of the sentence of banishment without
trial. Sanctuary seekers who abjured the realm chose this punishment instead of punishment after trial. In this sense, the abjuration
of the realm was a refinement of the law of outlawry. Now outlaws
were permanently exiled from the country.

Fortunately, there are many cases of abjuring the realm in English legal records, so it is fairly easy to reconstruct the elaborate
procedure involved.[45] Initially, a fugitive arriving at a sanctuary had
to comply with formal entrance procedure. While the protection of
the sanctuary privilege theoretically began the moment the fugitive
stepped onto church property, there were often elaborate admission
procedures when the fugitive actually reached the church building.
For example, in Durham, there were two special chambers at the
north door of St Cuthbert's[46] where church officials could sleep and
receive fugitives at any hour of the day or night. When the fugitive
was admitted,[47] the Galilee bell was tolled as a sign that someone

was seeking sanctuary. The fugitive then had to declare before credible witnesses why sanctuary was taken or the nature of his offense. The sanctuary seeker then tolled another bell as a token of his or her request for sanctuary. It was then the custom at Durham to give the fugitive a black gown with a yellow cross upon the left shoulder (the cross of St. Cuthbert) to wear while under sanctuary protection. At Durham, sanctuary seekers were lodged in a graete or bedstead near the south door (the door farthest from the door of entry, where pursuers may arrive). Food and bedding were provided for a maximum of thirty-seven days at Durham.[48]

At St. John's of Beverly, another great chartered sanctuary, the sanctuary seeker was administered the following oath:

> Ye shall be true and faithful to the Archbishop of York, Lord of this, to the Provost of the same, to the Canons of this Church, and all others its Ministers.
>
> Ye shall bear good heart to the Baille and 12 Governors of this town, to all Burgesses, and Commoners of the same.
>
> Ye shall bear no pointed weapon, dagger, knife, and no other weapon against the King's peace.
>
> Ye shall be ready at all your power if there be any debate or strife, or not so, then in the case of fire within the town to help to suppress it.
>
> Also ye shall be ready at the Obit of King Aethelstone, at the Dirge, and the Messe, at such time as it is done at the warning of the belman of the towne, and do your good duty in ringing and for to offer the Messe on the morrow, so help you God and their Holy Evangelists.[49]

After this oath, the fugitive "kissed the book" (presumably the Bible but perhaps the register) and then paid the bailiff a fee of two shillings and four pence, and the clerk a fee of four pence. These seem to be the only fees paid by any fugitives. The clerk then entered a description of the sanctuary seeker (class or occupation), residence, and the place and mode of the crime involved into the church register.[50] Unlike Durham, the fugitive at Beverly was not allowed to put on any religious habit.[51] Lodging was provided in the dormitory and food in the refectory for thirty days.[52]

Conditions varied at the different sanctuaries. Sometimes lodging was provided in a house within the church precincts.[53] At least one church, St. Gregory's at Norwich, had spacious lodgings (in the porches of the church) set apart for sanctuary men and women.[54] On the other hand, conditions could be very harsh in the parish churches, where the watch and ward was very strict[55] and the fugitives were fed only if the parish priest was charitable. There is some evidence that friends of the fugitive were sometimes able to supply him or her with food.[56]

The watch and ward consisted of a guard of men from the four neighboring villages.[57] This guard was summoned by the church and was fined if the fugitives escaped from the sanctuary.[58] It was also the duty of the church officials to summon the local coroner.[59] It took an average of three to four days for the coroner to arrive, and sometimes it took as long as a fortnight. When the coroner arrived, he entered the name of the fugitive in the coroner's rolls and took the fugitive's confession, in the presence of representatives of the four neighboring villages and other witnesses.[60]

After the sanctuary seeker confessed to the coroner, he or she had several options: either surrender to trial or abjure the realm. However, the fugitive generally had forty days to make the decision.[61] In other words, the sanctuary protection lasted forty days (or longer, if there was a charter). At the end of the forty days, if the sanctuary seeker still did not make any decision, the church officials were forbidden to provide food to the fugitive and he or she was starved out of the church.[62] Bracton writes of those in a sanctuary who did not come out after the forty days:

> But what if he refuses to leave it; may he not be dragged out forcibly by the lay power? No, as is evident, for to do so would be abominable and impious. It seems therefore that the ordinary of the place, the archdeacon or his official, dean or parson, may and ought to do so, that is compel him to come out for sword ought to aid sword, nor does the execution of law constitute a wrong. Since he has refused to come out unless compelled there is a strong presumption as to his guilt (especially if he is a known thief) and to protect him in the church (at least after he has been there for one night or more), will be to act contrary to the peace

and the king himself, who ought to safeguard the peace for the security of all.[63]

There are many instances where the fugitive was taken out of sanctuary by other means: by fire, by violence (violating the sanctuary with arms), by persuasion, and by beguilement (false promises of pardon or escape).[64]

If the fugitive decided to abjure the realm, then the coroner was again summoned. The fugitive knelt before the door of the church,[65] sometimes clothed in sackcloth.[66] Before witnesses[67] the fugitive took a form of the following oath:

> This hear, thou Coroner, that I, M. of H., am a robber of sheep or any other beast, or a murderer of one or more, and a felon of our Lord the King of England, and because I have done many such evils or robberies in the land, I do abjure the land of our Lord Edward King of England, I shall haste me towards the port of such a place which thou hast given me; and that I shall not go out of the highway, and if I do, I will be taken as a robber and a felon of our Lord the King; and that at such a place I will diligently seek for passage, and that I will tarry there but one flood and ebb, if I can have passage; unless I can have it in such a place, I will go every day into the sea up to my knees, assaying to pass over; and unless I can do this within 40 days, I will put myself again into the Church as a robber and a felon of our Lord the King, so help me God and His holy judgment.[68]

After the oath, there was a ritual in which the fugitive gave up all his clothing to the sacristan but then had it returned.[69] This ritual was apparently a symbol that when the fugitive abjured the realm, he or she was left without any rights or public privileges and it was only through the charity of the church officials that he or she even had any means of sustenance. The chattels and land of the abjurer were also automatically forfeited to the king.[70]

There is considerable confusion among historians as to the mode of dress of the abjurers as they traveled to their ports of embarkation. The abjurers were either clothed in a white robe with a red cross of mercy,[71] plain sackcloth,[72] or white sackcloth.[73] During the fourteenth century, it is recorded that the abjurers were clothed in shirt and breeches.[74] Some note that the abjurers traveled bareheaded and barefooted.[75] It was also customary for abjurers to carry a cross.[76] Regardless of how they were precisely dressed, abjurers on the highway must have been a very striking image.

It seems that the early practice may have been to allow the abjurer to choose a port[77] but it was the general practice, at least since the time of Henry III, that the coroner assigned a port to the abjurer.[78] The time given for the journey varied, perhaps considering the age and health of the abjurer and the season of the year.[79] The most popular port seemed to be Dover (to go to either France or Flanders), a journey of eight to fifteen days from anywhere in England, with twelve days being the most common travel time allotted.[80] There is some evidence that some coroners meticulously planned the abjurer's itinerary, detailing specific directions and stopping points.[81]

While on their journey, the abjurers were able to stop overnight but never at any one place longer than two nights.[82] They were not allowed to use the roads or hospices for pilgrims.[83] It is not completely clear but at least some abjurers were escorted by the guard from the four neighboring villages,[84] and others by local constables.[85] If the abjurers strayed from the main highway or tried to escape, they could be (and usually were) immediately executed when caught.[86]

When the abjurer reached the port, he or she was to stay at the beach and wade into the water to the knees each day as an expression of the need for passage abroad.[87] If no ship appeared or was willing to take the abjurer as a passenger within forty days (or some other fixed interval established by the coroner), the abjurer was to return to the original place of sanctuary, presumably to set out again at a later date.[88] It is unknown how abjurers paid for the passage if a ship was found; either the abjurers received money from friends or the ships were somehow bound to take the abjurers without charge.[89] Since abjuration of the realm was a lifelong exile or banishment,[90] the abjurers could not return to England unless pardoned by the king. While some abjurers were pardoned and returned to England,[91] it is unknown what happened to most of the abjurers who ended up on the shores of continental Europe.[92]

Fortunately, there are several reliable primary sources detailing the operation of sanctuaries and the abjurations of the realm. One source is the records of St. Cuthbert's in Durham. Between the years 1464 to 1524, 332 persons sought sanctuary at Durham for 243 different crimes. The overwhelming majority of the crimes, 195 of them, were homicides and 16 were by debtors. While there is only an occasional mention of the social status or occupation of the sanctuary seekers, there is much primary source material regarding the type of murder weapons used—principally daggers (56) and swords (21).[93] It is also interesting to note that most of the sanctuary seekers came from outside the county of Durham, reflecting the national character of this great chartered sanctuary.[94]

Similar statistics can be compiled for the sanctuary at Beverly. In the years 1478–1539, 469 persons sought sanctuary at St. John's. There were 173 cases of murder, with 52 of the 186 persons involved being tailors. There were over 200 cases involving debt, with 31 butchers being the most numerous among occupations. At Beverly, the occupations of the sanctuary seekers were generally recorded and reflected the predominance of the farmer or agricultural labor class in the contemporary society. It is unknown why tailors were so murderous but the fact that debtors outnumbered murderers at Beverly evidenced the growing commercialization of England and the emerging power of the merchant class. In contrast to Durham, the weapons used in the crimes were seldom recorded at Beverly. However, like Durham, Beverly attracted sanctuary seekers from counties throughout England.[95]

Finally, one historian estimates that there was an average of twenty sanctuary cases in each county every year (based on thirteenth century records for a "typical" county). Based on this estimate, the historian calculates about one thousand cases of sanctuary each year.[96] Later historians disagree about the accuracy of this estimate.[97] Regardless of what the actual number was, it is evident that sanctuaries were widely used during the fourteenth, fifteenth and sixteenth centuries.

It is also evident that the institution of sanctuary in medieval England was radically different from either the Hebrew cities of refuge or the early Christian sanctuaries in the late Roman Empire. Combined with the abjuration of the realm, the sanctuary protection had become a drastic alternative sentence of banishment. The institution had also become secularized, where the church officials were acting more as royal officers of justice than as intercessors or mediators. However, the widespread use of sanctuary soon led to widespread abuse.

The Demise of Sanctuary in English Law

Abuses by Debtors

One reason for the demise of sanctuary was its growing abuse within an increasingly commercial society. While the original conceptions of sanctuary protected fugitives from blood revenge, debtors now fled to city churches to escape their creditors.[98] One common scheme was for debtors to assign all their property to friends and then flee to a sanctuary. The creditors were then forced to settle their claims at a much reduced value or lose them altogether (if the debtor was in a secular or chartered sanctuary, he could often stay indefinitely while the creditor could not afford to wait). Once the debtors were free of the claims of their creditors, they left the sanctuary and then retrieved their property. Westminster Cathedral and St. Martin le Grand's in London were popular sanctuaries to carry out these schemes. While Parliament ruled in 1377 under Edward III that creditors could take their full claims against such collusive schemes, abuses persisted.[99]

The next year, Parliament again considered the problem of debtors abusing the sanctuary privilege. It was the opinion of the Justices and Doctors of both the canon and civil laws in the Privy Council that neither God, the Pope, or any king could grant a sanctuary privilege to debtors because "sin it is and occasion for sin expressly to delay a creditor in his claim for a debt."[100] After much testimony and debate, it was decided that sanctuary would only be provided to non-fraudulent debtors, or those "who by fortune of sea or fire, robbers or other mischief without fraud or collusion shall have been so impoverished as to be unable to pay their debts."[101] The following year, 1379, a procedure was established where the sheriff would go to the site of the sanctuary for five successive weeks with a summons for a debtor to appear before the king's justices when creditors' claims were outstanding. If no appearance was made by the debtor, judgment was entered in favor of the creditor and execution against the goods and land of the debtor was carried out.[102] Henry V enacted legislation to protect the claims of creditors when debtors abjured the realm by subjecting any debtors "going beyond the seas" to the full claims of their creditors.[103] While all legislative attempts to control the use of sanctuaries by debtors were never totally successful, they played an important role in questioning the privilege before the King and his legislative bodies and in providing a forum for arguments for the ultimate abolition of the privilege.

London Sanctuaries

There were other more serious abuses of the sanctuary privilege at St. Martin le Grand in London. In 1402 the Commons complained that thieves were taking their loot to the church, that vendors were not paid for goods sold to those within the sanctuary, and that criminals were using the church as a base from which to commit further crime in the city of London.[104] The petition by the Commons asked that the sanctuary privilege be reduced in London but such relief was not granted.[105] Instead, Henry IV only ordered the church to produce proof of its right to exercise the privilege before the Privy Council.[106] Meanwhile, the abuses continued.[107]

The complaint of the Londoners did not arise as much from fear of the criminal raids on the city as from purely economic interests in controlling craftspersons who took sanctuary there. In the 1440's and 1450's, there were repeated challenges to both the exemption of craftspersons within the protection of St. Martin's from the supervision of the wardens of the guilds and the general exemption of all the inhabitants of the sanctuary from taxation. A thriving alternate market developed in St. Martin's Lane, which encouraged the production of inferior wares, especially counterfeit plate and jewelry. Foreigners who could not join the craft guilds also found St. Martin's to be a profitable place to carry on their trades. The kings of the period generally had little sympathy for the London guilds, and so the abuses continued.[108] There were also many legal battles over the taxation of the inhabitants of St. Martin's. London sheriffs routinely violated the sanctuary and distrained goods of the inhabitants for the non-payment of taxes. However, the officials of St. Martin's often protested—usually successfully—such violations of the sanctuary and the goods were often restored.[109] Thus, St. Martin's represented the erosion of a legal privilege intended to protect fugitives into a setting for commercial enterprise.

Ecclesiastical and Judicial Regulation

There were several ways that the privilege of sanctuary was attacked during the fifteenth century. Henry VII was able to enlist the aid of papal authority to restrict the privilege when Pope Innocent VIII granted a bull providing (1) that a fugitive who left the sanctuary lost its protection, (2) that the sanctuaries were only to protect the loss of life or limb (and therefore, by implication, not debtors threatened only with the loss of personal property) and (3) that the king could send his soldiers to the sanctuary to guard any fugitives who had committed treason.[110] There are too many complex motivations involving the relationships between church and state, between popes and kings, to provide a simple explanation for the papal cooperation with the secular restriction of an ecclesiastical privilege. However, it is clear that the church authorities were not blind to the erosion of the privilege and hoped to maintain some control over it by continuing to redefine it.[111] The concessions made through these papal bulls might be worthwhile sacrifices if the privilege itself could be preserved.

The judicial branch of the English government provided another method of restricting the sanctuary privilege. One writer describes the efforts of the justices as the "most successful campaign against sanctuary before the break with Rome."[112] By the time of Henry VIII, no sanctuary could be maintained in law unless the one who claimed the privilege could show (1) a royal grant or charter, (2) usage of the privilege and (3) prior allowance or recognition of the privilege in the courts. After 1486, the standard of proof for a charter became the Westminster charter, which had specifically defined the sanctuary privilege. This standard of evidence was ironical because most recognized that the Westminster charter was a forgery.[113] However, the justices successfully encroached upon the privilege through this rigid definition of the circumstances in which sanctuary might be claimed.

The justices also restricted the privilege through the application of rigid rules of judicial procedure. A person who had taken refuge in a sanctuary could still be arrested and removed from the sanctuary if the proper pleading was not made to the king's officers. The fugitive could not simply plead a defense of sanctuary for the protection of his or her life but had to expressly confess the commission of a felony. The extreme application of this requirement occurred during Henry VII's reign, when sanctuary would be denied if the fugitive's victim had suffered a mortal wound but had not yet died (since the technical felony of murder had not yet been committed).[114] Thus, the justices gave those in sanctuary a very clear and difficult choice: surrender to arrest and trial or confess guilt and be forced to abjure the realm. While such a choice had always faced the fugitive, the decision was now made in the presence of the waiting sheriffs. Arrest and trial became a much more imminent and threatening alternative. Furthermore, any mistake in pleading made by the fugitive could result in the loss of the sanctuary protection altogether.

Similarly, when a fugitive had been wrongfully removed from a sanctuary, he or she had to meet rigid pleading requirements in order to assert a violation of sanctuary as a defense. If the pleading requirements were not met, the accused would be subject to full criminal prosecution without any claim to sanctuary protection. The justices construed the privilege narrowly and did not allow any privilege in the church gardens, barns or stables. Further, the justices did not recognize the privileges of the independent jurisdictions or secular sanctuaries.[115] Presumably, these restrictions by the justices resulted in greater numbers of violations of sanctuary and the loss of the privilege by many fugitives. Widespread use and abuse had necessitated increasing judicial limitations.

Henry VIII

The attack on the sanctuary privilege soon became more direct under Henry VIII. First, the king began to burden the exercise of the privilege by regulating it nationally. In 1529, Henry VIII enacted a statute whereby abjurers were to be branded on the brawn of the right thumb with an "A" (for abjurer) after their confession to the coroner and just before their oath of abjuration, "to the intent that he might be the better known among the king's subjects to have abjured."[116] Since the abjurer was about to go into exile anyway, the requirement seems largely punitive and also a disincentive for those who might see sanctuary and abjuration as an attractive course of action. A sanctuary seeker would be subject not only to exile but a painful, permanent maiming.

In 1536, the king enacted rigid regulations for life within the sanctuary. First, all fugitives had to wear a distinctive badge on the upper garment, measuring ten inches by ten inches, to be assigned by the governor or the head of the sanctuary. Failure to wear such a badge resulted in the loss of the sanctuary protection. Second, the sanctuary men and women could not leave their lodgings—even if still within the sanctuary grounds—between sunset and sunrise. This regulation was equivalent to placing all those in sanctuary under house arrest during the evenings. The sanctuary protection would be lost upon the third violation of the curfew regulation. Finally, those in sanctuary could not carry any weapons, except a meat knife and then only at mealtimes.[117]

While all these regulations of the sanctuary privilege probably deterred some from seeking sanctuary, it took Henry VIII many more years to abolish the privilege altogether. Parliament's first attempt in 1512 to reduce the privilege lapsed because of strong clerical opposition to the parallel reduction of the privilege of the benefit of clergy.[118] It was not until the 1530–1531 session of Parliament that Henry VIII was finally able to substantively limit the privilege. An enactment during that session required abjurers to stay in England, resulting in lifetime imprisonment in the sanctuaries. The only method of release was through a pardon. Furthermore, if the fugitive was captured outside the sanctuary, there would be no further sanctuary protection and he or she would stand trial for the original offense. The preamble to the statute notes that many abjurers were expert mariners, able soldiers or trained archers. Henry VIII wanted to keep these persons in England since their mass exile would expose important military information and personnel to foreign enemies.[119] The result of the statute was to end the practice of abjuration of the realm. Without the abjuration practice as a method of limiting the sanctuary protection, the privilege of sanctuary itself became vulnerable to direct attack.[120]

That direct attack came in 1540, when Parliament abolished all the chartered sanctuary privileges, preserving the privilege only for parish churches and churchyards, cathedral churches, hospitals, collegiate churches and dedicated chapels used as parish churches. Furthermore, no sanctuary protection was available at all for the crimes of murder, rape, burglary, robbery, arson and sacrilege. (Severe restrictions had already been placed on debtors and those accused of treason.) Finally, Henry VIII designated eight cities—Wells, Westminster, Manchester, Northampton, York, Derby, Launceston and Norwich—as sanctuary towns where fugitives could also gain sanctuary protection.[121] While some historians have been quick to draw an analogy to the six Hebrew cities of refuge, Henry VIII's motivations seemed to have sprung less from an imitation of Mosaic law than from his desire to continue to limit the flight of sanctuary seekers abroad, an exodus that posed a military drain and threat to England.[122] Thus, while the comparison between the Hebrew cities of refuge and Henry VIII's cities of refuge is tempting, it is probably more coincidental than substantive. Henry VIII was interested in abrogating the sanctuary privilege, not in resurrecting its ancient Hebrew origins.[123]

As noted above, the attack on the sanctuary privilege of the churches came at a time when the English monarchy was consolidating its general power over the independent jurisdictions.[124] The extension of the king's writ into the northern counties of Tynedale, Redesdale and Hexham under the reign of Henry V in 1414 and 1421 directly resulted from complaints about the abuse of the secular sanctuary privileges in those jurisdictions.[125] In the 1490's all jurisdictions were made subject to the king's law for any crimes of treason.[126] Thus, the great palatine liberties suffered a gradual erosion of their independence.

Henry VIII was active in consolidating the royal jurisdiction over the the independent counties. First, he imposed penalties on those liberties that did not hand over fugitives to the king's officers. Then, he extended the king's writs to most of the independent jurisdictions in the north.[127] At the same time, Henry VIII incorporated Wales and the Percy lands into English rule.[128] Thus, the demise of the privilege of sanctuary must be understood in its historical context:

> . . . sanctuaries and their fate had been drawn into the stream
> of two great movements: the anti-clerical wave which preceded
> and facilitated the break with Rome, and the Tudor policy—in-

evitable in the drawing of a modern age—of destroying all jurisdictions which could rival or resist the power of the king. [129]

Indeed, it was not until Henry VIII broke the bonds with
Rome that the direct attack on the sanctuary privilege was successful. [130] When Henry VIII had established the monarchy as the supreme authority in the land—both religious and secular—then the
church could no longer protest the abrogation of its privilege of sanctuary.

Final Abolition

Despite Henry VIII's efforts, a privilege of sanctuary continued to survive for at least another century. Henry's successor, Edward VI, restored the privilege for anyone who committed a felony
other than treason, willful murder or aggravated theft. While the use
of the eight cities of refuge was abandoned during Edward VI's
reign, the 1540 Act was never expressly repealed. [131]

Even the chartered sanctuaries were not quite destroyed. References to the Westminster sanctuary in the 1556–1557 Acts of the
Privy Council evidence its continued use during Queen Mary's
reign. [132] There were bills introduced against the sanctuary privilege
in 1558, 1563 and 1566, so the privilege must have still been viable
during Elizabeth I's reign as well. [133] In 1569, the Privy Council pronounced that no sanctuary would be available to fraudulent debtors,
but there is evidence that sanctuary was still available to anyone who
took an oath against fraud and the non-payment of debts. [134]

It was not until the reign of the first Stuart king, James I, that
the sanctuary privilege was finally abolished by statute. First, the
1603–1604 session of Parliament enacted the following:

> . . . That so much of all Statutes as concerneth abjured Persons
> and Sanctuaries, or ordering or governing of Persons abjured or
> in sanctuaries, made before the five and thirtieth yeere of the late
> Queene Elizabeth's Reigne, shall also stand repealed and be
> voide. [135]

However, this first legislation seemed only to be a part of the
general repeal of Elizabethan law. Presumably some sanctuary privilege persisted because numerous bills were introduced by both the

Houses of Lords and Commons to abolish the privilege beginning from 1606.[136] Finally, in 1624, a one sentence statute ended at least eleven centuries of sanctuary privilege in England:

> And Be it alsoe enacted by the authoritie of this present Parliament, that no Sanctuarie or Privilege of Sanctuary shalbe hereafter admitted or allowed in any case.[137]

CHAPTER SEVEN

Sanctuary in United States History

"What is sanctuary? In feudal times, both in medieval Europe and old Hawaii, sanctuary was a guarantee of refuge and protection, usually under the auspices of the Church or in the locale of a certain city (Honaunau, for instance). Refugees from prosecution and persecution could be harbored indefinitely in places of guaranteed safety. But in "democratic" twentieth-century America, where the courts are supposed to afford justice and uphold human rights, sanctuary is not recognized or respected, however often it is invoked. Yet as a symbol of resistance to injustice, sanctuary remains effective today in stirring the consciences of men."[1]

—Statement of Resistance Group
at the University of Hawaii
November 1968

The First Colonists

It was soon after the final abolition of the sanctuary privilege during the reign of James I that the Pilgrims and Puritans first settled in America. To these first colonists, their entire journey to the North American continent was a new Exodus to a new Promised Land away from religious and social persecution and oppression. Thus, the entire continent was viewed as a sanctuary, a refuge from

158

the upheaval in the aftermath of the Protestant Reformation and the Catholic Counter-Reformation.[1a] One could almost say that these first colonists had abjured their realms and were now living lives of exile in North America. To these first European settlers, it would have been redundant to revive the institution of sanctuary as a legal privilege. Furthermore, with the recent abuses of the privilege still fresh in their memories, these colonists were probably reluctant to transplant connotations of corruption and outlawry to their new home. In any case, the law of sanctuary was not adopted as part of the colonial common law.

There is at least one anecdotal account of the provisions of sanctuary in the early colonial history. The events are recorded by Rollin G. Osterweis in the history entitled *Three Centuries of New Haven, 1638–1938*.[2] Osterweis describes the scenario as colonial New Haven in the 1660's, when Charles II had ascended to the English throne. The same ship which brought the news of the new reign to Boston in July 1660 also carried two regicides—two officers of the Cromwellian army and members of the High Court of Justice that had tried Charles I and issued his death warrant. The two officers became fugitives four months later when Charles II sent his officers to find them and bring them back to England for trial. The fugitives fled to New Haven and were received by the Rev. John Davenport. The king's officers were in hot pursuit but were delayed by the governor of New Haven Colony, who was sympathetic to the Cromwellians. Thus, the king's officers were forced to first attend Sabbath services where the Rev. Davenport deliberately preached on the text of Isaiah 16:3, which reads in part, "Hide the fugitives, do not betray the refugees." It became readily apparent to the congregation—including the king's officers—what the preacher intended and encouraged. The governor further aggravated the frustration of the king's officers by having the royal arrest warrants read aloud in a public meeting instead of treating them as secret documents. It was no accident that the king's officers were unable to find the fugitives in New Haven. Osterweis then records that the fugitives were able to hide in New Haven for three years, and then in Massachusetts for seven more years, until they died of natural causes.[3] Thus, neither the Rev. John Davenport nor any of the colonial officials invoked the privilege of sanctuary; one shrewd pastor simply outwitted the king's officers.

The Underground Railroad
for Fugitive Slaves

The first practical provision of sanctuary in the United States on any widespread scale occurred in the years before the Civil War, during the operation of the Underground Railroad. However, even during this period, there was still no express invocation of the defunct English privilege. Instead, preachers such as the Rev. Charles Bush of Norwich, Connecticut[4] used texts such as Deuteronomy 23:16–17 ("If a slave has taken refuge with you, do not hand him over to his master. Let him live among you wherever he likes and in whatever town he chooses. Do not oppress him") to support their work for the abolition of slavery. The churches providing sanctuary did not seek to claim a legal privilege but only sought to respond to religious commands regarding hospitality. For example, after the *Dred Scott* decision,[5] the Rev. Leverett Griggs of Bristol, Connecticut preached on the topic of "Fugitives from Slavery":

> Fugitives from American Slavery should receive the sympathy and aid of all lovers of freedom. If they come to our door, we should be ready to feed, clothe, and give them shelter, and help them on their way. If we make the bible our rule of life, if we are willing to do to others as we would they should do to us, we can have no difficulty on this subject.[6]

The Underground Railroad operated in the face of the Fugitive Slave Act of 1850 (as well as its predecessors) which prohibited harboring or assistance of fugitive slaves. Indeed, there were many prosecutions against members of the Underground Railroad for violating the Act.[7] It is unclear whether any of these prosecutions were targeted at churches but it is well documented that churches and church communities formed integral parts of the Underground Railroad.[8] However, the churches and clergy that participated in the Underground Railroad seemed less interested in reviving any legal privilege of sanctuary in the United States than in providing practical assistance to the fugitive slaves. As abolitionists, they where willing to violate what they perceived as an unjust and immoral law and did not claim any special privileges or immunities because of their religiosity. In other words, these churches and clergy did not see the protection they provided as any different from that afforded by the other participants in the Underground Railroad.

Sanctuary During the Vietnam War

In the East

The only explicit invocation of church sanctuary in the United States prior to its current manifestation for Central American refugees occurred during the Vietnam War. On October 16, 1967, at a "Service of Conscience and Acceptance" at the Arlington Street Unitarian Church in Boston, Massachusetts, nearly three hundred draft resisters turned over their draft cards to members of the clergy and some fifty of them burned their draft cards as a protest against the war. Rev. William Sloane Coffin, Jr., chaplain at Yale University, preached the sermon:

> Now if the Middle Ages churches could offer sanctuary to the most common of criminals, could they not today do the same for the most conscientious among us? And if in the Middle Ages they could offer forty days to a man who had committed both a sin and a crime, could they not today offer an indefinite period to one who had committed no sin?

> The churches must not shrink from their responsibility in deciding whether or not a man's objection is conscientious. But should a church declare itself a "sanctuary for conscience" this should be considered less a means to shield a man, more a means to expose a church, an effort to make a church really a church.

> For if the state should decide that the arm of the law was long enough to reach inside a church there would be little church members could do to prevent an arrest. But the members could point out what they had already dramatically demonstrated, that the sanctity of conscience was being violated.[9]

Coffin clearly expressed a new conception of church sanctuary. First, the motivation for providing sanctuary was not so much to protect the sanctuary seeker as to be truthful to the role of the church in society—"to make a church really a church." The underlying rationale for church sanctuary was theological and political rather than legal. Second, there was no claim to any legal recognition of the privilege. Indeed, it was precisely the illegality of the act—an act of civil disobedience—that gave the concept of sanctuary its symbolic power as a confrontation with an unjust and illegal war. The speaker knew and suffered the consequences of his words. For his sermon and his role in the October 16 service, Coffin was found guilty of conspiring to counsel, aid and abet those refusing induction into the army and was sentenced to two years' imprisonment and a $5,000 fine. The conviction was eventually overturned on appeal in 1969.[10]

Other churches were quick to answer the call to provide sanctuary to those protesting mandatory military service in Vietnam. In November 1967, the session of the St. Andrew United Presbyterian Church of Marin City, California declared the church as a sanctuary:

> The offer of sanctuary means what the medieval church offered to individuals who were being persecuted, namely the moral protection of the Christian community. The doors of the building are open to those who have taken a conscientious stand of non-cooperation with the Selective Service System. Food and lodging will be offered so that if there is to be an arrest, it can take place in the church building where the moral confrontation will be obvious.[11]

Such a provision of sanctuary had obvious parallels to the medieval institution, namely, the provision of food and lodging. However, because the privilege was not formally recognized by United States law, the strength of the sanctuary rested in its moral and political symbolism rather than upon its legal protection against arrest.

On the first day of the trial of Coffin and the other members of the "Boston Five" for the October 16 service, the Arlington Street church put into practice what had been preached the previous October. On May 20, 1968 Robert A. Talmanson, 21, of Boston, whose appeal to overturn his conviction for induction refusal had just been denied by the United States Supreme Court,[12] and Specialist 4 William Chase, 19, of Dennis, Massachusetts, Absent Without Leave (AWOL) from Fort Lewis, Washington, took sanctuary in the church. Victor Jokel, the Executive Director of the church, declared:

> While the invocation of sanctuary can have no legal force—nor should it have—in our society, this historical concept, as renewed today, has the force of a moral imperative on the side of life and man. . . .[13]

Thus, Jokel expressly rejected any legal basis for sanctuary. It was an act of civil disobedience, not a legal privilege. The federal authorities were in agreement because three days later, United States Marshals carried Talmanson away from the pulpit of the church. Only clubs and mace from Boston police reinforcements enabled the Marshals to pass through the crowd of protestors gathered outside the church.[14]

Talmanson was taken to the federal correctional institution at Petersburg, Virginia, to serve his three-year sentence.[15] On May 29, nine days after he first took sanctuary, Chase surrendered himself to Army authorities at Boston's Federal Building following guarantees of the recognition of his conscientious objections to the war.[16]

Meanwhile, other churches in New York, Detroit and San Francisco declared themselves as sanctuaries.[17] In June 1968, the Unitarian Universalist Church of the Mediator in Providence, Rhode Island announced that Anthony W. Ramos, 24, of East Providence, Rhode Island, and Ron P. Moyer, 23, of White Plains, New York, who had both been indicted for refusing induction, had taken sanctuary at the church.[18] Ramos had returned from Toronto to enter the sanctuary. Albert Q. Perry, the minister of the church, told the press:

> They are permitted to stay here as long as the state honors and respects the traditions of the religion which have universally maintained that a person's first duty was obedience to his conscience or to his god.

> We . . . would remind it [the state] that it must either respect the principles of this place or frankly violate them. We cannot forbid, but can condemn the latter.[19]

Again, the church official recognized that the sanctuary only had the moral and political force of dramatizing the confrontation between the church and state, between individual conscience and government. The Federal Bureau of Investigation apparently had little respect for the position of conscience because after three nights, its agents broke through a locked door and arrested Ramos and Moyer in the church, along with nine other protesters who were attempting to non-violently obstruct the FBI.[20]

The same month, June 1968, Donald C. Baty, 22, of Huntington, Long Island, refused to appear in a federal court after refusing induction and was arrested in the sanctuary of the Washington Square United Methodist Church in Greenwich Village. The church board, which had voted to offer Baty sanctuary, joined a crowd of one hundred friends, family and other supporters at the arrest.[21] Baty was convicted of refusing induction[22] and was sentenced for up to four years in federal prison.[23] Although the number of churches offering sanctuary was growing, so were the lengths of the prison sentences given the sanctuary seekers.

The provision of sanctuary was an ecumenical movement, involving a wide range of denominations. Specialist 4 Frederick N. Rutman, 22, of Quincy, Massachusetts, was given sanctuary at the Friends Meeting house in Cambridge on August 11, 1968. Rutman had been AWOL from Fort Monmouth, New Jersey since June 9.[24] That same month, Private Victor M. Bell, 19, from Ohio, was sheltered at the Friends Meeting near the University of Chicago as part of the work of the Mobilization Committee to End the War in Vietnam. Bell had been AWOL from Fort Meade, Maryland for over two weeks before he presented himself at the Rockefeller Chapel of the University of Chicago seeking sanctuary. Local and national draft resisters met and decided to give Bell sanctuary.[25] Thus, the sanctuary movement, rooted in the churches, became part of the growing anti-war movement.

In the Universities

In November 1968, two Marine NCO candidates, Tom Met and Gary Gray, AWOL from Kaneohe Marine Base, took sanctuary in the student lounge of the University of Hawaii and then at the University YMCA. On the third day, a Sunday, after a "Service in

Celebration of Conscience" at the Unitarian Church, the two Marines led a march of about two hundred persons to the Marine base where they turned themselves in.

The sanctuary at the University of Hawaii was a radically different kind of sanctuary since it was centered at a university rather than at a church. The idea of an academic sanctuary first emerged at the Harvard Divinity School in the early fall of 1968 when protection was given to an AWOL Marine.[27] Later, the students from the Boston University School of Theology organized a sanctuary for Private Raymond Kroll, 18, of Walla Walla, Washington, at Marsh Chapel at the university. Kroll was eventually arrested when federal agents and the Boston police invaded the sanctuary.[28] Kroll had been AWOL from Fort Benning, Georgia, and was sentenced to three months of hard labor at Fort Devens, Massachusetts.[29]

In October 1968, the Massachusetts Institute of Technology Student Center became a sanctuary for Private Jack Michael O'Conner, 19, of Presque Isle, Maine. O'Conner had been AWOL from Fort Bragg, North Carolina since September 14.[30] An editorial in the student paper explicitly rejected the religious basis of sanctuary:

> Another aspect of the situation which may at first seem strange is the idea of claiming sanctuary in a non-religious area. For those who don't know, the term sanctuary is derived from the old custom of seeking political refuge in holy places, where the rules of the game said it would be safe. The action in the Student Center appears to be a case more of political asylum than sanctuary. At Marsh Chapel, where Ray Kroll claimed sanctuary for several days earlier this year, the religious aspects were overplayed to the detriment of the political. The latter, is after all, the central issue involved. It is appropriate, therefore, that the Resistance chose the Student Center rather than the Chapel for the confrontation with the system.[31]

Thus, at least one sanctuary perceived itself as offering a type of political asylum within the United States rather than claiming any religious sanctuary privilege. Indeed, O'Conner had been brought to the sanctuary by the M.I.T. Resistance, a political, not religious organization.[32] O'Conner was arrested in the early morning of November 10, after twelve days in the sanctuary.[33] He was later convicted of being absent without leave and was fined and sentenced to four months of hard labor at Fort Devens, Massachusetts.[34]

The provision of sanctuary at academic institutions continued through the last months of 1968 and through 1969. On October 31, 1968, Private William Steven Brakefield, 19, took sanctuary in the ballroom of the Finley Student Center at City College of New York. Brakefield had been AWOL from Fort Devens since October 2. Again, there were no invocations of any religious privilege; the sanctuary was organized by the New York Resistance, with support from the campus chapter of Students for a Democratic Society, the City College Commune, and the executive committee of the student government.[35] On November 4, local police entered the ballroom to arrest Brakefield, but when the crowd of about one hundred supporters presented non-violent resistance, the police removed their handcuffs from Brakefield and left.[36] However, the police returned, now numbering about two hundred and fifty, on November 7 and arrested Brakefield and all the students—over one hundred and twenty-five in all. The police made the arrests only after a reluctant request from the Associate Dean of the college. The criminal charges brought against the students were only for trespassing, not for harboring the AWOL Brakefield.[37] The arrests were followed by a series of further anti-war protests at the school.[38] Brakefield was convicted of criminal trespass in the third degree and sentenced to time already served in jail, seven days. He was then returned to Fort Devens to face military discipline.[39]

Specialist 4 John D. Rollins, 20, of Wilmington, North Carolina, took sanctuary at Brandeis University in Waltham, Massachusetts on December 4, 1968. Rollins, AWOL from Fort Clayton in the Canal Zone since November 12, stayed at Brandeis until he was arrested on December 19. He, too, was taken to Fort Devens after his arrest.[40] Private Jorge Caputo, 17, from Schenectady, New York, took sanctuary at St. Paul's Chapel at Columbia University on October 15, 1969. Caputo had been AWOL from Fort Dix since September 19 and left Columbia after five days to go underground. The sanctuary at Columbia was an interfaith effort, based in the Protestant chapel but strongly supported by the Radical Jewish Union.[41]

In the West

In 1971 and 1972, several California churches became involved in the sanctuary movement, providing refuge primarily for Navy personnel (as opposed to those AWOL or refusing Army induction on the East Coast). On September 30, 1971, six enlisted men from the attack aircraft carrier *USS Constellation* took sanctuary in San Diego's Christ the King Roman Catholic church. The men were Airman John Daniel Hoag, 18, from St. Louis, Missouri; Airman Charles W. Andrews, 22, from Greensburg, Pennsylvania; Fireman James A Mikell, Jr., 20, from Screven, Georgia; Seaman Ronald P. McLeod, 23, from Little Rock, Arkansas; Fireman Darryl L. Larrabee, 20, from Duluth, Minnesota; and Electronics Technician 3C Carl Scott Flanagan 22, from San Diego.[42] These six were later joined by three others: Seaman Apprentice David N. Clay, 19, from Stockton, California; Seaman John C. Obe, 19, from Ellsworth, Iowa; and Petty Officer 3C Charles M. Lawson, 21, from Midlothian, Texas.[43]

While the church consciously sheltered the sailors as a sanctuary, there was no legal privilege invoked. Instead, the provision of sanctuary was intended to be primarily symbolic. The pastor of the church, Fr. James Gallas, was quoted as saying, "We believe that because of our Christian heritage, we cannot turn anyone away. We certainly weren't concealing them."[44] Indeed, then San Diego Auxiliary Bishop John R. Quinn (now Archbishop of San Francisco) was quick to disclaim the action of the church: "The concept of sanctuary does not apply in the United States, where church buildings do not have jurisdictional exemption from civil law."[45]

After three nights in the church, the nine sailors were arrested by federal agents wearing civilian clothing in a pre-dawn 4:40 A.M. raid of the church. At the time, some thirty to forty anti-war sympathizers were also sleeping in the church but none were arrested.[46] The sailors were first taken to the North Island Naval Air Station and then flown by Navy plane to their ship, the *Constellation*, already more than three hundred miles offshore.[47] The nine men were first sentenced to thirty days in corrective custody.[48] Then, in December, eight of the nine sailors were flown to Treasure Island Naval Base in San Francisco and given "general discharges under honorable conditions." The ninth sanctuary-seeker, Airman Daniel Hoag, chose to remain on board the *Constellation*.[49]

Meanwhile, ten church communities from the San Francisco Bay Area declared themselves as sanctuaries on November 9, 1971, hoping to attract sailors from the aircraft carrier *USS Coral Sea*, berthed at the Alameda Naval Air Station and ready to set sail for Vietnam. The participating congregations were the University Lutheran Chapel, Berkeley; Sacred Heart Catholic Church, San Francisco; St. Benedictine's Catholic Church, San Francisco; Mary Help of Christians Catholic Church, Oakland; the Session of the First Presbyterian Church, Palo Alto; St. Andrew's Presbyterian Church, Marin City; the Community of St. Ann's (the Catholic chapel at Stanford University), Palo Alto; Hayward Area Friends; Palo Alto Friends; Berkeley Friends; and the Jesuits for Peace at the Jesuit School of Theology, Berkeley.[50] Again, a spokesperson for the sanctuary churches acknowledged that "sanctuary does not have the support of civil law" but emphasized the benefits of providing a church forum for the anti-war protests.[51]

On November 10, the day following the announcement by the churches, the Berkeley City Council voted 6-1 to "provide a facility for sanctuary" for "any person who is unwilling to participate in military action." The novel city council resolution banned city employees, including police officers, from aiding the investigation or arrest of anyone protected by the city's sanctuary.[52] United States Attorney James Browning was quick to denounce the city council's resolution and to threaten federal prosecution for any actual provision of sanctuary. In addition, Berkeley City Manager William Hanley announced his refusal to comply with the city council's resolution, creating further tension in the local political scene.[53] In the midst of all the public controversy, the *Coral Sea* did depart as scheduled, with no crew member seeking sanctuary.[54] Nevertheless, this incident marked the first time that a subgovernmental body in the United States had ever declared itself a sanctuary.

In 1972, two Naval servicemen did enter sanctuaries in California. First, in January, Douglas J. Nelson, 22, failed to return to his ship, the aircraft carrier *USS Hancock*, and took sanctuary at the LaJolla Friends Meeting house.[55] Later that same month, Richard R. "Ric" Larson, 19 of Detroit, Michigan, from the aircraft carrier *USS Midway* stayed in a sanctuary co-sponsored by three Palo Alto churches (St. Ann's at Stanford, First Presbyterian and the Friends Meeting). Larson stayed in the sanctuaries for four days before the Navy arrested him. He was eventually court-martialed and served a sentence of thirty days for unauthorized absence but then was honorably discharged as a conscientious objector.[56]

In all, over twenty churches in California declared themselves as sanctuaries: at least fifteen in the San Francisco Bay Area and five in San Diego. One pastor estimates that there were about nineteen public and about fifty private sanctuary seekers in California during the Vietnam War. However, all were either arrested or surrendered voluntarily. In addition, the sanctuary churches in California counseled over two hundred men who were considering conscientious positions on the war.[57]

Analysis

While it is difficult to draw conclusions about the sanctuary movement during the Vietnam War, several themes seem to emerge. First, the sanctuaries on the East Coast were distinct from the ones on the West Coast. On the East Coast, the sanctuary seekers were all from the Army while those on the West Coast came from the Navy. At first, the East Coast sanctuary seekers were men who refused Army induction, but later they were those AWOL from Army bases across the nation. Perhaps this trend simply reflected the focus of anti-war protests as the war continued, from induction refusal to active desertion. Although the first sanctuary seekers went to churches, college campuses soon became the common sanctuary sites. This change in the location of sanctuaries reflected a change in how they operated. At first, there was still some invocation of the ancient religious privilege even though the sanctuary churches acknowledged that such a privilege would not be recognized by the law. However, the primary purpose of proclaiming and offering sanctuary was to emphasize the moral objections to the war in Vietnam. As the war continued, the anti-war movement became a stronger independent political force and that movement began to use sanctuary as an accepted or, perhaps more accurately, tolerated form of political protest. School officials at City College of New York, Brandeis and Columbia insisted that the sanctuary activity was a matter between the servicemen and the military authorities and declined to intervene. Only when the students began to become disruptive were there any arrests. However, the arrests were only for trespassing rather than for the more serious felony charges of aiding desertion or other conspiracy offenses. Thus, while the sanctuaries were all eventually invaded by the civil or military authorities, they introduced a new form of resistance in a community other than in a church. It was a form of resistance that required the total involvement of its supporters, with many students moving into the sanctuaries with their sleeping bags to maintain a continuous vigil around the sanctuary seeker. Again, while there were no legal barriers to prevent governmental intrusion into the sanctuary, the police often had to confront human barriers who offered non-violent resistance to any arrests. Furthermore, all the sanctuary seekers were prosecuted by civil and/or military courts. There was no testing of any sanctuary privilege in any of these proceedings; the sanctuary seekers accepted their sentences as consequences of their protest activities. Finally, none of the sanctuaries themselves were ever prosecuted for their sanctuary activity.

On the West Coast, the sanctuaries again were provided by churches but they also took on new characteristics. First, the sanctuaries were often declared before there were any specific sanctuary seekers to take refuge in them. Therefore, the sanctuaries often became centers of more generalized anti-war activities, offering counseling and other lawful assistance. Again, the idea of sanctuary had been expanded to a broader meaning than merely a refuge for fugitives. The success or failure of the sanctuary movement during the Vietnam War must be measured in terms other than the number of war resisters who were protected from arrest. The focus of national and local attention on the sanctuaries raised many important moral and political issues about the war. In turn, churches and universities emerged as centers for continued public witnesses against the war. Third, the declaration by the Berkeley City Council created a new form of sanctuary unknown in the United States history. However, the question of whether a local government could shelter a person from the operation of federal law was never tested in any court.

The experiences and lessons of the sanctuary movement during the Vietnam War provide important sources of reflection for the current sanctuary movement. It was a remarkably diverse movement, involving sanctuary seekers of all draftable ages, from all over the nation. The churches and universities that offered sanctuary were also diverse in size and denomination. The provision of sanctuary for Central American refugees today continues that diversity and that history.

CHAPTER EIGHT

Application of the History
of the Sanctuary to
Central American Refugees Today

"Public sanctuary for Central American refugees takes a stand on behalf of a particularly powerless and vulnerable group of people, who have fled persecution in their own country only to face possible prosecution in ours. Whether or not public sanctuary can be justified in any particular congregation, the sanctuary movement calls the church to reexamine its fundamental commitment to the poor and powerless. Is practice in accord with mission? Sanctuary asks the church to seek to be holy, not only in the ritual within the "sanctuary" of worship, but also in its faithfulness to its mission. Worship and social ministry are united in the concept of sanctuary."[1]

—Eric Jorstad, St. James
Lutheran Church, Detroit, Michigan

It is interesting to note the parallels and distinctions between sanctuary today and sanctuary as it has existed throughout history. The authority for any provision of sanctuary today is clearly moral and religious rather than legal. There is no legal privilege, no charter from the king, no claim to legal independence from the king's jurisdiction as there was in England. The sanctuary movement today does not even derive authority from church-based institutions; it is a spontaneous and ecumenical movement, without any centralized or hierarchial directives. The sole basis for a church or congrega-

172

tional declaration of sanctuary today is its own moral and religious beliefs and convictions.

From Holy Places to Communities of Faith

The current manifestation of church sanctuary has given new meaning to the concept of sanctuary as it has been understood throughout history. Sanctuary for Central American refugees, while rooted historically in the sacredness of the church, is no longer limited to the geographic boundaries of church buildings. Modern skepticism no longer respects the sanctity of territory—there are few "holy places" in the United States. While historians and the tourist industry maintain many landmarks and monuments, churches have been reduced in the common mentality to being merely buildings. Indeed, economic survival has required many churches to become community centers, often renting out space to other groups and organizations for purely secular uses. The geographic spaces that churches occupy do not command any special reverence in the United States. Churches are not free from vandalism, graffiti and physical erosion. Thus, it is difficult to speak of sanctuary today with the same understanding of its inviolability and sacredness as the ancient Hebrews, Greeks and Romans.

For example, the sanctuary offered by both the ancient Canaanite altars and the Hebrew cities of refuge derived primary meaning from the sanctity of the place where they were located. While a modern mind may dismiss the legendary and mythic quality of these sanctuaries, their effectiveness was premised on the assumption that all—including the governmental authorities—would respect the sanctity of these sites and not violate the invisible protection they offered to sanctuary seekers.

In contrast, the current provision of sanctuary for Central American refugees is distinctly a community event. Most of the churches and other organizations that have publicly declared themselves as sanctuaries have made a conscious decision to become one—their actions create the holiness of the sanctuary. By declaring sanctuary, the church communities have consecrated their church building and made their church ground holy. Perhaps a few have only publicly ratified or acknowledged what was already occurring in their church but the overwhelmingly majority of the churches have engaged in a lengthy process of education, dialogue, debate, and prayer prior to deciding whether to become a sanctuary. No community has claimed that their building is exempt from the operation of law. The absence of any geographic justification for sanctuary simply shifts the emphasis away from the *place* to the *people*. Thus, the concept of sanctuary has taken on an entirely new meaning. It is the active community or the congregation, not the passive church building, that now offers sanctuary.

A Movement of Common People

Furthermore, the current sanctuary movement is a grassroots movement of ordinary people, not a movement focused on a few visible, charismatic leaders. There is clearly a network of church-people, lawyers and social workers coordinating the movement. However, there are no hierarchies, no formal organizations, no regulations regarding membership. There is no requirement of either uniformity or conformity. Churches do not join any formal structure to become part of the movement; their public declaration of sanctuary is sufficient.

Thus, this is not a movement akin to the intercessory skills of individual bishops nor part of the favoritism by English kings for chartered sanctuaries in English history. It is a profoundly democratic movement, where commitment is demonstrated by one's actions, not rhetoric. Leaders can talk, but it takes many committed volunteers to transport, house, feed and otherwise assist the refugees. While there have been several visible figures and spokespersons in the movement as well as endorsements and position statements by national denominational bodies and organizations,[2] much of the momentum for the work still emerges from the grassroots. While the mass media has focused on the big-city churches and those criminally prosecuted, literally hundreds of local churches and communities have taken a quiet, but critical part in this new underground railroad.

It is also critical to examine to *whom* sanctuary is being offered. Central American refugees are not murderers like those who fled to the Hebrew cities of refuge. They cannot be easily compared to the fugitive slaves who sought sanctuary in the early Christian times. While the churches continue to play an intercessory role in lobbying for foreign policy changes and providing basic social services to the refugees, the church no longer commands the authority of the early Christian bishops. While the church's voice against deportation is a clear one, it has no authority to secure pardons or oaths of good treatment for the refugees. The Central American sanctuary seekers are also not like the debtors of England, fleeing to sanctuaries as economic havens. However, refugees today—called "illegal aliens"— are often used as scapegoats for the failures of the United States economy and as targets of legislative efforts to "regain control of our borders."[3]

In historical sanctuaries, there was always some confession of guilt required of the sanctuary seeker. In England, this confession reached its extreme form in the oath of self-exile of the abjurer of the realm. Today, there is no parallel confession of guilt required. Rather, the only requirement is a confession of faith; the faith of the refugee in the protection of the sanctuary church, and the faith of the church that inspires and sustains the provision of sanctuary. Furthermore, the sanctuary seekers of today are not returned, as fugitive slaves were, or confined, as the Hebrew fugitives were, nor exiled, as the abjurers of the realm were. The goal of sanctuary is to protect these refugees until they can safely return to their homes in Central America.

The Central American refugees are and remain distinctly outsiders in the United States, distinguishable by race, language, culture and class. How is it then that predominantly white, English-speaking, middle-class North Americans have made such a commitment to poor, Spanish-speaking Central Americans? Perhaps the answer lies in the experience of the Underground Railroad for fugitive slaves, where the abolitionists realized that solidarity with the slaves was the only appropriate response to the abomination of slavery. By providing haven for the slaves, the abolitionists took on risks and dangers that enabled them to truly understand the plight and experiences of the fugitive slave.

A Theology of Liberation

In contemporary theological language, this identification has been expressed as a preferential option for the poor.[4] It is no coincidence that the same conditions that have created articulate theological reflection from Latin America are also responsible for the flight of many refugees from Central America. As the refugees share their lives and their struggles, they incarnate this new theology of liberation for the North American church. Jim Corbett writes:

> This vitalization of religious community is now arriving among us in Anglo America. It is not arriving as a new theology or creed or ritual but in a person, as a Central American refugee. . . . We can become illegals alongside the refugee or we can be obedient subjects of the U.S. government; we can serve the rule of love or we can serve the rule of money and violence; but we must choose to serve one or the other.[5]

Dan Dale of the Chicago Religious Task Force on Central America explains this ministry that the refugees have taken up: "By telling their story, it turns a senseless, meaningless experience into something that has some meaning. The Salvadorans and Guatemalans are the real evangelists. They have a mission of teaching."[6] In being ministered to by the refugees, the people of the North American church are invited to join a journey of faith. Professor Renny Golden and Rev. Michael McConnell from Chicago proclaim: "Undocumented refugees and outlawed Christians and Jews are together forming a new exodus community that takes seriously a God who acts in history."[7] This new solidarity between churchpeople of North and South is based upon a partnership of shared struggle rather than any prior models of dependency and condescension.[8] Thus, in providing sanctuary to refugees from Central America, the church of North America discovers its own need for conversion. Golden and McConnell articulate a vivid theology of sanctuary:

> Through public sanctuary the North American church is allowing its own conversion to happen. It is the same conversion that happened to Saul in Damascus. The refugees from Central America are like Ananias, called by God to risk their own safety

and go to the source of persecution. Ananias knew that Saul was harming Christians just as Salvadorans know that the United States is supplying arms to their government. Ananias went to Saul, laid his hands upon the persecutor's head and "immediately it was as though scales had fallen from Saul's eyes and he could see again." . . . For the truth to be heard in North America, it must be spoken by the people of Latin America themselves. They come to us as prophets and missionaries, laying their hands upon us, so that the scales can fall from our eyes. . . . Our own liberation is inextricably bound to the liberation of our sisters and brothers in Central America.[9]

Sister Darlene Nicgorski, who was indicted for her sanctuary work in Arizona, has written:

The message of the prophets from the South is often hard for us to hear—we who love so much and live in a sense of righteousness and with the illusion of power and control. The spirit is moving in the church, but it is now a movement from the South to the North. Again it comes in forms hard to recognize— another language, culture, experience. It is all changed—what appears to be religious is politics, what appears to be political is faith lived in the public forum. Sanctuary is one of the clearest ways the North American church has to identify with the spirit, life and future.[9a]

The emerging theology of sanctuary draws from the continuing experience of the sanctuary churches but it is also deeply rooted in the Scriptures. The themes of exodus and liberation are remembered in the persistent biblical injunction to care for the alien in one's midst:

When a stranger sojourns with you in your land, you shall not do him wrong. The stranger who sojourns with you shall be to you as the native among you, and you shall love him as yourself; for you were strangers in the land of Egypt; I am the Lord your God (Leviticus 19:33–34).

In the Hebrew understanding, such responsibility to the alien is deeply rooted in the people's identity as aliens in Egypt, liberated from bondage through Moses, and also in their ancestor Abraham's identity as a sojourner in an alien land, seeking the land of promise secured by Yahweh's covenant. Other Near Eastern cultures used the care of widows and orphans as a standard for measuring the humanitarianism of a ruler, but Israel was unique in articulating the duty to love and care for strangers.[10] The command calls forth Israel's empathy and memory of her own experience as aliens:

> You shall not pervert the justice due to the sojourner[11] or to the fatherless, or take a widow's garment in pledge; but you shall remember that you were a slave in Egypt and the Lord your God redeemed you from there; therefore I command you to do this (Deuteronomy 24:17–18).

At the same time, the command also reminds Israel of God's salvation of the lowly and the oppressed—lest Israel turn oppressor:

> You shall not wrong a stranger or oppress him, for you were strangers in the land of Egypt. You shall not afflict any widow or orphan. If you do afflict them, and they cry out to me, I will surely hear their cry; and my wrath will burn, and I will kill you with the sword, and your wives shall become widows and your children fatherless (Exodus 22:21–24).

This warning clearly establishes Yahweh's advocacy on behalf of the orphan, the widow and the alien:

> For the Lord your God is God of gods and Lord of lords, the great, the mighty, and the terrible God, who is not partial and takes no bribe. He executes justice for the fatherless and the widow, and loves the sojourner, giving him food and clothing. Love the sojourner therefore; for you were sojourners in the land of Egypt (Deuteronomy 10:17–19).

Feeding and sheltering the alien became part of the Jubilee economic order established in the Old Testament.[12] (See Deuteronomy 14:28–29 and 26:12–13.) For example, the gleanings from the harvest were to be left for the aliens. (See Leviticus 19:9–10 and 23:22 and Deuteronomy 24:19–22.)[13]

In offering sanctuary to the aliens of Central America, the churches are responding to this recurring biblical command to care

for the alien in their midst. In doing so, the churches are also rediscovering their own identity as sojourners and aliens, seeking a heavenly kingdom. (See Hebrews 11:13–16.)[14] The themes of exodus
and liberation are reclaimed, creating a solidarity within the universal church that has seldom been experienced.[14a]

This new exodus community that provides sanctuary to aliens
can also draw upon the rich biblical image of God as a refuge or
sanctuary. The image is often found in the Psalms:[15]

> He who dwells in the shelter of the Most High,
>   who abides in the shadow of the Almighty,
> Will say to the Lord, "My refuge and fortress;
>   my God, in whom I trust" (Psalm 91:12).

This image of God as refuge is not limited to a spiritual meaning but is rooted in the historical experience of the Israelites, who
were often surrounded by enemies, both externally and from
within.[16] Thus, the image is not one of a passive place of shelter but
of a God who actively rescues the people of Israel:

> In thee, O Lord, do I take refuge;
>   let me never be put to shame!
> In thy righteousness deliver me and rescue me;
>   incline thy ear to me, and save me!
> Be thou to me a rock of refuge,
>   a strong fortress, to save me,
>   for thou art my rock and fortress.
> Rescue me, O my God, from the hand of the wicked,
>   from the grasp of the unjust and cruel man (Psalm 71:1–4).

As a community of faith, each sanctuary church incarnates this
rescuing God that gives refuge. The sanctuary churches have in-
clined their ears to the refugees and rescued them from deportation
and death. In New Testament language, the sanctuary churches
have thus claimed their identity as the new temple of God, now
made visible in the Christian community. (See Ephesians 2:19–20;
1 Corinthians 3:16; 1 Peter 2:5; 2 Corinthians 6:16.) The God of refuge dwells in their midst.[17]

Accountability and Liability

If the growing sanctuary movement is part of a deeper response of the North American church to its role as an agent for justice, then new questions and issues are raised. There is a consistent historical trend that sanctuaries were regulated and limited whenever and wherever they became a threat to the established governmental authority. Thus, in Greece and Rome, the sanctuaries were limited when they became refuges for common criminals who sought to escape punishment for their crime. In England, sanctuaries were restricted only at the height of their efficient processing of fugitives through the abjuration of the realm, a legal alternative to the criminal justice system of trial and punishment. Certainly, the limited experience of sanctuary in the United States has been connected to two of the most defiant protest movements in United States history: the abolitionist and anti-Vietnam War movements.

The current movement strikes even deeper, challenging the wisdom of decades of United States influence in Central America.[18] The history and rationale of United States intervention in that region must be examined and debated elsewhere. For the sanctuary movement, it is enough to note that sanctuary presents more than a counter-cultural protest against the government. These are not political activists and fringe extremists taking up the protest but rather respected, ordinary, churchgoing citizens.[19]

Today, the sanctuary movement also presents a significant challenge to the assumption that government is sovereign regarding immigration policy. Now individual citizens are implementing their own alien admission system and offering asylum outside the usual governmental processes.[20] In a recent analysis of United States immigration law and policy, one expert cites the sanctuary movement as a threat to the effective enforcement of current immigration law and therefore, part of the erosion of what he calls the "classical" theory of immigration policy, based upon governmental exclusion, restriction, and unmitigated power to classify, detain, and deport:

> By regarding all who arrive here not as strangers but as members, along with Americans, of a universal moral community in which abstract principles of exclusion yield to the more palpable claims of actual and potential human linkage, communitarian

values deprive administrative deportation efforts of the moral le-
gitimacy that the classical order managed to sustain for so long.[21]

It should therefore not be surprising if the governmental response will eventually be severe and widespread. As churches struggled to understand the many political and theological dimensions of
sanctuary, the governmental reaction had been confused and skeptical. For many months, every public statement by the INS denied
the strength of the movement, casually dismissing it as a publicity
stunt by the well-meaning but uncommitted and uninformed. Such
statements have underestimated the spirit with which the sanctuary
movement has not only endured but also matured. Indeed, the
movement has grown and deepened after the initial arrests of the
sanctuary workers in Texas and Arizona. A dozen religious leaders
representing several denominations issued a joint statement after the
Arizona indictments that articulates well the reaction of the sanctuary movement to government prosecution:

> Sanctuary is not a building. It is not one man or one woman or
> 16 of them. It is a response rooted in faith and nurtured by
> prayer and conscience that has captured the hearts of tens of
> thousands of persons across the country. It is a sign of hope and
> compassion that is springing forth from an ever-growing num-
> ber of faithful every day. To prosecute those who have shown
> leadership in this ministry will not bring it to a halt but rather
> is likely to swell the ranks of those who will stand firmly in their
> place.[22]

Every week, more and more churches take up the issue of sanctuary
for discussion, debate and prayer.

However, the confrontation between the government and the
sanctuary churches raises difficult questions of accountability and
liability. Whenever legal authorities have recognized and accepted
the provision of sanctuary throughout history, there had always
been a governmental definition and regulation of the scope of the
privilege. Thus, the caretakers of the Greek and Roman temples, the
early Christian bishops, or the English church hierarchy could always be held responsible for any abuses of the sanctuary privilege.
It is no coincidence that it was Henry VIII who was finally able to
undermine the privilege at the same time that he was asserting the

power of the English throne over the power of the church in England.

It is far more difficult to assign responsibility to members of today's sanctuary movement. There are no national leaders or formal organizations. While clergy and other church officials have endorsed or taken part in the movement, they are not always the critical people behind the movement. The government is thus faced with a dilemma: how to stop the movement without fueling it. The government cannot simply prosecute those with higher social status or a religious title because such persons are not necessarily essential to the continuation of the movement and the resulting adverse publicity would be too costly. On the other hand, prosecuting individuals within the sanctuary movement demands a high level of resources that the government simply does not have. Despite the public nature of the movement, participants are not naive about their legal liabilities. Since it is much more difficult to prove guilt for single acts of transporting or harboring undocumented aliens, responsibility and liability is shared and delegated. Thus, as the movement broadens, it becomes more difficult for the government to pinpoint legal liability in a way that will effectively stop the movement. The sanctuary movement is creating a type of mass civil disobedience that the government simply cannot curtail with individual prosecutions.

The Future of Sanctuary

Despite the risks of prosecution that face the sanctuaries and their supporters, those dangers remain minuscule compared to the dangers facing the refugees who seek sanctuary. While these modern day sanctuary seekers do not face exile or physical branding as did the English abjurers of the realm, they do face the stigma of being "illegal aliens" in a foreign land. While not physically confined within their sanctuaries, these modern day fugitives can never be completely at home in a strange land, among strange people. They often leave behind all they have—their families, jobs, homes and land. They must struggle to eke out a living and learn a new language, a new culture, a new way of life. They do not have to wear the white robes and carry the crosses of the abjurers of the realm but they wear a new uniform—bandanas and cowboy hats—that clearly sets them apart. Ironically, these disguises—worn to protect relatives and friends still in Central America—are trademarks of the stereotyped images of the North American frontier. These images are now rudely forced upon these newest Americans. The refugees also carry their personal crosses—testimonies and memories and experiences of horror and pain that emerges from the daily reality of Central America. As long as the violence in their homelands continues, new refugees will seek sanctuary with similar tales of despair and desperation.

Hopefully, the fate of these refugees is more promising than those of historical sanctuary seekers who were starved, tricked, or violently dragged from their sanctuaries. Today, the threat of arrest and deportation remains very real to each of these refugees. As long as the United States government refuses to abide by international and domestic law and recognize these people as legal refugees, they will continue to seek sanctuary in the churches. Many of the refugees who have found such sanctuary speak eloquently of their own continuing conversion, and their discovery of genuine communities of faith. The provision of sanctuary has created and revived hope and faith for all those involved. Perhaps this hope and faith can serve as the beginning of the repentance of the United States for its complicity in the violence in Central America and help to heal the bitterness of death and injustice that burns so deeply in the hearts of the Central American people.

It is this same hope and faith that is also creating a conversion in the North American church, challenging and provoking the church to be a community of faith, to be an advocate and minister of justice, to be a prophetic voice in its society. Regardless of the future of the sanctuary movement, hundreds of churches and thousands of lives have been touched and changed. The future of those churches and of those individuals is the real future of sanctuary.

APPENDIX
Numbers 35:6–34

"... The cities which you give to the Levites shall be the six cities of refuge, where you shall permit the manslayer to flee, and in addition to them you shall give forty-two cities. All the cities which you give to the Levites shall be forty-eight, with their pasture lands. And as for the cities which you shall give from the possession of the people of Israel, from the larger tribes you shall take many, and from the smaller tribes you shall take few; each, in proportion to the inheritance which it inherits, shall give of its cities to the Levites."

And the Lord said to Moses, "Say to the people of Israel, When you cross the Jordan into the land of Canaan, then you shall select cities to be cities of refuge for you, that the manslayer who kills any person without intent may flee there. The cities shall be for you a refuge from the avenger, that the manslayer may not die until he stands before the congregation for judgment. And the cities which you give shall be your six cities for refuge. You shall give three cities beyond the Jordan, and three cities in the land of Canaan, to be cities of refuge. These six cities shall be for refuge for the people of Israel, and for the stranger and for the sojourner among them, that any one who kills any person without intent may flee there.

"But if he struck him down with an instrument of iron, so that he died, he is a murderer; the murderer shall be put to death. And if he struck him down with a stone in the hand, by which a man may die, and he died, he is a murderer; the murderer shall be put to death. Or if he struck him down with a weapon of wood in the hand, by which a man may die, and he died, he is a murderer; the murderer shall be put to death. The avenger of blood shall himself put the murderer to death; when he meets him, he shall put him to death. And if he stabbed him from hatred, or hurled at him, lying in wait, so that he died, or in enmity struck him down with his hand,

184

so that he died, then he who struck the blow shall be put to death; he is a murderer; the avenger of blood shall put the murderer to death when he meets him.

"But if he stabbed him suddenly without enmity, or hurled anything on him without lying in wait, or used a stone, by which a man may die, and without seeing him cast it upon him, so that he died, though he was not his enemy, and did not seek his harm; then the congregation shall judge between the manslayer and the avenger of blood, in accordance with these ordinances; and the congregation shall rescue the manslayer from the hand of the avenger of blood, and the congregation shall restore him to his city of refuge, to which he had fled, and he shall live in it until the death of the high priest who was anointed with the holy oil. But if the manslayer shall at any time go beyond the bounds of his city of refuge to which he fled, and the avenger of blood finds him outside the bounds of his city of refuge, and the avenger of blood slays the manslayer, he shall not be guilty of blood. For the man must remain in his city of refuge until the death of the high priest; but after the death of the high priest the manslayer may return to the land of his possession.

"And these things shall be for a statute and ordinance to you throughout your generations in all your dwellings. If any one kills a person, the murderer shall be put to death on the evidence of witnesses; but no person shall be put to death on the testimony of one witness. Moreover you shall accept no ransom for the life of a murderer, who is guilty of death; but he shall be put to death. And you shall accept no ransom for him who has fled to his city of refuge, that he may return to dwell in the land before the death of the high priest. You shall not thus pollute the land in which you live; for blood pollutes the land, and no expiation can be made for the land, for the blood that is shed in it, except by the blood of him who shed it. You shall not defile the land in which you live, in the midst of which I dwell; for I the Lord dwell in the midst of the people of Israel."

NOTES

Introduction

1. The information for this account is compiled from "Small Band of Springs Catholics Aids Salvadorans," *Denver Post*, February 21, 1984; "Government Crackdown on Sanctuary Movement," *Central American Refugee Defense Fund Newsletter*, June 1984, pp. 1, 4, 8; "Activist working with Salvador refugees doesn't regret choosing to live her faith," *Contra Costa Times*, October 21, 1984, "Times-Plus," p. 2; "Refugee tells of repression," *Contra Costa Times*, October 21, 1984, p. 7; "Basta! National Sanctuary Newsletter," July 1984 (Chicago: Chicago Religious Task Force on Central America, 1984), p. 2; "National Sanctuary Mailing," May 1984 (Chicago: Chicago Religious Task Force on Central America, 1984), p. 6; "Conspiracy of Compassion," *Sojourners*, vol. 14, March 1985, pp. 14–18; "Merkt, Elder await jail for doing 'what was legal,' " *National Catholic Reporter*, vol. 21, April 15, 1985, p. 5 and from appearances by and conversations with Stacey Merkt in Berkeley, California, October 6 and 9, 1984.

2. Quoted in "Basta! National Sanctuary Newsletter," July 1984 (Chicago: Chicago Religious Task Force on Central America, 1984), p. 2.

3. *Ibid.*

4. Quoted in "National Sanctuary Mailing," May 1984 (Chicago: Chicago Religious Task Force on Central America, 1984), p. 6.

5. Quoted in "Conspiracy of Compassion," *Sojourners*, vol. 14, March 1985, p. 18.

6. Quoted in "Merkt, Elder await jail for doing 'what was legal,' " *National Catholic Reporter*, vol. 21, April 5, 1985, p. 5.

7. *Ibid.*

1.   The Provision of Sanctuary for Central American Refugees

1.   Quoted in Michael McConnell and Renny Golden, "Theology of Sanctuary," "Basta! Sanctuary Organizers' Nuts and Bolts Supplement

No. 1" (Chicago: Chicago Religious Task Force on Central America, undated [Fall 1983]) p. 39.

2. While this writing focuses on the sanctuary movement in the United States, it is interesting to note that St. Andrew's United Church in Beloeil, Quebec in Canada declared itself a sanctuary church in January 1984, with the support of fourteen Protestant and Catholic congregations in the Montreal area. See Robert Block, "Sanctuary and the defiant churches," *MacLean's*, vol. 97, January 30, 1984, p. 43. The sanctuary was created when the Canadian government began to systematically deport Guatemalan refugees. After the declaration of sanctuary, the Canadian government stopped the deportations.

In addition, this writing will emphasize the Christian churches and Christian theology involved in the sanctuary movement while recognizing that an increasing number of Jewish synagogues and congregations are joining the movement and claiming the entire Judaeo-Christian nature of the sanctuary tradition. Notably, the Conservative Rabbinical Council of the United States passed a resolution on May 22, 1984, stating: "Whereas millions of Jews were murdered by the Nazis because nations, including the United States, would not open their gates, the National Assembly endorses the concept of sanctuary and urges the government of the United States to grant extended voluntary departure status to those fleeing the violence in Central America." See "Government Crackdown on Sanctuary Movement," *Central American Refugee Defense Fund Newsletter*, June 1984, p. 4.

3. Quoted in "Conspiracy of Compassion," *Sojourners*, vol. 14, March 1985, p. 16. See, also Karen Matthews, "Sanctuary," *The Berkeley Monthly*, vol. 15, no., 3, December 1984, pp. 23–29; "Churches offer sanctuary to Salvadorean refugees," *National Catholic Reporter*, vol. 18, April 12, 1982, pp. 1, 22; Dale Maharidge, "Escape from El Salvador," reprinted from *The Sacramento Bee*, August 26–30, 1984.

4. Quoted in "Conspiracy of Compassion," *Sojourners*, vol. 14, March 1985, p. 17.

4a. See footnote 3 and Paul Burks, "The Caravan: Sanctuary Goes Public," *Sequoia*, October–November 1984, pp. 3–7; "Sanctuary movement leaders under surveillance, they think," *The Daily Californian*, March 15, 1985, pp. 1, 4, 19.

5. June 1984 list of sanctuary sites, compiled by the Chicago Religious Task Force on Central America.

6. "Basta! Sanctuary Organizers' Nuts and Bolts Supplement No. 1" (Chicago: Chicago Religious Task Force on Central America, undated [Fall 1983]) p. i. At first, many churches and religious organizations were reluctant to follow the lead of the Tucson and Berkeley churches in pro-

claiming public sanctuary. Many were uncertain or fearful of the legal consequences of such a declaration. See "Churches offer sanctuary to Salvadorean refugees," *National Catholic Reporter*, vol. 18, April 12, 1982, pp. 22.

Some churches and church leaders remain opposed to the sanctuary movement. Notably, in 1983, Roman Catholic Archbishop John Roach of the Archdiocese of Minneapolis-St. Paul, and then president of the National Conference of Catholic Bishops, forced his archdiocesan urban affairs commission to revoke an earlier resolution endorsing the sanctuary at St. Luke's Presbyterian Church in Wyzata, Minnesota. (Subsequently, Roach has moderated his position: "It's my style, however, that we work better within the system than outside. . . . I am very sympathetic to the people who believe and practice sanctuary. I can't do it. It's not where my head is: it is where my heart is." See, Willmar Thorkelson, "Roach backs those who offer refuge, but 'it's not for me,' " *National Catholic Reporter*, vol. 21, February 1, 1985, p. 20).

Auxiliary Bishop Anthony J. Bevilacqua of Brooklyn, chairman of the National Conference of Catholic Bishops' Committee on Migration and Tourism, has said: "I am opposed to sanctuary because it is illegal. . . . I do not feel at the present time that this is an unjust law." See "Churches Give Sanctuary to Illegal Refugees Who Face Deportation," *New York Times*, April 18, 1983, p. A16. Bevilacqua fears more than illegal conduct: "There's a nativist movement—a mood against refugees. We've had enough. People get tired of feeling sorry. . . . In offering sanctuary, we're really arousing people into stronger opposition." See "A Refugee Outside the Law," *Newsday*, July 24, 1983. Washington D.C.'s Archbishop James Hickey and Chicago Cardinal Joseph Bernardin have also declined to endorse the concept of sanctuary. See "Urge Refugee Asylum," *Christian Century*, vol. 100, no. 12, April 20, 1983, "Events and People," p. 361.

On the Protestant side, the National Association of Evangelicals has refused to endorse the movement. See Randy Frame, "Churches Violate Federal Law to Shelter Illegal Aliens," *Christianity Today*, vol. 28, March 16, 1984, p. 35. However, some seventy-five other American and Canadian churches, coordinated by Julius Belser of Reba Place Fellowship in Evanston, Illinois, have sought to create an "overground railroad" to help Central American refugees get to Canada. Begun by Jubilee Partners in January 1983 from their two and a half year old ministry to Southeast Asian refugees, the overground railroad has given sanctuary to over two hundred Central American refugees. The refugees first apply for asylum in the United States and then continue to Canada to apply for asylum there. However, even its organizers acknowledge that the overground railroad operates only with the cooperation of the Immigration and Naturalization Service, which declines to arrest or detain these particular refugees en route to Canada. Furthermore, although Canada has made provisions for granting asylum to refugees from Central America, there is no guarantee that such status will be actually given to these refugees. See Randy Frame, "Churches Violate Federal Law to Shelter Illegal Aliens," *Christianity Today*, vol. 28, March 16, 1984, p. 35 and Don Mosley, "Waystations on a Journey," *Crucible of Hope* (Washington, D.C.: Sojourners, 1984) pp. 115–117; *Central American Refugee Fund Newsletter*, December 1984, p. 2.

Finally, it should be acknowledged that some churches have considered becoming a sanctuary but have ultimately decided against such a declaration." See, e.g., "Ames Church Votes Against Providing 'Sanctuary,' " *Des Moines Register*, September 12, 1983 [Collegiate Presbyterian Church in Ames, Iowa and the Knox Presbyterian Church in Des Moines, Iowa]; Willmar Thorkelson, "Sanctuary? No!" *National Catholic Reporter*, vol. 21, March 15, 1985, p. 6. [St. Mark's Catholic Church in St. Paul, Minnesota]; "Church balks at giving sanctuary to refugees," *The Oakland Tribune*, March 25, 1985, p. A10 [St. Mary Magdalen Parish, Berkeley, California].

7. "Sanctuary Movement Updates" in "Basta! Sanctuary Organizers' Nuts and Bolts Supplement No. 1" (Chicago: Chicago Religious Task Force on Central America, undated [Fall 1983]).

8. June 1984 list of sanctuary sites, compiled by the Chicago Religious Task Force on Central America; "More Churches Join in Offering Sanctuary for Latin Refugees," *New York Times*, September 21, 1983, p. A18 [up to thirty thousand church members involved]; and Renny Golden, " 'Coyote,' " *Witness*, vol. 67, January 1984, p. 8.

While the sanctuary movement remains a distinctly religious movement, other places have declared themselves sanctuaries. The Graduate Student Council at the University of California, Riverside declared its campus a sanctuary in May 1984. Since that time, students at the University of California campuses at Berkeley and Irvine, Brown University and the University of Colorado have also declared their support for the sanctuary movement. Representatives from over ten California universities gathered in Riverside, California in February 1985 to discuss and plan future efforts to support the sanctuary movement in the universities. University chapels at Rutgers University and Tufts University have declared public sanctuary. See, "UC Riverside first school to offer sanctuary," *Los Angeles Herald-Examiner*, May 16, 1984 and "Students Vow to Expand Campus Sanctuary Efforts," *Los Angeles Times*, February 10, 1985, Part I, p. 27. On February 19, 1985, the City Council of Berkeley, California declared the city of Berkeley a sanctuary. The resolution, passed by a 6-1 vote, forbids Berkeley police and other city officials from assisting agents of the INS during the investigations or arrests of Central American refugees. The resolution is similar to the sanctuary declaration passed by the Berkeley City Council in 1971 during the Vietnam War (see Chapter Seven). On the same day, the City Council of St. Paul, Minnesota unanimously (7-0) adopted a resolution endorsing the sanctuary movement and directing that no city agency "take any action contrary to the safety and welfare of a refugee." The resolution was passed without knowledge of Berkeley's declaration. The Madison, Wisconsin Common Council passed a resolution similar to the Berkeley declaration on March 5, 1985. On April 8, 1985, the City Council of Cambridge, Massachusetts voted 5-4 to declare the city a sanctuary. The resolution prohibits city agencies and employees from cooperating with federal efforts to deport refugees from El Salvador, Guatemala and Haiti and extends city services to all Cambridge residents regardless of their immigration status. Similar sanctuary declarations are being considered in the cities of Tucson, Arizona; Duluth, Minnesota; and Seattle, Washington. See, "All Berkeley is 'sanctuary,' " *The Oakland Tribune*, February 20, 1985, p. A1; "Berkeley Becomes a 'Sanctuary,' " *San Francisco Chronicle*, February 20, 1985, pp. 1, 14; "Berkeley's 'sanctuary' greeted by praise, yawns," *The Oakland Tribune*, February 21, 1985, p. A1: "INS Assails Berkeley's Latin Sanctuary," *San Francisco Chronicle*, February 21, 1985, p. 7; "Cambridge Now A Sanctuary for Refugees," *San Francisco Chronicle*, April 9, 1985, p. 13.

9. Renny Golden, "Churches Confront INS, Offer Refugees Sanctuary," *Witness*, vol. 65, no. 12, December 1982, p. 6; Renny Golden, "Sanctuary," *Sojourners*, vol. 11, December 1982, p. 26; "A Haven for Salvadorans," *Newsweek*, vol. 99, April 5, 1982, p. 32; and "Presbyterians Honor Tucson Congregation," *Arizona Daily Star*, June 3, 1984.

10. "An Underground Railroad Set Them Free," *Providence Journal*, April 15, 1984.

11. "Sanctuary: Churches' Way to Protest," *U.S. News and World Report*, vol. 97, September 24, 1984, p. 45; "Why Illegal Aliens Get Sanctuary," *San Francisco Chronicle*, April 11, 1984, p. F–3; "When Churches Smuggle Aliens," *U.S. News and World Report*, vol. 98, January 28, 1985, p. 14.

12. Eric Jorstad, "Sanctuary for Refugees: A Statement on Public Policy," *The Christian Century*, vol. 101, March 14, 1984, p. 275.

13. *Ibid.*, at p. 274; Greg Cahill, "Covenanting to Provide Sanctuary," *The Christian Century*, vol. 100, August 3–10, 1983, p. 720.

14. See, e.g., the experiences of St. Benedict Moor of Milwaukee, Wisconsin, in Renny Golden and Michael McConnell, "Sanctuary: Choos-

ing Sides," *Christianity and Crisis*, vol. 43, February 21, 1983, p. 31 and the University Baptist Church, Seattle, Washington, in Carey Quan Gelernter, "Salvadorans' Lives and Seattle Faith Make a Long Journey," *Seattle Times*, January 15, 1983, reprinted in *Church and Society*, vol. 73, March/April 1983, pp. 51–54.

15. One distinction is that the refugees from Southeast Asia were encouraged by the United States government to come to the United States and entered legally, while many refugees from Central America today enter or remain in the United States without proper immigration documentation. However, the similarities between the two groups of refugees are perhaps more striking: both flee countries where there has been a history of United States military involvement and where the United States-backed government has been under attack from internal political forces. The continued involvement of the United States in these countries has been justified by similar characterizations of the internal political forces as communist or leftist guerrillas.

16. Matthew 22:35–40; Luke 10:25; Mark 12:28–34.

17. See, e.g., Jim Wallis, *The Call to Conversion* (San Francisco: Harper and Row, 1981); Waldron Scott, *Bring Forth Justice* (Grand Rapids: Wm. B. Eerdmans Publishing Co., 1980); John C. Haughey, ed., *The Faith That Does Justice: Examining the Christian Sources for Social Change* (New York: Paulist Press, 1977); Ronald J. Sider, ed., *Cry Justice* (New York: Paulist Press and Downers Grove: InterVarsity Press, 1980); Donal Dorr, *Option For the Poor: A Hundred Years of Vatican Social Teaching* (Maryknoll: Orbis Books, 1984); Nicholas Wolterstorff, "Until Justice and Peace Embrace," *The Other Side*, vol. 20, May 1984, pp. 20–23.

18. See, e.g., Gustavo Gutierrcz, *A Theology of Liberation* (New York: Orbis Books, 1973); Jose Miguez-Bonino, *Doing Theology in a Revolutionary Situation* (Philadelphia: Fortress Press, 1975); Juan Luis Segundo, *The Liberation of Theology* (New York: Orbis Books, 1976). See, generally, Robert McAfee Brown, *Theology in a New Key* (Philadelphia: Westminster Press, 1978).

19. See, e.g., *Lumen Gentium* (Dogmatic Constitution on the Church), in Walter M. Abbott, ed., *The Documents of Vatican II* (Chicago: Follett Publishing Company, 1966).

20. Quoted in Renny Golden, " 'Coyote,' " *Witness*, vol. 67, January 1984, p. 8. See also Christine K. Thompson, "The Liberating Quality of Truth: Churches and the Sanctuary Movement," *Engage/Social Action*, vol. 12, February 1984, p. 43 [quotes from Rev. Thomas B. Norwood of St. Francis House, Madison, Wisconsin].

21. Renny Golden and Michael McConnell, "Sanctuary: Choosing Sides," *Christianity and Crisis*, vol. 43, February 21, 1983, p. 31.

22. "Underground Railroad to go public," *Seattle Times*, May 19, 1984.

23. See, e.g., Jim Wallis, "The Court Prophets," *Sojourners*, vol. 13, September 1984, pp. 3–4.

24. National Conference of Catholic Bishops, *The Challenge of Peace: God's Promise and Our Response* (Washington, D.C.: United States Catholic Conference, 1983) and Ad Hoc Committee on Catholic Social Teaching and the U.S. Economy, National Conference of Catholic Bishops, First Draft of Pastoral Letter on Catholic Social Teaching and the U.S. Economy, November 11, 1984, reprinted in *National Catholic Reporter*, vol. 21, November 23, 1984, pp. 9–32.

25. Jim Wallis, "The President's Pulpit," *Sojourners*, vol. 13, September 13, 1984, pp. 11–21.

26. See, e.g., "Politics and the Pulpit," *Newsweek*, vol. 104, September 17, 1984, pp. 24–27.

27. See, e.g., the confrontation between Elijah and the prophets of Baal who served the wicked Queen Jezebel (1 Kings 18:17–40) or the bold prophecy of Micaiah to King Jehoshaphat (1 Kings 22:5–28). See, generally, Jim Wallis, "The Court Prophets," *Sojourners*, vol. 13, September 1984, pp. 3–4.

28. In this sense, the analysis comes full circle. The church itself is facing a problem of defining its own refugee status; it, too, seeks sanctuary as an alien in a foreign land. Reflecting upon the plight of the Central American refugee can provide theological insight into what it means for the North American church to be outcast and persecuted by the world around it. See Chapter Eight.

29. Eric Jorstad, "Sanctuary for Refugees: A Statement on Public Policy," *The Christian Century*, vol. 101, March 14, 1984, p. 276.

30. *Ibid.*, pp. 275–276.

31. "Scores of Churches Take In Illegal Aliens Fleeing Latin America," *Wall Street Journal*, June 21, 1984, p. 27.

32. The Israelite mothers who saved Moses' life violated Pharaoh's law to kill all the Israelite babies. Moses' defiance against Pharaoh— the exodus—was also an act of civil disobedience. So, too, Daniel's resistance against Nebuchadnezzar. See, generally, David Daube, *Civil-Disobedience in Antiquity* (Edinburgh: Edinburgh University Press, 1972). One modern pastor has noted that Jesus' resurrection, in breaking the Roman seal on his tomb, was itself an act of civil disobedience. Jim Wallis, *The Call to Conversion* (San Francisco: Harper and Row, 1981) p. 162.

33. Jim Corbett, "Sanctuary and the Covenant Community," unpublished paper, June 1984. Jim Wallis of the Sojourners community in Wash-

ington, D.C. writes about the movement from protest to faithful resistance: "Protest is speaking; resistance is acting. To protest is to say that something is wrong; resistance means trying to stop it. To protest is to raise your voice; to resist is to stand up with your body. To protest is to say you disagree; to resist is simply to say no." Jim Wallis, "From Protest to Resistance," *Crucible of Hope* (Washington, D.C.: Sojourners, 1984) p. 119. Rev. William Sloane Coffin, Jr., pastor of Riverside Church in New York City, declares: "It is not enough to resist with confession, we must confess with resistance." "Sanctuary," *The Christian Century*, vol. 101, October 17, 1984, "Events and People," p. 951.

34. Tim McCarthy, "Sanctuary movement: crucible of crisis," *National Catholic Reporter*, vol. 21, February 1, 1985, p. 20.

35. See, Joyce Hollyday, "A Spirit of Resolve," *Sojourners*, vol. 14, March 1985, p. 10; Tim McCarthy, "Sanctuary: a crucible of crisis," *National Catholic Reporter*, vol. 21, February 1, 1985, p. 20.

36. See, "Foreign, domestic policies tied, Coffin says," *Arizona Daily Star*, January 24, 1985 and Tim McCarthy, "Sanctuary: a crucible of crisis," *National Catholic Reporter*, vol. 21, February 1, 1985, p. 20. This call was later repeated by Elsa Talmez, a theologian from Puerto Rico, who urged greater solidarity with the "underside" of the world.

36a. William Sloane Coffin, "Sanctuary for refugees—and ourselves," *Christianity and Crisis*, vol. 45, March 18, 1985, pp. 75–76.

37. See, "Sanctuary: rooted in values that confront American way," (editorial), *National Catholic Reporter*, vol. 21, February 1, 1985, p. 12. This goal parallels the emerging understanding of missionary work: to be so effective in promoting indigenous leadership that foreign missionaries work themselves out of a job.

38. See, Joyce Hollyday, "Wayfare," *Sojourners*, vol. 14, March 1985, p. 23.

39. See, also statements of Raul Gonzalez and Alejandro Rodriquez, Antonio, Francisco, and Felipe and Elena Excot in "Basta!", Tucson edition, January 1985, pp. 15–17 and Larry Cohen, "Statement on Sanctuary" in "Basta!", Tucson edition, p. 33. Cohen also points out that not all Salvadoran and Guatemalan refugees—even among those in sanctuary—are alike in needs and personalities.

40. Yvonne Dilling, "Opened Hearts and Homes," *Sojourners*, vol. 14, March 1985, p. 22.

41. See, also statement of Pedro and Sylvia, in "Basta!", Tucson edition, January 1985, p. 17.

42. December 1984 Letter from Jim Corbett, "Basta!", Tucson edition, January 1985, p. 23.

43. *Id.*, at p. 24.

44. "Conspiracy of Compassion," *Sojourners*, vol. 14, March 1985, p. 18.

44a. The National Sanctuary Defense Fund will use the following criteria for the distribution of the money raised: 1) defendants should be either sanctuary workers affiliated with the Public Sanctuary Movement or with its Underground Railroad, or refugees arrested in situations directly involving the movement; 2) any money that is distributed should be to support cases with the greatest potentiality for furthering opposition to unjust U.S. immigration policies regarding Central American refugees and to those policies which create refugee flight; 3) defendants would be willing to allow the case to be used publicly to strengthen the Public Sanctuary Movement; and 4) funds will be allocated to local defense committees rather than to individual attorneys or law firms. "Basta!" National Newsletter of the Chicago Religious Task Force on Central America, April 1985, p. 26.

45. See, e.g., Tim McCarthy, "Sanctuary activists unite, despite tensions," *National Catholic Reporter*, vol. 21, February 8, 1985, p. 6.

46. December 1984 Letter from Jim Corbett, "Basta!", Tucson edition, January 1985, p. 23.

47. *Id.*, at p. 30.

48. *Id.*, at p. 22.

49. Editor's Note, "Basta!", Tucson edition, January 1985, p. 19.

50. *Id.*

51. CRTFCA Statement of Faith, "Basta!", Tucson edition, January 1985, p. IV. The *National Catholic Reporter* has also commented:

For most of the people involved [in the sanctuary movement], there is no overriding political ideology, but there may well be an underlying dynamic of faith. At bottom, it is not so much a political confrontation between church and state as it is a religious challenge to what has become the American way.

"Sanctuary: rooted in values that confront the American way," (editorial), *National Catholic Reporter*, vol. 21, February 22, 1985, p. 12.

52. December 1984 Letter from Jim Corbett, "Basta!", Tucson edition, January 1985, p. 24.

53. Jim Corbett, "A View From the Border," (unpublished), September 8, 1984, pp. 1–2.

54. *Id.*

55. *Id.*, at p. 3.

56. "Some Considerations on Direction for the Sanctuary Movement," "Basta!", Tucson edition, January 1985, p. V.

57. TEC Task Force Letter, "Basta!", Tucson edition, January 1985,

p. 20 and Jim Corbett, "A View From the Border," (unpublished), September 8, 1984, p. 1.

58. "Some Considerations on Direction for the Sanctuary Movement," "Basta!", Tucson edition, January 1985, p. VII.

59. *Id.*

60. Jim Corbett, "A View From the Border," (unpublished), September 8, 1984, p. 1 and TEC Task Force Letter, "Basta!", Tucson edition, January 1985, p. 20.

61. CRTFCA Statement of Faith, "Basta!", Tucson edition, January 1985, p. IV.

62. *Id.*

63. Gil Dawes, "Sanctuary Solidarity," "Basta!", Tucson edition, January 1985, p. 35.

64. Letter From Jim Corbett to Basta!, "Basta!", Tucson edition, January 1985, p. 21.

65. Editor's Note, "Basta!", Tucson edition, January 1985, p. 21.

66. Jim Corbett, "A View From the Border," p. 3.

67. "Some Considerations on Direction for the Sanctuary Movement," "Basta!", Tucson edition, January 1985, p. VI.

2. U.S. Immigration Law Concerning Refugees

1. Peter H. Schuck, "The Transformation of Immigration Law," *Columbia Law Review*, vol. 84, no. 1, January 1984, p. 1.

2. Renny Golden, "Churches Confront INS, Offer Refugees Sanctuary," *Witness*, vol. 65, no. 12, December 1982, p. 5; Renny Golden and Michael McConnell, "Sanctuary: Choosing Sides," *Christianity and Crisis*, vol. 43, February 21, 1983, p. 36; Pat Samples, "The Church as Sanctuary," *The Other Side*, vol. 37, February 1983, p. 18 and Gary MacEoin and Nivita Riley, *No Promised Land: American Refugee Policies and the Rule of Law.* (Boston: Oxfam America, 1982) p. 41.

3. MacEoin and Riley, pp. 42–46; Carey Quan Gelernter, "Salvadorans' Lives and Seattle Faith Make a Long Journey," *Seattle Times*, January 15, 1983, reprinted in *Church and Society*, vol. 73, March/April 1983, pp. 51–52 [thirty percent reported by Amnesty International and Archdiocese of San Salvador]; Kay Miller, "Church Shelters Salvadoran Refugee," *The Minneapolis Tribune*, December 12, 1982, reprinted in *Church and Society*, vol. 73, March/April 1983, p. 56 [ten percent reported by Oxfam].

In 1984 the House Subcommittee on Immigration tried to follow up on 482 randomly selected deportees to El Salvador. Although the U.S. Embassy found no violations of the human rights of any of the deportees located, they only located about half—233—of the persons on the list. The sample group was taken from lists of Salvadorans deported from Los Angeles at the end of 1983. The short time these deportees were in El Salvador and the questionable methods of contacting them (by mail & phone) also cast doubt upon the study's validity. A comprehensive study is now being conducted by the American Civil Liberties Union, comparing the names of deportees obtained from the INS after a Freedom of Information Act lawsuit with the lists of those killed, disappeared or tortured recorded by various human rights organizations. So far, 112 persons have been identified on both sets of lists but further investigation is being continued. "The Fates of Salvadorans Expelled From the United States," "Basta!" National Newsletter of the Chicago Religious Task Force on Central America, April 1985, pp. 23–25; "Despite a Crackdown, 7 Guatemalans Are Smuggled Into U.S." New York Times, January 20, 1985; and Michael J. Farrell, "Sanctuary: part of a bigger picture," National Catholic Reporter, vol. 20, September 14, 1984, p. 14. See also "Ouster of Salvadorans Defended," New York Times, January 26, 1984, p. A6; and "1 in 50 Deported Salvadorans May Be Dead, Study Shows," Los Angeles Times, January 25, 1984; and "Scores of U.S. Churches Take In Illegal Aliens Fleeing Latin America," Wall Street Journal, June 21, 1984, p. 27.

4. "Ouster of Salvadorans Defended," New York Times, January 26, 1984, p. A6.

5. Pub. L. No. 96-212, 94 Stat. 102, now codified in scattered sections of 8 U.S.C. (1982). The Act was signed by President Jimmy Carter on March 17, 1980.

6. This section is compiled from information from a variety of sources, including: John Higham, "American Immigration Policy in Historical Perspective," Law and Contemporary Problems, vol. 21, Spring 1956, pp. 213–235; Immigration and Naturalization Service, "Our Immigration: A Brief Account of Immigration to the United States" (Washington, D.C.: U.S. Government Printing Office, 1980); Charles Gordon and Harry N. Rosenfield, Immigration Law and Procedure, revised edition, vol. 1 (New York: Matthew Bender and Co., 1984); The Immigration Project of the National Lawyers Guild, Immigration Law and Defense, Second Edition (New York: Clark Boardman Company, 1981).

7. Act of June 25, 1798, 1 Stat. 570 (expired 1800). This Act was part of the Alien and Sedition Law.

8. The Immigration Act of March 2, 1875, 18 Stat. 477, prohibited the importation of prostitutes and barred the entry of convicts.

9. Act of May 6, 1882, 22 Stat. 58 (repealed, Act of December 17, 1943, 57 Stat. 600).

10. Act of August 3, 1882, 22 Stat. 214.

11. See, e.g., 8 U.S.C. § 1182 (a)(15) ("public charge"). Other exclusion grounds are derived from laws passed in 1891, Act of March 3, 1891, 26 Stat. 1084, compare, 8 U.S.C. § 1182(a)(8) ("paupers") and § 1182(a)(6) ("persons with loathsome or dangerous contagious diseases") and § 1182(a)(9) ("those previously convicted of a criminal offense involving moral turpitude") and § 1182(a)(11) ("polygamists"); in 1903, Act of March 3, 1903, 32 Stat. 1213, compare 8 U.S.C. § 1182(a)(28)(A) ("anarchists") and § 1182(a)(2) and (3) ("insane persons") and § 1182(a)(8) ("professional beggars"); in 1907, Act of February 20, 1907, 34 Stat. 898, compare 8 U.S.C. § 1182(a)(7) ("persons suffering from mental or physical conditions that might affect their ability to earn a living") and § 1182(a)(1) ("feeble-minded") and § 1182(a)(6) ("tuberculosis" but see 42 C.F.R. § 34.2 for recent amendment) and § 1182(a)(12) and (13) ("woman coming to the United States for prostitution or other immoral purposes"); and in 1918, Act of October 16, 1918, 40 Stat. 1012, compare 8 U.S.C. § 1182(a)(28)(F) ("members of, or those affiliated with, organizations seeking to overthrow the government by force or violence").

12. Act of October 19, 1888, 25 Stat. 566.

13. Act of March 3, 1891, 26 Stat. 1084 and Act of March 3, 1903, 32 Stat. 1213.

14. Act of February 5, 1917, 39 Stat. 874.

15. Act of May 19, 1921, Pub. L. No. 67-5, 42 Stat. 5.

16. Immigration and Naturalization Service, "Our Immigration: A Brief Account of Immigration to the United States" (Washington, D.C.: U.S. Government Printing Office, 1980) p. 6 and John Higham, "American Immigration Policy in Historical Perspective," *Law and Contemporary Problems*, vol. 21, Spring 1956, pp. 222–223.

17. Immigration Act of May 26, 1924, Pub. L. No. 68-139, 43 Stat. 153.

18. Immigration and Naturalization Service, "Our Immigration," p. 6.

19. Note that the base date for the national origins quota was first moved *back* to 1890 to further favor the immigration of northern Europeans and exclude southern and eastern Europeans.

20. Over 4.5 million Mexicans participated in the *bracero* program initiated in 1951 under the Migratory Labor Agreement with Mexico, Pub. L. No. 78, 65 Stat. 119, and extended six times until 1964. Galarza, *Merchants of Labor: The Mexican Bracero Story* (Santa Barbara: McNally and Loftin, 1964), Julian Samora, *Los Mojados: The Wetback Story* (Notre Dame: University of Notre Dame Press, 1971); Richard B. Craig, *The Bracero Program: Interest Groups and Foreign Policy* (Austin: University of Texas Press, 1971); Ernesto Galarza, *Farmworkers and Agri-Business in California 1947–*

1960 (Notre Dame: University of Notre Dame Press, 1977); Otey M. Scuggs, "The United States, Mexico and the Wetback, 1942–1947," *Pacific Historical Review*, vol. 30, May 1961, pp. 316–329.

21. Act of June 28, 1940, 54 Stat. 670.

22. Compare, 8 U.S.C. § 1254. The Act did also provide the first statutory relief from deportation, a suspension of deportation for resident aliens of good moral character.

23. Act of September 23, 1950, 64 Stat. 987. Compare 8 U.S.C. § 1182(a)(27).

24. Indicative of the ambivalance of the federal government's attitude toward immigrants was the shift of the Bureau of Immigration from the jurisdiction of the Treasury Department (Act of March 3, 1891, 26 Stat. 1084) to the Department of Commerce and Labor in 1903 (Act of February 14, 1903, 32 Stat. 825; see, also Act of April 28, 1904, 33 Stat. 591) and then to the new Labor Department in 1913 (Act of March 4, 1913, 37 Stat. 737) and then the final transfer to the Department of Justice in 1940 (President Franklin D. Roosevelt's Reorganization Plan V, May 22, 1940, 5 Federal Register 2223). The authors of the law text *Immigration Law and Defense* comment: "The progression reflects the government's evolving view of the immigrants as monetary investments, then as wage earners, and finally as legal problems." Immigration Project of the National Lawyer's Guild, *Immigration Law and Defense*, second edition (New York: Clark Boardman Co., Ltd., 1981) pp. 2–6.

25. Absolute Chinese exclusion was repealed in 1943 and Chinese were eligible for the "generous" allocation of one hundred and five annual visas and for naturalization. In 1946, the quota for Filipinos was doubled by Presidential proclamation: from fifty to one hundred annual visas. Filipinos and immigrants from India were also made eligible for naturalization in 1946. The War Brides Act of December 28, 1945, 59 Stat. 659 and the Fiancees Act of June 29, 1946, 60 Stat. 339, admitted alien spouses and children of members and veterans of the U.S. Armed Forces. About 118,000 and 5,000, respectively, entered the country under these two acts.

26. Act of June 27, 1952, Pub. L. No. 82-414, 66 Stat. 163, now codified, as amended, at 8 U.S.C. § 1101 *et seq.*

27. Immigration and Nationality Act Amendments, Act of October 3, 1965, Pub. L. No. 89-236, 79 Stat. 911.

28. There were other amendments to the 1952 Immigration and Nationality Act, changing the right of judicial review (Act of September 26, 1961, Pub. L. No. 87-301, 75 Stat. 650), extending the 20,000 per country limit to the Western Hemisphere quota and creating quotas for colonies and dependent areas (Act of October 20, 1976, Pub. L. No. 94-571, 90 Stat. 2703) and consolidating the hemispheric quotas into a worldwide

quota of 290,000 annual visas (Act of October 5, 1978, Pub. L. No. 95-412, 92 Stat. 907).

29. Immigration and Nationality Act, § 203(a)(7), 79 Stat. 911, 912–915, codified as 8 U.S.C. § 1153(a)(7), superseded by 8 U.S.C. § 1157 (1980). 17,400 persons (6% of the worldwide ceiling of 290,000) were allowed to enter the United States annually under this new section. After two years residence in the United States, such conditional entrants could adjust their immigration status to lawful permanent residents. 8 U.S.C. § 1153(g)–(h).

30. Information for this section was extracted from: Deborah E. Anker and Michael H. Posner, "The Forty Year Crisis: A Legislative History of the Refugee Act of 1980," *San Diego Law Review*, vol. 19, no. 1, December 1981, pp. 12–20; Note, "U.S. Immigration and Refugee Reform: A Critical Evaluation," *Virginia Journal of International Law*, vol. 22, no. 4, Summer 1982, pp. 809–813; Note, "The Endless Debate: Refugee Law and Policy and the 1980 Refugee Act," *Cleveland State Law Review*, vol. 32, no. 1 1983–1984, pp. 121–124; Note, "The Right to Asylum under United States Immigration Law," *University of Florida Law Review*, vol. 33, no. 4, Summer 1981; pp. 540–543; Comment, "Political Asylum and Withholding of Deportation: Defining the Appropriate Standard of Proof Under the Refugee Act of 1980," *San Diego Law Review*, vol. 21, no. 1, December 1983, pp. 174–175.

31. Act of September 23, 1950, 64 Stat. 987, at 1010. The new § 20(a) of the Immigration Act of 1917 read: "No alien shall be deported under any provisions of this Act to any country in which the Attorney General shall find that such alien would be subjected to physical persecution."

32. Section 243(h) of the Immigration and Nationality Act, 66 Stat. 163, at 214. The section read: "The Attorney General is authorized to withhold deportation of any alien within the United States to any country in which in his opinion the alien would be subject to physical persecution and for such period of time as he deems to be necessary for such reason." For background on the withholding of deportation provision, see Note, *Cleveland State Law Review*, pp. 138–148 and Scott M. Martin, "Non-refoulement of Refugees: United States Compliance with International Obligations," *Harvard International Law Journal*, vol. 23, no. 2, Winter 1983, pp. 370–371.

33. Arthur C. Helton, "Political Asylum Under the 1980 Refugee Act: An Unfulfilled Promise," *University of Michigan Journal of Law Reform*, vol. 17, no. 2, Winter 1984, pp. 246, 248.

34. Pub. L. No. 89-236, 79 Stat. 911, at 918.

35. Revision in the regulations permitted an application for the withholding of deportation before, during or even after a deportation hearing.

8 C.F.R. § 108.1 (1976); 8 C.F.R. § 108.3 (1980). However, withholding of deportation was still understood as relief from deportation rather than an affirmative method of admitting refugees.

36. Act of June 25, 1948, Pub. L. No. 80-774, 62 Stat. 1009. A Presidential directive dated December 22, 1945 had admitted 40,324 displaced persons. INS, "Our Immigration," p. 13. While the authority for such executive action is unclear, no one at the time challenged such a humanitarian gesture.

37. INS, "Our Immigration," p. 13.

38. Act of July 29, 1953, Pub. L. No. 83-162, 67 Stat. 229.

39. Act of August 7, 1953, Pub. L. No. 82-203, 67 Stat. 400. The Act was extended under the 1957 Refugee-Escape Act, Act of September 11, 1957, Pub. L. No. 85-316, 17 Stat. 639. The 1957 Act also expunged the mortgages on the national origins quotas from the 1948 Displaced Persons Act and provided for some waivers of the exclusion grounds for the incoming refugees.

40. INS, "Our Immigration," p. 13.

41. Act of September 2, 1958, 72 Stat. 1712.

42. Act of July 25, 1958, 72 Stat. 419. The Attorney General's parole power was based on Immigration and Nationality Act § 212(d)(5), codified at 8 U.S.C. § 1182(d)(5).

43. Act of July 14, 1960, Pub. L. No. 86-648, 74 Stat. 704.

44. INS, "Our Immigration," p. 17. Despite these admissions, many refugees still remained in the UN refugee camps.

45. Pub. L. No. 87-510, 76 Stat. 121. The Act was made applicable to Southeast Asian refugees under the Indochina Migration and Refugee Assistance Act of 1975, Pub. L. No. 94-23, 89 Stat. 87.

46. The parole power was also used to admit Chinese nationals in Hong Kong in 1962 and Vietnamese and Cambodian refugees in the mid-1970's.

47. Act of November 2, 1966, Pub. L. No. 89-732, 80 Stat. 1161 and Act of October 20, 1976, Pub. L. No. 94-571, 90 Stat. 2703.

48. Act of October 5, 1978, Pub. L. No. 95-412, 92 Stat. 907, 909. This date was moved forward to April 1, 1980 by the 1980 Refugee Act. § 208(g) of the Immigration and Nationality Act, 94 Stat. 102.

49. For more extensive analyses of the United Nations Convention and Protocol, see Note, "Alien's Rights: The Refugee Act of 1980 as Response to the 1967 Protocol Relating to the State of Refugees: The Final Test," *Vanderbilt Journal of Transnational Law*, vol. 14, Summer 1983, pp. 569–577; Martin, *Harvard International Law Journal*, pp. 357–366; Arthur C. Helton, "Persecution on Account of Membership in a Social Group as a Basis for Refugee Status," *Columbia Human Rights Law Review*, vol. 15,

no. 1, Fall 1983, pp. 53–59; Diana Vincent-Daviss, "Human Rights Law: A Research Guide to the Literature. Part 2: International Protection of Refugees and Humanitarian Law," *New York University Journal of International Law and Policy*, vol. 14, Winter 1982, pp. 496–499.

50. See, e.g., Havana Convention Fixing the Rules to Be Observed for the Granting of Asylum, 1928. 132 L.N.T.S. 323–343. See, generally, Vincent-Daviss, *New York University Journal of International Law and Policy*, pp. 489–499.

51. 13 LoNCM 53, 246 (1921).

52. Article 3, Convention adopted October 28, 1933, entered into force, June 1935. 159 L.N.T.S. 199.

53. Constitution of the International Refugee Organization, opened for signature, December 15, 1946, entered into force, August 20, 1948. 18 U.N.T.S. 3. The United States ratified this document in 1947.

54. Statute of the Office of the United Nations High Commissioner for Refugees. G.A. Res. 428. 5 U.N. GAOR, Supp. (No. 20) 46, U.N. Doc. A/1775 (1950).

55. Adopted July 28, 1951, entered into force April 22, 1954. 19 U.S.T. 6260, T.I.A.S. No. 6577, 189 U.N.T.S. 137. The full name of the Convention is the "Final Act and Convention of the United Nations Conference of Plenipotentiaries on the Status of Refugees and Stateless Persons," U.N. Doc. A/CONF 2/108, U.N. Sales No. 1951. IV. 4 (1951).

Nearly eighty states are parties to the Convention. See Office of the United Nations High Commission for Refugees, *Handbook on Procedures and Criteria for Determining Refugee Status* (Geneva: UNHCR 1979), Annex IV, pp. 86–87.

56. Helton, *Columbia Human Rights Law Review*, pp. 41–42.

57. However, economic migrants and refugees are often difficult to distinguish. *UNHCR Handbook*, 62–64, pp. 16–17.

58. See, David A. Martin, "The Refugee Act of 1980: II. Past and Future," *1982 Michigan Yearbook of International Legal Studies:* Transnational Legal Problems of Refugees, p. 101.

59. See Article 1(2)(C)(1)–(6) and (D) of the Convention.

60. Article 42(1) provides: "At the time of signature, ratification or accession, any State may make reservations to articles of the Convention other than to articles 1, 3, 4, 16(1), *33*, 36–46 inclusive" (emphasis added). See, Martin, *Harvard International Law Journal*, pp. 360–361.

61. G. A. Res. 2312, 22 U.N. GAOR Supp. (No. 16) 81, U.N. Doc. A/6716 (1968).

62. Article 3(2).

63. P. Weiss, "The United Nations Declaration on Territorial Asylum," *The Canadian Yearbook of International Law*, vol. 7, 1969, p. 117.

64. See, generally, Atle Grahl-Madsen, *Territorial Asylum* (Stockholm: Almquist and Wiksell International, 1980); Atle Grahl-Madsen, "International Refugee Law Today and Tomorrow," *Archiv des Völkerrechts*, vol. 20, 1982, pp. 413–415.

65. See, e.g., Geoffrey S. Gilbert, "Right of Asylum: A Change of Direction," *International and Comparative Law Quarterly*, vol. 32, July 1983, pp. 633–650.

66. Many nations have provided for advisory roles for a representative of the UNHCR in their domestic refugee legislation. See *UNHCR Handbook*, 193–194, p. 46; Grahl-Madsen, *Archiv des Völkerrechts*, p. 433; and Jean-Francois Durieux, "Refugee Status Determination Procedure in Germany, France, the U.S.A. and Australia," *Refugee*, vol. 3, no. 4, June 1984, p. 5–7. Several United States commentators have proposed a greater role for the UNHCR in United States refugee and asylum processing. See Anker and Posner, *San Diego Law Review*, pp. 77–79; Note, "Protecting Aliens from Persecution Without Overloading the INS: Should Illegal Aliens Receive Notice of the Right to Apply for Asylum?" *Virginia Law Review*, vol. 69, no. 5, June 1983, pp. 927–929; and Arthur C. Helton, "Political Asylum Under the 1980 Refugee Act: An Unfulfilled Promise," *University of Michigan Journal of Law Reform*, vol. 17, no. 2, Winter 1984, pp. 263–264.

67. This problem is aggravated by the fact that the individual refugee is caught between two nations. Certainly, the persecuting country is not about to intervene on behalf of the individual refugee to enforce the principle of *nonrefoulement* against the country of asylum. Any third party or country would not have legal standing nor any incentive to intervene on behalf of the individual refugee.

68. The Convention articulates many rights for refugees, including the right to freedom of religion (Article 4), freedom of association (Article 15), access to courts (Article 16), to employment (Article 17), to education (Article 22) and public assistance (Article 23) on the same basis as citizens of the country of asylum.

69. Article 1(B). Nine states—Argentina, Brazil, Italy, Madagascar, Malta, Monaco, Paraguay, Peru and Turkey—have exercised this option.

70. Adopted January 31, 1967, entered into force October 4, 1967. 19 U.S.T. 6223, T.I.A.S. 6577, 606 U.N.T.S. 267. Over seventy states are signatories to the Protocol. All the states which are signatories to the Convention are also parties to the Protocol, except Columbia, Jamaica, Kenya, Liberia, Madagascar, Monaco, and Peru. Two countries, the United States and Swaziland, are parties to the Protocol only. *UNHCR Handbook*, Annex IV, pp. 86–87. There were other minor changes made to the Convention (regarding the right of reservation and the jurisdiction of

the UNHCR and the International Court of Justice) by the Protocol. See P. Weiss, "The 1967 Protocol Relating to the Status of Refugees, and Some Questions of the Law of Treaties," *The British Year Book of International Law*, 1967, vol. 42, pp. 39–70.

71. Article 7(1).

72. The information in this section is drawn from the sources listed in footnote 49. See also Office of the United Nations High Commissioner on Refugees, *Collection of International Instruments Concerning Refugees*, 2nd ed. (Geneva: UNHCR, 1979) and Grahl-Madsen, *Archiv des Völkerrechts*, pp. 412–416.

73. This analysis will not explore the complex question of how such international law should or should not be applied by United States courts. See Kathryn Burke, Sandra Coliver, Connie de la Vega and Stephen Rosenbaum, "Application of International Human Rights Law in State and Federal Courts," *Texas International Law Journal*, vol. 18, no. 2, Spring 1983, pp. 291–328; Jeffrey M. Blum and Ralph G. Steinhardt, "Federal Jurisdiction over International Human Rights Claims: The Alien Tort Claims Act after *Filartiga v. Pena-Irala*," *Harvard International Law Journal*, vol. 22, no. 1, Winter 1981, pp. 53–113; Note, "The Domestic Application of International Human Rights Law: Evolving the Species," *Hastings International and Comparative Law Review*, vol. 5, no. 1, Fall 1981, pp. 161–209; and the entire issues of the *Houston Journal of International Law*, vol. 4, no. 1, Autumn 1981 and the *Hofstra Law Review*, vol. 9, no. 2, Winter 1981.

Much of the commentary has focused on the cases *Filartiga v. Pena-Irala*, 630 F.2d 876 (2d Cir. 1980) (federal court jurisdiction under the Alien Tort Claims Act over a wrongful death allegedly resulting from a Paraguayan government official's use of torture) and *Fernandez v. Wilkinson*, 505 F.Supp. 787 (D. Kan. 1980) (indefinite detention without an exclusion hearing of a Cuban alien a violation of international law as exemplified by the Universal Declaration of Human Rights and the American Convention of Human Rights) *aff'd sub nom, on other grounds, Rodriguez-Fernandez v. Wilkinson*, 654 F.2d 1382 (10th Cir. 1981).

74. Article 13, G.A. Res. 217, 3 U.N. GAOR, Annex, 3, U.N. Doc. A/80 (1948). The United States has not ratified this document but it may be binding upon the United States as part of the customary international law. *Filartiga v. Pena-Irala*, 630 F.2d 876, 882–883 (2d Cir. 1980).

75. G.A. Res. 2200A, 21 U.N. GAOR, Supp. (No. 16) 52, U.N. Doc. A/6316 (1966). Opened for signature December 19, 1966, entered into force March 23, 1976. The United States President has submitted this treaty to the Senate for ratification, but the Senate has not yet acted upon it. See Martin, *Harvard International Law Journal*, p. 364, n. 44.

76. OAS Official Recs. OEA/Serv. K/XVI/I.I., Doc. 65, Rev. 1,

Corr. 2, January 7, 1970. The United States Senate has also received this treaty for ratification. Martin, *Harvard International Law Journal*, p. 362, n. 33.

77. Article 22(7).

78. 1949 Geneva Convention Relative to the Protection of Civilian Persons in Time of War, 6 U.S.T. 3516, T.I.A.S. No. 3365, 75 U.N.T.S. 287, in force October 21, 1950, entered into force for United States February 2, 1956. The Convention is sometimes known as Geneva Convention IV because of the three other 1949 Conventions relating to the wounded in the field, the wounded at sea, and prisoners of war, respectively. See also *UNHCR Handbook*, 164, p. 39.

79. Protocol Additional to the Geneva Conventions, and Relating to the Protection of Victims of International Armed Conflict, opened for signature, December 7, 1977, in force December 12, 1978, U.N. Doc. A/32/144 Annex I (1977) and Protocol Additional to the Geneva Conventions, and Relating to the Protection of Victims of non-International Armed Conflict, in force December 12, 1978, U.N. Doc. A/32/144 Annex II (1977). The United States has not yet acceded to either of these Protocols. See also *UNHCR Handbook*, 164, p. 39.

80. The following analysis of international humanitarian law is based upon Karen Parker, "Geneva Convention Protections for Salvadoran Refugees," *Immigration Newsletter* (of the National Immigration Project of the National Lawyers Guild, Inc.), vol. 13, no. 3, May–June 1984, pp. 1, 5–13.

81. *UNHCR Handbook*, 164, p. 39.

82. In addition, Article 30 of the 1949 Convention establishes the right of civilian victims of civil war to seek protection in other countries.

83. Article 10 also sets forth the right of civilian initiative to aid persons protected by this humanitarian law. This right guarantees international law protection for those citizens or humanitarian organizations of other countries who seek to aid the victims of armed conflict. One scholar has argued that this right of civilian initiative might be the basis for an affirmative defense to a United States criminal prosecution of sanctuary church or worker for sanctuary activities that assist Salvadorans and Guatemalans fleeing the civil wars in those countries. See Parker, *Immigration Newsletter*, pp. 8–9.

84. See also *The Paquette Habana*, 175 U.S. 677, 708 (1900).

85. See, e.g., Burke, Coliver, *et al.*, *Texas International Law Journal*, pp. 291–328; Note, *Hastings International and Comparative Law Review*, vol. 5, no. 1, Fall 1981, pp. 161–209.

86. See, e.g., *Pierre v. United States*, 547 F.2d 1281, 1288 (5th Cir. 1977) and *In re Dunar*, 14 I & N Dec. 310 (BIA 1973).

87. For an extensive analysis of the legislative history of the 1980 Refugee Act, see Deborah Anker and Michael Posner, "The Forty Year Crisis: A Legislative History of the Refugee Act of 1980," *San Diego Law Review*, vol. 19, no. 1, December 1981, p. 9–89.

88. *Ibid.*, p. 39.

89. *Ibid.*, pp. 40–41.

90. *Ibid.*, pp. 37–38.

91. *Ibid.*, p. 23.

92. S. Rep. No. 256, 96th Congress, 1st Session 3 (1979).

93. H. R. Conf. Rep. No. 781, 96th Congress, 2d Session 19 (1979), reprinted in 1980 U.S. Code Cong. and Admin. News 160.

94. Act of March 17, 1980, Pub. L. No. 96-212, 94 Stat. 102, codified in scattered sections of 8 U.S.C. § 1101 *et seq.* (1980).

95. There were two other major Congressional battles over any proposed legislation involving refugees. First, the executive branch wanted to retain its flexible parole power to admit groups of aliens into the United States but Congress sought to end this discretion. Anker and Posner, *San Diego Law Review*, pp. 28–29, 34, 45, 53, 61–62. Second, Congress wanted an extensive consultation procedure and even a legislative veto over the numerical limits to be established for regular or annual refugee admissions while the President refused to submit to such accountability. Anker and Posner, *San Diego Law Review*, pp. 34–36, 44, 49–50, 53–54, 58–60, 63.

96. Section 101(a)(42)(B) actually provides a broader definition of a refugee than the Convention definition since the President may, after appropriate consultation with Congress, recognize persons as refugees while they are still in their own countries. However, the exclusion of persons who have participated in the persecution of others is not found in either the 1951 Convention nor the 1967 Protocol.

97. S. Rep. No. 256, 96th Congress, 1st Session, 4, 9, 14–16, 20 (1979), and S. Rep. No. 590, 96th Congress, 1st Session 19–20 (1979), and H. R. Rep. No. 608, 96th Congress, 1st Session, 9, 17–18 (1979) and H. R. Rep. No. 781, 96th Congress, 2d Session 19-20 (1979), reprinted in 1980 U.S. Code Cong. and Admin. News 160–161.

98. Section 207 of the INA, now codified at 8 U.S.C. § 1157. Refugees still in their countries of nationality could also apply for refugee status if the President specifically designated such persons as refugees under 8 U.S.C. § 1101(a)(42)(B).

99. 8 C.F.R. § 207.1(a) (1981).

100. 8 U.S.C. § 1157(a).

101. 8 U.S.C. § 1157(a)(1) and (2).

102. 8 U.S.C. § 1157(b).

103. 8 U.S.C. § 1151(a).

104. Section 212(d)(5)(A), now codified at 8 U.S.C. § 1182(d)(5)(A).

105. 8 U.S.C. § 1182(5)(B). See also 8 C.F.R. § 212.5 (1982). Ironically, the 1980 Refugee Act was disregarded almost immediately after its passage. Prior to 1980, refugees had generally come to the United States through third countries or through refugee camps. The few that came directly were usually individual defectors. However in 1980–1981, hundreds of thousands of Cubans and Haitians landed in Florida seeking asylum in the United States. This was the United States' first experience with mass first asylum: refugees fleeing to the United States as a group. The refugees were not admitted under the emergency provisions of 8 U.S.C. § 1157(b). After much confusion, most of the Cubans and some of the Haitians were given a new status created by fiat by the Carter Administration called "Cuban/Haitian entrants (status pending)." Announced by Ambassador Victor H. Palmieri, U.S. Coordinator of Refugee Affairs, White House Fact Sheet, June 20, 1980, reprinted in Department of State Bulletin, vol. 80, August 1980, p. 81. See also *New York Times*, January 13, 1981, p. 7. The status was extended on December 29, 1980. Such executive action seems to be in direct contravention of the statutory scheme for the admission of refugees. The treatment of the Cubans and Haitians has generated a flood of commentary. See, e.g., Peter H. Schuck, "The Transformation of Immigration Law," *Columbia Law Review*, vol. 84, no. 1, January 1984, pp. 39–40; Note, "Aliens' Rights: The Refugee Act of 1980 as Response to the 1967 Protocol Relating to the Status of Refugees: The Final Test," *Vanderbilt Journal of Transnational Law*, vol. 14, Summer 1981, pp. 561–584; David A. Martin, "Due Process and Membership in the National Community: Political Asylum and Beyond," *University of Pittsburgh Law Review*, vol. 44, no. 2, Winter 1983, pp. 165–235; John A. Scanlan, "Regulating Refugee Flow: Legal Alternatives and Obligations Under the Refugee Act of 1980," *Notre Dame Lawyer*, vol. 56, no. 4, April 1981, pp. 618–643.

106. 8 U.S.C. § 1253(h)(1).

107. 8 U.S.C. § 1253(h)(1) and (2). The exceptions relating to criminal convictions and danger to the national security are based on Article 33 of the 1951 Convention. The other exceptions relating to Nazi war criminals and those who persecuted others are not based on the international Convention and Protocol, but are consistent with the new United States statutory definition of refugee found at 8 U.S.C. § 1101(a)(42).

108. _____ U.S., _____ 104 S.Ct. 2489 (1984).

109. Section 208 of the INA, now codified at 8 U.S.C. § 1158.

110. See Maureen O'Brien, "The Kudirka Affair: Bringing Sanity to the Law of Asylum, *Human Rights*, vol. 8, no. 4, Winter 1980, pp. 38–43; Comment, "Political Asylum and Withholding of Deportation: Defining the Appropriate Standard of Proof Under the Refugee Act of 1980," *San*

Diego Law Review, vol. 21, no. 1, December 1983, pp. 178–179, Note, "The Right to Asylum under United States Immigration Law," *University of Florida Law Review,* vol. 33, no. 4, Summer 1981, pp. 545; and James Z. Pugash, "The Dilemma of the Sea Refugee: Rescue Without Refuge," *Harvard International Law Journal,* vol. 18, no. 3, Summer 1977, p. 594, no. 110.

111. *Department of State Bulletin,* vol. 66, 1972, p. 124 [adopted by the INS at 37 Fed. Reg. 3447 (1972)].

112. 39 Fed. Reg. 41, 832 (1974) (superseded by 1980 Refugee Act). The status was only created under the broad power of the Attorney General to promulgate immigration regulations. 8 U.S.C. § 1103. Regulations passed in 1979 allowed asylum applications to be made to immigration judges and the Board of Immigration Appeals in deportation proceedings. 44 Fed. Reg. 21, 253 (1979).

113. 8 U.S.C. § 1158(a). See also 8 C.F.R. § 208.3(a)(2) (1984).

114. The Attorney General may delegate this discretionary power to officers of the INS. 8 U.S.C. § 1103(a). The Attorney General has delegated the discretionary determination of asylum applications to the INS District Directors. See, 8 C.F.R. § 103.1(n) and 8 C.F.R. §§ 208.1 and 208.8 (1980).

115. 8 C.F.R. § 208.8(f)(i).

116. See footnote 97. Several courts have acknowledged this express legislative intent. See, e.g., *Immigration and Naturalization Service v. Stevic,* 104 S.Ct. at 2499; *Yiu Sing Chun v. Sava,* 708 F.2d 869, 870, n. 2 (2d Cir. 1983); and *Orantes-Hernandez v. Smith,* 541 F.Supp. 351, 374–375 (C.D. Cal. 1982).

117. See *Moser v. United States,* 341 U.S. 41, 45–46 (1951).

118. See *Whitney v. Robertson,* 124 U.S. 190, 194 (1888).

119. INS Statistics reprinted in U.S. Committee for Refugees, *The Asylum Challenge to Western Nations,* December 1984, p. 13. The INS also reports the following statistics for Salvadorans for prior years:

Asylum Applications

Fiscal Year (10/1–9/30)	Made	Granted	Denied	Backlog
1981	5,570	2	154	6,043
1982	11,126	65	978	22,134
1983	2,712	71	2,914	13,501

Reprinted in American Friends Service Committee, Church World Service Immigration and Refugee Program, Inter-Religious Task Force on El Salvador and Central America and Lutheran Immigration and Refugee

Service, *Seeking Safe Haven: A Congregational Guide to Helping Central American Refugees in the United States*, undated [1984].

Furthermore, none of the 11,792 asylum applications made in 1980 were approved. Renny Golden, "Sanctuary," *Sojourners*, vol. 11, December 1982, p. 26. See other statistics in Patty Somlo, "A Sanctuary for Salvadorans," *America*, vol. 148, March 19, 1983, pp. 211–212 [26 of 12,000]; "Sanctuary for Salvadorans," *Newsweek*, vol. 102, July 11, 1983, p. 27 [74 out of 15,800 in 1981 and 1982]; "1 in 50 Deported Salvadorans May Be Dead, Study Shows," *Los Angeles Times*, January 25, 1984 [18,400 applications; 306 granted; 5,400 denied for 1981–1983]; Mark Gibney, "Seeking Sanctuary: A Special Duty for the U.S.?" *Commonweal*, vol. 111, May 18, 1984, p. 295 [200 out of over 3,300 in 1983]; Fred Krueger, "Land of the free, home of the eligible," *Christianity and Crisis*, vol. 44, July 9, 1984, p. 276 [65 out of 25,000 in 1982].

120. 8 C.F.R. § 208.1(a) (1984).

121. 8 C.F.R. § 208.2.

122. 8 C.F.R. § 208.6.

123. 8 C.F.R. § 208.7.

124. 8 C.F.R. § 208.8(a) and (b). The advisory opinion becomes part of the record in the case. 8 C.F.R. 208.10(b).

125. 8 C.F.R. § 208.8(c). The regulations specify six grounds for denial:

> The alien i) Is not a refugee within the meaning of section 101(a)(42) of the Act;
>
> ii) Has been firmly resettled in a foreign country;
>
> iii) That the alien ordered, incited, assisted or otherwise participated in the persecution of any person on account of race, religion, nationality, membership in a particular social group, or political opinion;
>
> iv) The alien, having been convicted by a final judgment of a particularly serious crime, constitutes a danger to the community of the United States;
>
> v) There are serious reasons for considering that the alien has committed a serious non-political crime outside the United States prior to the arrival of the alien in the United States; or
>
> vi) There are reasonable grounds for regarding the alien as a danger to the security of the United States.

8 C.F.R. § 208.8(f)(i).

126. 8 C.F.R. § 208.9. This procedure enables an asylum applicant who is lawfully present in the United States to get a second chance at asylum status. Some have called this procedure "two bites at the apple." See, e.g. *Jean v. Nelson*, 727 F.2d 957, 981 (11th Cir. 1984) (en banc).

127. 8 U.S.C. § 1159 and 8 C.F.R. § 209.2.

128. 8 C.F.R. §§ 208.3(b) and 208.10(a).

129. 8 C.F.R. § 208.3(b).

130. 8 C.F.R. § 208.5.

131. 8 C.F.R. § 208.10(b).

131a. 8 C.F.R. § 208.10(e).

132. 8 C.F.R. § 208.10(f).

133. 8 C.F.R. § 3.1(b). The BIA was created by the Attorney General. See 8 C.F.R. § 3.1.

134. 8 U.S.C. § 1105a(a).

135. For example, see Note, "Basing Asylum Claims on a Fear of Persecution Arising From a Prior Asylum Claim," *Notre Dame Lawyer*, vol. 56, no. 4, April 1981, pp. 719–730; Arthur C. Helton, "Persecution on Account of Membership in a Social Group as a Basis for Refugee Status," *Columbia Human Rights Law Review*, vol. 15, no. 1, Fall 1983, pp. 39–67; Note, "The Right to Asylum under United States Immigration Law," *University of Florida Law Review*, vol. 33, no. 4, Summer 1981, p. 545.

136. Due process challenges have also been raised regarding the mass detention of and denial of access to the asylum process to Cubans and Haitians. See *Fernandez v. Wilkinson*, 505 F.Supp. 787 (D. Kan. 1980) (indefinite detention of Cubans not a permissible alternative to exclusion order), *aff'd sub nom. on other grounds, Rodriguez-Fernandez v. Wilkinson*, 654 F.2d 1382 (10th Cir. 1981); *Vigile v. Sava*, 535 F.Supp. 1002 (S.D. N.Y.) (detention of Haitians pending decision on parole status unconstitutionally discriminatory), *rev'd and remanded sub nom., Betrand v. Sava*, 684 F.2d 204 (2d Cir. 1982); *Fernandez-Roque v. Smith*, 91 F.R.D. 239 (N.D. Ga. 1981) (no indefinite detention of Cubans without exclusion hearings), *appeal dismissed*, 671 F.2d 426 (11th Cir. 1982), *on remand*, 539 F.Supp. 925 (N.D. Ga. 1982) (classwide review of asylum claims by habeas corpus).

See, also, *Haitian Refugee Center v. Civiletti*, 503 F.Supp. 442 (S.D. Fla. 1980), *aff'd as modified sub nom., Haitian Refugee Center v. Smith*, 676 F.2d 1023 (5th Cir. 1982) (Haitians have due process rights in asylum and deportation proceedings). Some of the factual conclusions of the Fifth Circuit regarding the accelerated INS processing of Haitians are especially distressing: "Under the circumstances described, we conclude that INS had knowingly made it impossible for Haitians and their attorneys to prepare and file asylum applications in a timely manner. . . . The results of the accelerated program adopted by INS are revealing. None of the over 4,000 Haitians processed during this program were granted asylum." [Footnote omitted.] 676 F.2d at 1031–1032.

The Fifth Circuit concluded: "In sum, via the Haitian program, the government created conditions which negated the possibility that a Haitian's asylum hearing would be meaningful in either its timing or nature. Under such circumstances, the right to petition for political asylum was effectively denied." 676 F.2d at 1040.

Finally, see also, the extremely complex case of *Louis v. Meissner*, 530 F.Supp. 924 (S.D. Fla. 1982) (preliminary injunction in Haitian detention cases, restraining INS from commencing or continuing exclusion hearings); 532 F.Supp. 881 (S.D. Fla. 1982) (jurisdiction questions); *Louis v. Nelson*, 544 F.Supp. 973 (S.D. Fla. 1983) (permanent injunction granted because INS detention policy not duly promulgated in accordance with the Administrative Procedure Act but no INS discrimination); *Jean v. Nelson*, 683 F.2d 1311 (11th Cir. 1982) (INS motion for partial stay of permanent injunction denied); 711 F.2d 1455 (11th Cir. 1983) (aff'd on grounds that INS detention policy violated the APA and also found prima facie claim of INS discrimination); 714 F.2d 96 (11th Cir. 1983) (rehearing en banc granted); 727 F.2d 957 (11th Cir. en banc 1984) (reversed APA violation as moot; reversed and remanded discrimination issue because excludable or unadmitted aliens have no equal protection rights under the Fifth Amendment and may be denied parole status for any facially legitimate and bona fide reason); and finally, *cert. granted*, 53 U.S.L.W. 3417 (12/3/84).

The en banc 11th Circuit also had reached the merits of the issue of what notice of the right to apply for asylum is required and had decided that no due process interests were implicated in the asylum application process and that no notice was required by the 1980 Refugee Act. 727 F.2d at 981–983. Much of the reasoning and conclusions of the 11th Circuit is therefore in conflict with *Nunez v. Boldin* and *Orantes-Hernandez v. Smith*. The en banc decision also limits the old Fifth Circuit's holding in *Haitian Refugee Center v. Smith*. The United States Supreme Court has granted certiorari in the case.

137. *Nunez v. Boldin*, 537 F.Supp. 578 (S.D. Tex. 1982), *appeal dismissed*, 692 F.2d 755 (5th Cir. 1982). This case was decided by the same United States District judge that would later preside over the first Stacey Merkt trial in May 1984 as well as the February 1985 trial of Merkt and Jack Elder. (See Chapter Three).

138. 537 F.Supp. at 584. The district court also quoted, with approval, the conclusion of the district court in *Haitian Refugee Center v. Civiletti*: "In a very graphic sense, the political asylum applicant who fears to

return to his homeland because of persecution has raised the specter of truly severe deprivations of life, liberty and property: in this case, harrassment, imprisonment, beatings, torture, and death." 503 F.Supp. at 455.

139. The test, articulated by the United States Supreme Court in *Matthews v. Eldridge*, 424 U.S. 319, 334–335 (1976), is quoted by the district court at 537 F.Supp. at 586: "[O]ur prior decisions indicate that identification of the specific dictates of due process generally requires consideration of three distinct factors: First, the private interest that will be affected by the official action; second, the risk of an erroneous deprivation of such interest through the procedures used, and the probable value, if any, of additional or substitute procedural safeguards; and finally, the Government's interest, including the function involved and the fiscal and administrative burdens that the additional or substitute procedural requirements would entail.

140. 537 F.Supp. at 586.

141. 537 F.Supp. at 580–581. Many of the issues were redressed by the preliminary injunction set forth at 537 F.Supp. at 580, n. 1, and extended by the order of the district court, 537 F.Supp. at 587.

142. 537 F.Supp. at 580–581 and 585. The statutory basis for voluntary departure is found at 8 C.F.R. § 1252(b) and (g).

143. 537 F.Supp. at 584.

144. 537 F.Supp. at 586.

145. 537 F.Supp. at 587.

146. *Orantes-Hernandez v. Smith*, 541 F.Supp. 351 (C.D. Cal. 1982). See, Order, set forth at 541 F.Supp. at 385–389.

147. 541 F.Supp. at 355–358.

148. 541 F.Supp. at 359.

149. 541 F.Supp. at 360–361 and n. 10.

150. 541 F.Supp. at 361. While the consent to voluntary departure is technically revocable at any time prior to actual departure, the district court noted that the aliens were generally ignorant of this right and that the aliens' attorneys were often not allowed to revoke the agreement on behalf of their clients. 541 F.Supp. at 362.

151. 541 F.Supp. at 362.

152. 541 F.Supp. at 363. Many of these conditions were also addressed by the injunction. 541 F.Supp. at 383–385, 386–387.

153. 541 F.Supp. at 366–372.

154. 541 F.Supp. at 373.

155. 541 F.Supp. at 375.

156. 541 F.Supp. at 376. Thus, the court technically based its conclusions on an involuntary waiver of rights analysis rather than the denial
of due process analysis used by the *Nunez* court.

157. 541 F.Supp. at 377–378. Such notice includes the notice of the
right to consult with legal counsel prior to signing a voluntary departure
agreement. 541 F.Supp. at 381.

158. 541 F.Supp. at 380.

159. See John A. Scanlan, "Regulating Refugee Flow: Legal Alternatives and Obligations Under the Refugee Act of 1980," *Notre Dame Lawyer*, vol. 56, no. 4, April 1981, pp. 618–643; David A. Martin, "Due
Process and Membership in the National Community: Political Asylum
and Beyond," *University of Pittsburgh Law Review*, vol. 44, no. 2, Winter
1983, pp. 165–235; T. Alexander Aleinkoff, "Aliens, Due Process and
'Community Ties': A Response to Martin," *University of Pittsburgh Law Review*, vol. 44, no. 2, Winter 1983, pp. 237–260; Note, "Protecting Aliens
From Persecution Without Overloading the INS: Should Illegal Aliens Receive Notice of the Right to Apply for Asylum? *Virginia Law Review*, vol.
69, no. 5, June 1983, pp. 901–930; Deborah M. Levy, "Detention in the
Asylum Context," *University of Pittsburgh Law Review*, vol. 44, no. 2, Winter 1983, pp. 297–328. The analysis in the *Nunez* and *Orantes-Hernandez*
cases was recently rejected in *Ramirez-Osorio v. INS*, 745 F.2d 939 (5th Cir.
1984).

160. ___U.S.___, 104 S.Ct. 2489 (1984). It is expected that much
commentary on this critical case will be forthcoming. See, e.g., Kip Steinberg, "The Standard of Proof in Asylum Cases after *I.N.S. v. Stevic*," *Immigration Newsletter* (of the National Immigration Project of the National
Lawyers Guild, Inc.), vol. 13, no. 4, July–August 1984, p. 1, 6–8.

161. *Stevic v. Sava*, 678 F.2d 401 (2d Cir. 1982).

162. Compare *Reyes v. INS*, 693 F.2d 597 (6th Cir. 1982); *cert denied*,
105S.Ct.—(4/22/85) and Augustin v. INS, 735 F.2d 32, 35 (2d Cir. 1984)
(well-founded fear of persecution standard), with *Marroquin-Manriquez v.
INS*, 699 F.2d 129 (3d Cir. 1983) *cert. denied*, 104 S.Ct. 3553 (1984) and
Rejaie v. INS, 691 F.2d 139 (3d Cir. 1982) (clear probability of persecution
standard). This conflict over the proper standard of proof in a withholding
of deportation and/or asylum application has been the subject of considerable commentary. See, e.g., Comment, "Political Asylum and Withholding of Deportation: Defining the Appropriate Standard of Proof
Under the Refugee Act of 1980," *San Diego Law Review*, vol. 21, no. 1, December 1983, pp. 171–194; Note, "The Right of Asylum Under United
States Immigration Law," *University of Florida Law Review*, vol. 33, no. 4,
Summer 1981, pp. 560–561; Ira J. Kurzban, "Restructuring the Asylum
Process," *San Diego Law Review*, vol. 19, no. 1, December 1981, pp. 107–

108; Carolyn Patty Blum, "The Half Open Door: U.S. Refugee Law and the *Stevic* Case," *Federal Bar News and Journal*, vol. 31, no. 5, May 1984 pp. 198–201.

163. 104 S.Ct. at 2495, n. 12.

164. 104 S.Ct. at 2493 and 2498.

165. 104 S.Ct. at 2494–2495.

166. 104 S.Ct. at 2496.

167. 104 S.Ct. at 2496, n. 15.

168. 104 S.Ct. at 2500, n. 22.

169. 104 S.Ct. at 2497–2498, 2501.

170. 104 S.Ct. at 2497, n. 18. There are distinctions between the two types of relief. For example, asylum will not be granted to an alien who is firmly resettled, 8 C.F.R. § 208.14, while irrelevant to withholding of deportation. See *In re Lam*, Interim Dec. No. 2857 (BIA 1981). However, the only pre-*Stevic* decisions to hold that the withholding of deportation required a clear probability of persecution were also premised on the assumption that the two standards were identical. *Rejaie v. INS*, 691 F.2d 139, 146 (3d Cir. 1982) and *Marroquin-Manriquez v. INS*, 699 F.2d 129, 133 (3d Cir. 1983), *cert. denied*, 104 S.Ct. 3553 (1984).

171. See *Carvajal-Munoz v. INS*, 743 F.2d 562, 575 (7th Cir. 1984); *Bolanos-Hernandez v. INS*, 749 F.2d 1316, 1322 (9th Cir. 1984); *Lemus v. INS*, 741 F.2d 765 (5th Cir. 1984); *Dally v. INS*, 744 F.2d 1191 (6th Cir. 1984); *Youkhanna v. INS*, 749 F.2d 360 (6th Cir. 1984). But see, *Sotto v. INS*, 748 F.2d 832, 836 (3d Cir. 1984) (standard same for both, clear probability).

The application of two standards to the same evidence is problematic upon review. A three-part analysis is utilized: first, whether there is reasonable, substantial, and probative evidence on the record as a whole to support a finding of a well-founded fear of persecution (an issue of fact); second, whether the exercise of discretion by the Immigration Judge in denying the application for asylum was arbitrary, capricious, or an abuse of discretion (an issue of law); and third, whether there is reasonable, substantial and probative evidence on the record as a whole to support a finding of a clear probability of persecution (an issue of fact) that would require the mandatory withholding of deportation. *Bolanos-Hernandez v. INS*, 749 F.2d 1316, 1321, n.9 (9th Cir. 1984), *Youkhanna v. INS*, 749 F.2d 360, 362, n.2 (6th Cir. 1984) (two-part review for asylum); *Carvajal-Munoz v. INS*, 743 F.2d 562, 569 (7th Cir. 1984); *Bolanos-Hernandez v. INS*, 749 F.2d 1316, 1320, n.8 (9th Cir. 1984); *Chavarria v. Dept. of Justice*, 722 F.2d 666, 670 (11th Cir. 1984) (substantial evidence standard of review for withholding of deportation). But see, *Sotto v. INS*, 748 F.2d 832, 837 (3d Cir. 1984) (abuse of discretion standard of review for withholding of deportation).

One court has suggested that immigration judges conduct separate evidentiary hearings when considering requests for asylum and the withholding of deportation. *Carvajal-Munoz v. INS*, 743 F.2d 562, 570 (7th Cir. 1984). However, several courts have suggested that the renewal of a prior asylum application filed with a District Director in a deportation proceeding will only be considered as an application for the withholding of deportation and not a separate application for asylum. *Dally v. INS*, 744 F.2d 1191, 1196, n.6 (6th Cir. 1984) and *Saballo-Cortez v. INS*, 749 F.2d 1354, 1355 (9th Cir. 1984).

172. 8 C.F.R. § 208.3(b).

173. 104 S.Ct. at 2497, n.18.

174. *Ibid.*, at 2501.

175. *Ibid.*, at 2498, n.19.

176. *Ibid.* See also *Bolanos-Hernandez v. INS*, 749 F.2d 1316, 1320, n.5 (9th Cir. 1984).

177. 104 S.Ct. at 2501.

178. *Ibid.*, at 2498.

179–181. Deleted in manuscript revision.

182. Office of the United Nations High Commissioner for Refugees, *Handbook on Procedures and Criteria for Determining Refugee Status*, (Geneva: UNHCR, 1979).

183. *UNHCR Handbook*, 38, p. 12.

184. See, e.g., *In re Rodriguez-Palma*, 17 I & N Dec. 465, 468 (BIA 1980), *In re Frentescu*, 18 I&N Dec. 244, 246 (BIA1982) (UNHCR Handbook used to define "serious crime"). See, also, *In re A———*, 60 Interpreter Releases 26 (before Immigration Judge Simpson, December 10, 1982).

185. See, e.g., *Stevic v. Sava*, 678 F.2d 401, 405–406 (2d Cir. 1982), *rev'd on other grounds sub nom. I.N.S. v. Stevic*, —U.S.—, 104 S.Ct. 2489 (1984), *McMullen v. INS*, 658 F.2d 1312, 1319 (9th Cir. 1981), *Zavala-Bonilla v. INS*, 730 F.2d 562, 567 (9th Cir. 1984) and *Hotel and Restaurant Employees Union v. Smith*, 594 F.Supp. 502, 512 (D.D.C. 1984).

186. The following analysis is based upon Comment, "Political Asylum and Withholding of Deportation: Defining the Appropriate Standard of Proof Under the Refugee Act of 1980," *San Diego Law Review*, vol. 21, no. 1, December 1983, pp. 188–190.

187. *UNHCR Handbook*, 37, p. 11.

188. *UNHCR Handbook*, 52, p. 14.

189. *UNHCR Handbook*, 40, p. 12.

190. *UNHCR Handbook*, 41, p. 12.

191. *UNHCR Handbook*, 53, pp. 14–15, and 201, p. 48.

192. *UNHCR Handbook*, 42, pp. 12–13.

193. *UNHCR Handbook*, 43, p. 13.

194. *Ibid.*

195. *UNHCR Handbook*, 42, p. 13, and 59, p. 16. See, also *Coriolan v. INS*, 559 F.2d 993, 1004 (5th Cir. 1977).

196. *UNHCR Handbook*, 196, p. 47. The courts are divided on this question of uncorroborated testimony. Compare, *Kashani v. INS*, 547 F.2d 376, 379 (7th Cir. 1977) and *Dally v. INS*, 744 F.2d 1191, 1195–1196 (6th Cir. 1984) (uncorroborated testimony discredited as self-serving) with *Carvajal-Munoz v. INS*, 743 F.2d 562 at 574–576, 577 and 579 (7th Cir. 1984) and *Youkhanna v. INS*, 749 F.2d 360, 362 (6th Cir. 1984) (uncorroborated testimony sufficient if credible, persuasive and specific).

197. *Ibid.*

198. *UNHCR Handbook*, 199, p. 47, and 203, p. 48.

199. *UNHCR Handbook*, 198, p. 47.

200. *UNHCR Handbook*, 199, p. 47.

201. *UNHCR Handbook*, 196, p. 47.

202. *UNHCR Handbook*, 202, p. 48.

203. Report of UNHCR Mission to Monitor INS Asylum Processing of Salvadoran Illegal Entrants, September 13–18, 1981, reprinted at 128 *Congressional Record* S827, daily edition, February 11, 1982.

204. *Ibid.* at S830.

205. Letter dated May 19, 1981. Such a group determination of prima facie refugee status is provided for in the *UNHCR Handbook:* "While refugee status must normally be determined on an individual basis, situations have also arisen in which entire groups have been displaced under circumstances indicating that members of the group could be considered individually as refugees. In such situations the need to provide assistance is often extremely urgent and it may not be possible for purely practical reasons to carry out an individual determination of refugee status for each member of the group." *UNHCR Handbook*, 44, p. 13.

206. 128 *Congressional Record* E5833 (1981). Bills introduced in November 1983 call upon the INS to halt the deportation of Salvadorans until the situation in El Salvador allows their safe return. However, this proposal (S. 2131, H.R. 4447), commonly named the DeConcini-Moakley bill, remained stalled in committee at the conclusion of the 98th Congress, despite having 18 co-sponsors in the Senate and 153 in the House. The bills were reintroduced as S.377 and H.R. 822 in early 1985.

207. See, e.g., letter of Alvin Paul Drischler, Acting Assistant Secretary of State for Congressional Relations, April 17, 1981, reprinted at 128 *Congressional Record* at S831.

208. See letter of David Crosland, Acting Commissioner of INS, May 1, 1981, reprinted at 128 *Congressional Record* at S832. Such status was

revoked for Nicaraguans in 1980 and created for refugees from Afghanistan in 1980 and from Poland in 1981. Some believe that the status, which is not based in any statute or regulation but created solely at the discretion of the Attorney General (with consultation from the Department of State), has been denied to Salvadorans and Guatemalans for political reasons. See, T. Alexander Aleinkoff, "Political Asylum in the Federal Republic of Germany and the Republic of France: Lessons for the United States," *University of Michigan Journal of Law Reform*, vol. 17, no. 2, Winter 1984, pp. 239–240. However, a legal challenge to the refusal of the Attorney General to grant the status to Salvadorans has been rejected. *Hotel and Restaurant Employees Union v. Smith*, 594 F.Supp.502 (D.D.C. 1984).

209. See, e.g., United States Department of State, *Country Reports on the World Refugee Situation*, August 1983, pp. 99–100; Elliot Abrams, "Extending Voluntary Departure for El Salvadorans," *Department of State Bulletin*, vol. 84, no. 2090, September 1984, pp. 48–49; Report of UNHCR Mission to Monitor INS Asylum Processing of Salvadoran Illegal Entrants, 128 *Congressional Record* at S830; *Orantes-Hernandez v. Smith*, 541 F.Supp. 351, 380, n. 37 (C.D.Cal. 1982). Others reject the contention that all Salvadorans are economic migrants. See, Aleinkoff, *University of Michigan Journal of Law Reform*, pp. 191–193, 231–232.

211. Immigration and Naturalization Service, "Asylum Adjudications: An Evolving Concept and Responsibility for the INS," June/December 1982 (unpublished report), p. 59; Arthur C. Helton, "Political Asylum Under the 1980 Refugee Act: An Unfulfilled Promise," *University of Michigan Journal of Law Reform*, vol. 17, no. 2, Winter 1984, p. 254; Note, "Behind the Paper Curtain: Asylum Policy Versus Practice," *New York University Review of Law and Social Change*, vol. 7, no. 1, Winter 1978, pp. 107–141; Georgetown University Institute for Public Representation, "The State Department Advisory Opinion: A Due Process Critique," *Immigration Law Reporter*, Spring 1984, pp. 20–21. See, also INS Operations Instruction 208.8 (requiring special procedures and "immediate action" on "politically sensitive" applications for asylum).

212. 8 C.F.R. §§208.7 and 208.10(b). The district court in *Orantes-Hernandez* questioned the need for such opinions in every asylum case. 541 F.Supp. at 379, n. 35.

213. Georgetown University Institute for Public Representation, *Immigration Law Reporter*, p. 13; Helton, *University of Michigan Journal of Law Reform*, p. 262; Aleinkoff, *University of Michigan Journal of Law Reform*, p. 193; John A. Scanlan, "Regulating Refugee Flow: Legal Alternatives and Obligations Under the Refugee Act of 1980," *Notre Dame Lawyer*, vol. 56, no. 4, April 1981, pp. 628–629; Ira Kurzban, "Restructuring the Asylum Process," *San Diego Law Review*, vol. 19, no. 1, December 1981, pp. 98–99;

John A. Scanlan, "Asylum Adjudication: Some Due Process Implications of Proposed Immigration Legislation," *University of Pittsburgh Law Review*, vol. 44, no. 2, Winter 1983, pp. 278–279; Report of UNHCR Mission to Monitor INS Asylum Processing of Salvadoran Illegal Entrants, 128 *Congressional Record* at S829.

These advisory opinions in Salvadoran and Guatemalan cases are generally form letters, with only the name, case number and date inserted. See, Georgetown University Institute for Public Representation, *Immigration Law Reporter*, pp. 18–19, n. 93. However, a legal challenge to their use in Salvadoran asylum cases has been rejected. *Hotel and Restaurant Employees Union v. Smith*, 594 F.Supp. 502 (D.D.C. 1984).

214. *Kasravi v. INS*, 400 F.2d 675, 677. n. 1. (9th Cir. 1968). See also *Zamora v. INS*, 534 F.2d 1055, 1061–1063 (2d Cir. 1976) and Aleinkoff, *University of Michigan Journal of Law Reform*, pp. 194–195, 235–236.

215. See note 213 and Note, "The Endless Debate: Refugee Law and Policy and the 1980 Refugee Act," *Cleveland State Law Review*, vol. 32, no. 1, 1983–1984, pp. 143–145.

216. See, e.g., *United States ex rel. Knauff v. Shaughnessy*, 338 U.S. 537, 543 (1950); *Harisiades v. Shaughnessy*, 342 U.S. 580, 589 (1952); *Kleindienst v. Mandel*, 408 U.S. 753, 770 (1972); *Fiallo v. Bell*, 430 U.S. 787, 792–793 (1977); *Hotel and Restaurant Employees Union v. Smith*, 594 F.Supp. 502 (D.D.C. 1984).

217. *Pollgreen v. Morris*, 496 F.Supp. 1042, 1049 (S.D. Fla. 1980).

218. *Haitian Refugee Center v. Smith*, 676 F.2d 1023, 1039 (5th Cir. 1982); *Pierre v. United States*, 547 F.2d 1281 (5th Cir. 1977).

219. "Amid Charges, Immigration Bill Dies," *New York Times*, October 12, 1984, p. A16. The Immigration Reform and Control Act of 1983 had been introduced into both houses on February 17, 1983. The Senate passed it by a vote of 76–18 on May 18, 1983 but the House did not pass it until June 20, 1984, by a vote of 216–211.

220. The proposals were §§ 121, 123 and 124 in S. 529 and H.R. 1510, reprinted at 130 *Congressional Record* H6154–H6156 and H6171–H6173, respectively. See Note, "The Endless Debate: Refugee Law and Policy and the 1980 Refugee Act," *Cleveland State Law Review*, vol. 32, no. 1, 1983–1984, pp. 153–159; Kurzban, *San Diego Law Review*, pp. 94–95; and Paul R. Verkuil, "A Study of Immigration Procedures," *UCLA Law Review*, vol. 31, no. 6, 1984, pp. 1187, 1198–1202.

3. The Confrontation Between Church and State

1. *San Antonio Light*, May 12, 1984, quoted in "INS official knocks refugee volunteers," *National Catholic Reporter*, vol. 20, May 25, 1984, p. 21.

2. For example, see the warnings in "Public Sanctuary for Salvadoran and Guatemalan Refugees: Organizers' Nuts and Bolts" (Chicago: Chicago Religious Task Force on Central America, undated) pp. 3, 9, 12; and Chicago Religious Task Force on Central America, the National Lawyers Guild, Proyecto Resistencia (Chicago) of AFSC, and Travelers and Immigrants Aid Society (Chicago), *Sanctuary and the Law: A Guide for Congregations* (Chicago, 1984) pp. 1–6, 13–15.

3. At the August 9, 1982, welcoming service at the Wellington Avenue United Church of Christ, the Rev. Michael McConnell proclaimed: "We cry 'Enough!' . . . We break the law and say, 'Enough to injustice!' " *Chicago Tribune*, August 9, 1982.

Perhaps the Reverend Sid Mohn has stated the position of the church most eloquently: "When a church has to break the law in order to provide refuge for homeless people, the struggle for justice has reached a new stage. Now the pastoral has merged with the political, service is prophetic and love is a subversive activity." Quoted in "Sanctuary: A Justice Ministry" (Chicago: Chicago Religious Task Force on Central America, undated), p. 1.

4. There was one incident where the INS followed an undocumented alien into a downtown Los Angeles church, chased the man through the church and arrested him in the church loft, in the fall of 1981, before the public sanctuary movement began. After this incident, there was word of an administrative order that INS agents were not to pursue aliens into churches, schools or hospitals. See "Sanctuary for Salvadorans," *Newsweek*, vol. 102, July 11, 1983, p. 27; Thomas Brom, "Church Sanctuary for Salvadorans," *California Lawyer*, vol. 3, no. 7, July 1983, p. 42; and an unpublished memorandum dated October 22, 1981 from Reverend John H. Wagner, Jr., executive director of the Lutheran Social Services of Southern California.

5–6. Deleted in manuscript revision.

7. This account is compiled from information in Patricia Scharber Lefevre, "On trial in Texas: is it legal or not to help refugees?" *National Catholic Reporter*, vol. 20, May 18, 1984, pp. 1, 21, 22; "Government Crackdown on Sanctuary Movement," *Central American Refugee Defense Fund Newsletter*, June 1984, pp. 1, 4, 8; Steven Hall-Williams, "Caught in the Net," *Sojourners*, vol. 13, September 1984, p. 8; "Small Band of Springs

Catholics Aids Salvadorans," *Denver Post*, February 21, 1984; and the motions and other legal documents filed in Merkt's case.

8. The refugees initially refused to cooperate with the prosecution and declined to testify against Merkt. They were eventually jailed for contempt of court for their silence but were again released on bond when they finally agreed to submit to cross-examination by the prosecution.

9. This account is compiled from information in Steven Hall-Williams, "Caught in the Net," *Sojourners*, vol. 13, September 1984, p. 8; "Basta! National Sanctuary Newsletter" (Chicago: Chicago Religious Task Force on Central America, July 1984); "Churches fear U.S. crackdown on refugees," *San Francisco Sunday Examiner and Chronicle*, June 10, 1984, p. A2; and the motions filed in Conger's case.

10. Arresting officers must have a reasonable suspicion based on articulable facts, together with rational inferences from those facts, that a vehicle contains aliens who may be illegally in the country. *United States v. Brigoni-Ponce*, 422 U.S. 873, 884 (1975).

11. Rob Cogswell, "Refugee Worker Arrested," *The Christian Century*, vol. 101, May 2, 1984, p. 454; "Refugee Center Operator Is Arrested in Texas," *New York Times*, April 14, 1984, p. A8; Patricia Scharber Lefevere, "Elder acquitted of transporting aliens," *National Catholic Reporter*, vol. 21, February 1, 1985, p. 19; "Acquittal in 'Sanctuary' Case Hailed," *San Francisco Chronicle*, January 26, 1985, p. 9; Patricia Scharber Lefevere, "Judge allows Elder's religious defense," *National Catholic Reporter*, vol. 21, January 25, 1985, p. 6; and "Despite a Crackdown, 7 Guatemalans Are Smuggled Into U.S.," *New York Times*, January 20, 1985. The District Court's decision on several pre-trial motions has now been reported at 601 F.Supp. 1574 (S.D. Tex. 1985).

12. The federal marshals changed their original plans to arrest Elder on April 12 when they saw worshippers and news media representatives waiting for them. Rob Cogswell, "Refugee Worker Arrested," *The Christian Century*, vol. 101, May 2, 1984, p. 454; "Are refugees 'illegal aliens'?" *Texas Catholic*, April 27, 1984.

13. Defense attorney Stephen Cooper, from the Neighborhood Justice Center in St. Paul, Minnesota, eloquently declared the defense's theory of the case during a pre-trial hearing:

> The religious community is watching, the international community is watching and the American public is watching, to see if our courts will really convict a man of federal felony crimes who has hurt no one, taken no one's property, turned no profit, sought no ill-gotten gains, demeaned no one's dignity and sought no personal benefit, simply be-

cause he could not sit idly by when other men's lives were in jeopardy, and all that was asked of him was a ride of a few miles.

Quoted in Patricia Scharber Lefevere, "Judge allows Elder's religious defense," *National Catholic Reporter*, vol. 21, January 25, 1985, p. 6.

Meanwhile, the three Salvadorans are now living in Long Island, New York, awaiting the completion of their deportation hearings.

14. This account is compiled from *Central American Refugee Defense Fund Newsletter*, December 1984 (Boston), p. 1; "Basta!," Newsletter of the Chicago Religious Task Force on Central America, January 1985, p. 3; "Two Go to Trial in Houston for Illegally Helping Aliens," *New York Times*, February 19, 1985, p. 7; "Leader in Movement to Harbor Aliens is Convicted," *New York Times*, February 22, 1985, p. 8; "Two Convicted of Smuggling Salvadorans, Vow to Continue Sanctuary Refugee Work," *Los Angeles Times*, February 22, 1985, Part I, p. 4; Patricia Scharber Lefevere, "Elder and Merkt guilty; attorney says he won't heed sanctuary 'setback,' " *National Catholic Reporter*, vol. 21, March 1, 1985, p. 7; "2 Sentenced in Aid to Illegal Aliens," *New York Times*, March 28, 1985, p. 13; "Sanctuary Worker Given A Lighter Sentence," *New York Times*, March 29, 1985, p. 8; "Sanctuary Worker Loses Her Probation," *San Francisco Chronicle*, March 27, 1985, p. 3; "Sanctuary Movement Workers Get Jail Terms," *San Francisco Chronicle*, March 28, 1985, p. 15; "Judge Relents on Sanctuary Worker's Term," *San Francisco Chronicle*, March 29, 1985, p. 14; Rob Cogswell, "Bishop Posts Bond," *The Christian Century*, vol. 102, January 2–9, 1985, "Events and People, p. 8.

15. Judge Vela had already refused to recluse himself from the case even though he had presided over the first Merkt case and had stated on the record during the first trial that he would put her in jail if she ever appeared before him again. "Two Go on Trial in Houston for Illegally Helping Aliens," *New York Times*, February 19, 1985, p. 7.

16. "U.S. Government vs. Sanctuary Movement," "Basta!," National Newsletter of the Chicago Religious Task Force on Central America, April 1985, pp. 6–10; "16 Indicted by U.S. in Bid to End Church Smuggling of Latin Aliens," *New York Times*, January 15, 1985, pp. 1, 7;

"Priests, Nuns Charged with Alien Smuggling," *Los Angeles Times*, January 15, 1985, Part I, pp. 1, 8;

"Sanctuary Leaders Get Support, Vow to Fight," *Los Angeles Times*, January 16, 1985, Part I, pp. 3, 13;

Tim McCarthy, "Crackdown butts church against state," *National Catholic Reporter*, vol. 21, January 25, 1985, p. 1;

"When Churches Smuggle Aliens," *U.S. News and World Report*, vol. 98, January 28, 1985, p. 14;

"Clerics Indicted For Sheltering Latin Refugees," *San Francisco Chronicle*, January 15, 1985, p. 9;

"U.S. sweeps down on churches accused of smuggling aliens," *Oakland Tribune*, January 15, 1985, p. A4.

17. "U.S. Asks Curb on Sanctuary Case Testimony," *New York Times*, January 27, 1985, p. 15.

18. "Use of Informants Questioned in Inquiry on Aliens," *New York Times*, March 2, 1985.

19. "Basta!", National Newsletter of the Chicago Religious Task Force on Central America, April 1985, pp. 1–2; "Two Go on Trial in Houston for Illegally Helping Aliens," *New York Times*, February 19, 1985, p. 7 and *National Catholic Reporter*, vol. 21, February 22, 1985, p. 3.

20. "U.S. Churches Defy Law and Harbor El Salvadoran Refugees." *Christian Science Monitor*, August 20, 1982, p. 6.

21. *The Berkeley Gazette*, March 24, 1983.

22. Michael J. Farrell, "Sanctuary: Part of the bigger picture," *National Catholic Reporter*, vol. 20, September 14, 1984, p. 11.

23. "Church Gives Sanctuary to Refugees," *Miami Herald*, March 29, 1983.

24. "Salvadoran Refugees Find Haven," *Sacramento Bee*, March 18, 1984.

25. "Why Illegal Aliens Get Sanctuary," *San Francisco Chronicle*, April 11, 1984, p. F–3.

26. *Ibid.*

27. " 'Underground railroad' still runs in the open," *The Arizona Daily Star*, December 25, 1982, p. B.1

28. "Churches Give Sanctuary to Illegal Refugees Who Face Deportation," *New York Times*, April 18, 1983, pp. A1, A16.

29. *Black's Law Dictionary*, 5th edition (St. Paul, Minnesota: West Publishing Co., 1979), p. 375 defines "*de facto*" as: "in fact, in deed, actually . . . a state of affairs which must be accepted for all practical purposes, but is illegal or illegitimate. . . . In this sense it is the contrary of *de jure*, which means rightful, legitimate, just, or constitutional." See also "*De facto*" and "*De jure*" in 25A *Corpus Juris Secundum* (Brooklyn: West Publishing Co., 1966), pp. 481–483.

4. Legal Implications for Sanctuaries and Sanctuary Workers

1. *United States v. Salinas-Calderon*, 585 F.Supp. 599, 602 (D. Kan. 1984).

2. 387 U.S. 294 (1967).

3. 387 U.S. at 321 (Douglas, dissenting).

4. 387 U.S. at 315–318. See also *Boyd v. United States*, 116 U.S. 616, 626–630 (1886); *Mapp v. Ohio*, 367 U.S. 643 (1961); *Chimel v. California*, 395 U.S. 752 (1969).

5. See, e.g., *Steagold v. United States*, 451 U.S. 204, 217–220 (1981) (subject of arrest warrant under "hot pursuit" cannot take sanctuary in home of another but home of a third party is protected where there is no search warrant, hot pursuit or exigent circumstances) and *Monroe v. Pape*, 365 U.S. 167, 208–210 (1961) (Frankfurter, dissenting) (there exists a realm of sanctuary surrounding every individual and infrangible, save in a very limited class of circumstances, by the agents of government).

6. 385 U.S. 323 (1966).

7. 385 U.S. at 346 (Douglas, dissenting). See also *Ker v. California*, 374 U.S. 23, 47–55 (Brennan, dissenting) (house is no sanctuary where proper notice and demand for entry given).

8. Any concept of a sanctuary privilege has been rejected in two other areas of law, namely the constitutional power of extradition between the states (cf. U.S. Constitution, Article IV, § 2, cl. 2; *Michigan v. Doran*, 439 U.S. 282, 287 [1978] [purpose of Extradition Clause was to preclude any state from becoming a sanctuary for fugitives from justice of another state and thus balkanize the administration of criminal justice among the several states]) and the reservation of limited concurrent jurisdiction by the states over land ceded to the federal government (see, e.g., *James, State Tax Commissioner v. Dravo Construction Co.*, 302 U.S. 134, 146–147 [1937] and *United States v. Unzeuta*, 281 U.S. 138, 143 [1930]).

9. T. Lincoln Bouscaren and Adam C. Ellis and Francis N. Korth, *Canon Law: A Text and Commentary*, 4th ed. (Milwaukee: The Bruce Publishing Company, 1963) p. 661.

10. James A. Coriden, Thomas J. Green and Donald E. Heintschel, eds., *The Code of Canon Law: A Text and Commentary* (Ramsey, N.J.: Paulist Press, 1984). There are only general provisions regarding the sanctity of each church.

11. Conversation with Professor Stephen Kuttner, Boalt Hall School of Law, February 23, 1984.

12. *Milwaukee Journal*, December 4, 1982. See also "Should Churches Provide Sanctuary?" Editorial, *Christian Century*, vol. 100, no. 2, April 27, 1983, p. 387.

13. 333 U.S. 483 (1948).

14. Act of February 5, 1917, 39 Stat. 874, at 880.

15. Act of February 20, 1907, 34 Stat. 898, at 900.

16. 333 U.S. at 486.

17. 333 U.S. at 488.

18. 333 U.S. at 495.

19. Act of June 27, 1952, Pub. L. No. 82-414, 66 Stat. 163, at 228. See also, 1952 U.S. Code Cong. and Admin. News 166.

20. 27 F.2d 223 (6th Cir. 1928).

21. 27 F.2d at 224.

22. 112 F.2d 83 (2d Cir. 1940).

23. 112 F.2d at 85.

24. *United States v. Mack*, 112 F.2d 290, 291 (2d Cir. 1940).

25. Comment, "Harboring of Illegal Aliens: New Meaning to the Concept of Shielding From Detection," *Suffolk Transnational Law Journal*, vol. 7, no. 1, Spring 1983, p. 258, n. 20.

26. *Susnjar v. United States*, 27 F.2d at 224.

27. 521 F.2d 437 (2d Cir.), *cert. denied*, 423 U.S. 995 (1975).

28. 521 F.2d at 441.

29. *Ibid.*

30. 521 F.2d at 440–441.

31. 521 F.2d at 441.

31a. See, generally, Wayne R. LaFave and Austin W. Scott, Jr., *Handbook on Criminal Law* (St. Paul: West Publishing Co., 1972), §24, pp. 175–176.

32. See also *United States v. Herrera*, 584 F.2d 1137 (2d Cir. 1978).

33. 531 F.2d 428 (9th Cir.), *cert denied*, 429 U.S. 836 (1976).

34. 531 F.2d at 430.

35. *Ibid.*, n. 4.

36. *Ibid.*, n. 3.

37. 557 F.2d 1173 (5th Cir. 1977), *rehearing denied*, 561 F.2d 831, *cert. denied*, 434 U.S. 1063 (1978).

38. 557 F.2d at 1180.

39. 557 F.2d at 1175–76.

40. 557 F.2d at 1180.

41. 557 F.2d at 1177.

42. 557 F.2d at 1180.

43. 645 F.2d 453 (5th Cir. 1981).

44. 645 F.2d at 455.

45. 674 F.2d 1067 (5th Cir. 1982).

46. 674 F.2d at 1060.

47. *Ibid.*

48. See, Comment, *Suffolk Transnational Law Journal*, pp. 255–266.

49. 674 F.2d at 1071.

50. 674 F.2d at 1072.

51. *Ibid.*

52. 674 F.2d at 1072.

53. Comment, *Suffolk Transnational Law Journal*, p. 265.

54. 674 F.2d at 1073.

55. 674 F.2d at 1073–1074, n. 5.

56. 531 F.2d at 430, n. 3.

57. 674 F.2d at 1073–1074, n. 5.

58. 674 F.2d at 1074, n. 5.

59. *United States v. Moreno*, 561 F.2d 1321, 1323 (9th Cir. 1977), *United States v. Corbett*, 215 U.S. 233, 242–243 (1909) and *United States v. Fruit Growers Express Co.*, 279 U.S. 363, 369 (1928).

60. *United States v. Orejel-Tejeda*, 194 F.Supp. 140, 143 (N.D. Cal. 1961) and *United States v. Corbett*, 215 U.S. 233, 242–243 (1909).

61. The Congressional discussion focused on the impact of the proposed employer sanctions provisions on the harboring section of the statute. The House amendment was introduced by Congresswoman Boxer (D.-Calif.), 130 *Congressional Record*, H5721–H5723, daily edition, June 13, 1984, and became § 112 of the final House bill (H.R. 1510), 130 *Congressional Record*, H6170, daily edition, June 20, 1984. A somewhat different amendment is found in the final Senate bill (S. 529), reprinted in 130 *Congressional Record*, H6153, daily edition, June 20, 1984.

62. 130 *Congressional Record*, H5722–H5723, daily edition, June 13, 1984.

63. The defendants in *Acosta de Evans* and *Rubio-Gonzalez* did not have pecuniary motivations but neither did they have the religious, humanitarian or political motivations of sanctuary workers.

64. A vagueness challenge had been raised and rejected in *Bland v. United States*, 299 F.2d 105, 109 (5th Cir. 1962) and *Martinez-Quiroz v. United States*, 210 F.2d 763 (9th Cir. 1954) but those decisions were rendered prior to the development of the "substantial facilitation" definition. The Fifth Circuit did consider a vagueness and overbreadth argument regarding the word "shield" in *Cantu*, 557 F.2d at 117, but dismissed it summarily without any discussion.

65. *United States v. Fierros*, 692 F.2d 1291, 1294 (9th Cir. 1982). However, the *Fierros* court rejected the proposition that § 1324(a) was so complex or so likely to ensnare innocent violators that it required intentional violation of a known legal duty. *Ibid.* at 1295.

66. *United States v. Pereira-Pineda*, 721 F.2d 137, 139 (5th Cir. 1983) and *United States v. Mt. Fuji Japanese Steak House, Inc.*, 435 F.Supp. 1194, 1197 (E.D. N.Y. 1977).

67. 509 F.Supp. 289 (S.D. Fla. 1980).

68. 509 F.Supp. at 295. The court held that the conduct of the refugees in attempting to land at Key West, Florida did not even constitute

an "entry" within the meaning of the statute since the Cubans were only seeking to request lawful entry as refugees. 509 F.Supp. at 295–296.

69. 509 F.Supp. at 295.

70. 509 F.Supp. at 299.

71. 509 F.Supp. at 298.

72. *United States v. Zayas-Morales*, 685 F.2d 1272 (11th Cir. 1982).

73. 685 F.2d at 1272 and 1277.

74. 685 F.2d at 1277.

75. 721 F.2d 137 (5th Cir. 1983).

76. 8 U.S.C. § 1324(a)(2).

77. 721 F.2d at 139.

78. *United States v. Kavazanjian*, 623 F.2d 730 (1st Cir. 1980), referred to in *United States v. Pereira-Pineda*, 721 F.2d at 140.

79. The aliens were to enter the United States under the transit without visa (TWOV) privilege which permits aliens traveling from one foreign country to another with a stopover in the U.S. to proceed in "immediate and continuous transit" through the United States without a passport or United States visa. 8 U.S.C. § 1182(d)(4)(C). The defendant met the aliens at the airport and either directed them to the INS officials at the airport to make applications for asylum/parole or smuggled the aliens out of the airport. 623 F.2d at 734–736.

80. This section prohibits the willful or knowing encouragement or inducement of the entry into the United States of any alien not duly admitted by an immigration officer or not lawfully entitled to enter or reside in the United States.

81. 623 F.2d at 736–738.

82. 623 F.2d at 739.

83. 721 F.2d 139–140.

84. 639 F.2d 194 (5th Cir. 1981).

85. See companion case, 639 F.2d 192, 193 (5th Cir. 1980).

86. 639 F.2d at 196.

87. 721 F.2d at 138, n. 2.

88. 721 F.2d at 138–139, n. 2 and at 140.

89. *Ibid.*

90. 721 F.2d at 139, n. 2.

91. *United States v. Periera-Pineda*, 721 F.2d at 137 and *United States v. Mt. Fuji Japanese Steak House, Inc.* 435 F.Supp. 1194, 1197 (E.D. N.Y. 1977).

92. Office of United Nations High Commissioner on Refugees, *Handbook on Procedures and Criteria for Determining Refugee Status* (Geneva: UNHCR, 1979), 28, p. 9.

93. See Frank E. Krenz, "The Refugee as a Subject of International

Law," *International and Comparative Law Quarterly*, vol. 15, 1966, p. 105 and Atle Grahl-Madsen, "International Refugee Law Today and Tomorrow," *Archiv des Völkerrechts*, vol. 20, 1982, pp. 426, 458.

94. If the Simpson-Mazzoli bills had been enacted, including sanctions for employers who hired undocumented aliens, this proviso would have been abandoned.

95. *United States v. Varkonki*, 645 F.2d 453, 460 (5th Cir. 1981).

96. 645 F.2d at 459 and *United States v. Mt. Fuji Japanese Steak House, Inc.*, 435 F.Supp. 1194, 1201–1202 (E.D. N.Y. 1977) and *United States v. Herrera*, 584 F.2d 1137, 1144 (2d Cir. 1978).

97. *United States v. Fierros*, 692 F.2d 1291, 1294 (9th Cir. 1982).

98. *United States v. Rubio-Gonzalez*, 674 F.2d 1067, 1073–1074, n. 5 (5th Cir. 1982).

99. *United States v. Lopez*, 521 F.2d 437, 441–442 (2d Cir. 1975); *United States v. Acosta de Evans*, 531 F2d. 428, 430 (9th Cir. 1976); and *United States v. Cantu*, 557 F.2d 1173, 1177–1178 (5th Cir. 1977).

100. 531 F.2d at 430.

101. An interesting dilemma would be presented to a court if a sanctuary church were also providing employment to the refugees.

102. *United States v. Shaddix*, 693 F.2d 1135, 1137–1138 (5th Cir. 1982); *United States v. Gonzalez-Hernandez*, 534 F.2d 1353, 1354 (9th Cir. 1976) and *United States v. Salinas-Calderon*, 585 F.Supp. 599, 601 (D. Kan. 1984). See, also, *United States v. Valenzuela-Bernal*, 458 U.S. 858, 885, n. 4 (1982) (Brennan, dissenting) (adopting *Gonzalez-Hernandez* formulation of elements without discussion).

103. 561 F.2d 1321 (9th Cir. 1977).

104. 561 F.2d at 1322. The government acknowledged this limited exception in *United States v. Fierros*, 692 F.2d 1291, 1293, n. 3 (9th Cir. 1982); *United States v. Salinas-Calderon*, 585 F.Supp. 599, 601 (D. Kan. 1984); and *United States v. Tindall*, 551 F.Supp. 161 (W.D. Tex. 1982). But compare *United States v. Gonzalez-Hernandez*, 534 F.2d 1353, 1354 (9th Cir. 1976) (that alien's ultimate purpose is to find employment does not constitute a defense); and *United States v. Shaddix*, 693 F.2d 1135, 1138 (5th Cir. 1982).

105. 561 F.2d at 1323 and *United States v. Salinas-Calderon*, 585 F.Supp. at 602.

106. 561 F.2d at 1322, n. 3.

107. 561 F.2d at 1323.

108. *United States v. Salinas-Calderon*, 585 F.Supp. 599, 602 (D. Kan. 1984) (following reversal of order granting motion to suppress, 728 F.2d 1298 (10th Cir. 1984), and trial to the district court).

109. *Ibid.*

110. U.S. Constitution, Amendment I. This restriction on governmental power has been extended to the states through the due process clause of the Fourteenth Amendment. *Cantwell v. Connecticut*, 310 U.S. 296, 303–304 (1940).

111. *Braunfeld v. Brown*, 366 U.S. 599, 603 (1961); *Cantwell v. Connecticut*, 310 U.S. at 303–304.

112. See, LaFave and Scott, *Handbook on Criminal Law*, §25, pp. 177–179. See also Paul Marcus, "The Forum of Conscience: Applying Standards Under the Free Exercise Clause," *Duke Law Journal*, vol. 1973, no. 6, January 1973, pp. 1233–1235; Note, "Religious Exemptions Under the Free Exercise Clause: A Model of Competing Authorities," *The Yale Law Journal*, vol. 90, no. 2, December 1980, p. 353, n. 18; Harrop A. Freeman, "A Remonstrance for Conscience," *University of Pennsylvania Law Review*, vol. 106, no. 5, March 1958, p. 826; Laurence H. Tribe, *American Constitutional Law* (Mineola, N.Y.: The Foundation Press, Inc., 1978), p. 838. But see Jonathan Weiss, "Privilege, Posture and Protection: 'Religion' in the Law," *The Yale Law Journal*, vol. 73, no. 4, March 1964, pp. 607–608.

113. See Stephen Pepper, "*Reynolds, Yoder,* and Beyond: Alternatives for the Free Exercise Clause," *Utah Law Review*, 1981, no. 2, pp. 311, 315–317; Donald A. Giannella, "Religious Liberty, Non-Establishment and Doctrinal Development, Part I: The Religious Liberty Guarantee," *Harvard Law Review*, vol. 80, no. 7, May 1967, p. 1382; Freeman, *University of Pennsylvania Law Review*, pp. 806–830.

At least three interpretations may be deduced from the legislative history: (1) an evangelical view, primarily associated with Roger Williams, that sought to protect religion from secular or "worldly" influences; (2) the "wall of separation" between church and state, a view of Thomas Jefferson that sought to protect secular public and private interests from the influence of religion; (3) a government abstention view of James Madison, where both religious and secular interests would be best served by competition among religions rather than government-supported dominance by any one religious sect. See Pepper, *Utah Law Review*, pp. 314–315; Tribe, *American Constitutional Law*, pp. 816–819; Philip B. Kurland, "The Irrelevance of the Constitution: The Religion Clauses of the First Amendment and the Supreme Court," *Villanova Law Review*, vol. 24, no. 1, November 1978, p. 11.

The only consensus among constitutional historians is that the First Amendment religion clauses were intended to prohibit the Congressional establishment of a national religion for the new nation. See Pepper, *Utah Law Review*, p. 312; Tribe, *American Constitutional Law*, p. 819; Kurland, *Villanova Law Review*, pp. 13–14.

114. J. Morris Clark, "Guidelines for the Free Exercise Clause," *Har-*

vard Law Review, vol. 83, no. 2, December 1969, pp. 329–330; Note, *The Yale Law Journal*, pp. 356–357; Marcus, *Duke Law Journal*, pp. 1240–1241.

115. *Reynolds v. United States*, 98 U.S. [8 Otto] 145 (1878). The law was passed by Congress to govern the Utah Territory. 98 U.S. at 146. The defendant in the case, George Reynolds, was the secretary to Mormon leader Brigham Young and had volunteered to be the defendant in this test case. See Orma Linford, "The Mormons and the Law: The Polygamy Cases, Part I," *Utah Law Review*, vol. 9, no. 2, Winter 1964, pp. 331–332.

116. 98 U.S. at 164.

117. *Ibid.*, at 163–164. See Pepper, *Utah Law Review*, pp. 319–322.

118. The Court used two extreme examples to support its conclusion:

> Laws are made for the government of actions, and while they cannot interfere with mere religious beliefs and opinions, they may with practices. Suppose one believed that human sacrifices were a necessary part of religious worship, would it be seriously contended that the civil government under which he lived could not interfere to prevent a sacrifice? Or if a wife religiously believed it was her duty to burn herself upon the funeral pyre of her dead husband, would it be beyond the power of the government to prevent her carrying her belief into practice?

98 U.S. at 166. These examples involving murder and suicide can hardly be equated with the practice of plural marriage by the Mormons. See Pepper, *Utah Law Review*, pp. 321–325. Several commentators have noted that since the Supreme Court clearly set out to condemn both polygamy and Mormonism, such an equivalence of evils seemed logical to the Court. See 98 U.S. at 164, 166 and Linford, *Utah Law Review*, pp. 340–341; Pepper, *Utah Law Review*, pp. 322–324; Freeman, *University of Pennsylvania Law Review*, p. 825; Tribe, *American Constitutional Law*, p. 854.

119. 98 U.S. at 166–167.

120. The Court had foreshadowed its conclusion by its characterization of the issue presented: "The inquiry is not as to the power of Congress to prescribe criminal laws for the Territories, but as to the guilt of one who knowingly violates a law which has been properly enacted, if he entertains a religious belief that the law is wrong." 98 U.S. at 162.

121. See, e.g., *Late Corporation of the Church of Jesus Christ of Latter-Day Saints v. United States*, 136 U.S. 1, 48–50 (1890); *Davis v. Beason*, 133 U.S. 333, 344 (1890).

122. 310 U.S. 296 (1940). The case also raised the question of the proper relationship between the free exercise clause and the First Amendment's protection of the freedom of speech. The United States Supreme

Court would be faced with several such cases in the years following *Cantwell.* Compare *West Virginia State Board of Education v. Barnette*, 319 U.S. 624 (1943) (no compulsory flag salute required of Jehovah's Witnesses because this would be compulsion to declare a belief) and *Murdock v. Pennsylvania*, 319 U.S. 105 (1943) (no license tax required of Jehovah's Witnesses distributing and soliciting sales of religious books and pamphlets), with *Prince v. Massachusetts*, 321 U.S. 158 (1944) (upholding statute prohibiting a girl under eighteen to sell literature in public places even though a child of Jehovah's Witnesses faith believed it was her religious duty to sell religious literature). See Note, *"Heffron v. International Society for Krishna Consciousness, Inc.:* Confusing Free Speech with Free Exercise Rights," *California Law Review*, vol. 71, no. 3, May 1983, pp. 1012–1029; John H. Mansfield, "The Religion Clauses of the First Amendment and the Philosophy of the Constitution," *California Law Review*, vol. 72, no. 5, September 1984, pp. 852–856; Pepper, *Utah Law Review*, pp. 326–329; Clark, *Harvard Law Review*, p. 336; Marc Galanter, "Religious Freedom in the United States: A Turning Point?" *Wisconsin Law Review*, vol. 1966, no. 2, Spring 1966, p. 236.

    123. 310 U.S. at 303–304.

    124. 366 U.S. 599 (1961).

    125. *Ibid.*, at 605.

    126. *Ibid.*, at 605–606.

    127. *Ibid.*, at 607–608.

    128. *Ibid.*, at 606–607.

    129. 374 U.S. 398 (1963).

    130. *Ibid.*, at 406.

    131. *Ibid.*, at 404.

    132. *Ibid.*, at 403, quoting *NAACP v. Button*, 371 U.S. 415, 438 (1963). The burden to show such an interest is on the government. See Giannella, *Harvard Law Review*, p. 1411.

    133. 374 U.S. at 406, quoting *Thomas v. Collins*, 323 U.S. 516, 530 (1945).

    134. 374 U.S. at 407–408. See Gail Merel, "The Protection of Individual Choice: A Consistent Understanding of Religion Under the First Amendment," *University of Chicago Law Review*, vol. 45, no. 3, Spring 1983, pp. 816–821. The least restrictive means test has been developed in *Moody v. Cronin*, 484 F. Supp. 270, 274 (C.D. Ill. 1979) and *Callahan v. Woods*, 736 F.2d 1269, 1272–1273 (9th Cir. 1984).

    The inquiry is not whether there is a sufficient governmental interest in the underlying statute but rather whether there is a compelling governmental interest in denying a religious exemption to *this* particular religious claimant. Otherwise, the governmental interest will almost always outweigh the interest of the single individual (or very small group of individuals) in a religious exemption. See Tribe, *American Constitutional Law*, p. 855; Note, *The Yale Law Journal*, pp. 358–359; Clark, *Harvard Law Review*, p. 331, Galanter, *Wisconsin Law Review*, p. 280; Stephen L. Pepper, "The Conundrum of the Free Exercise Clause: Some Reflections on Recent Cases," *Northern Kentucky Law Review*, vol. 9, no. 2, 1982, pp. 271–272; Shimon Shetreet, "Exemptions and Privileges on Grounds of Religion and Conscience," *Kentucky Law Journal*, vol. 62, no. 2, 1973–1974, p. 411. But see Giannella, *Harvard Law Review*, pp. 1409–1410.

135. 374 U.S. at 407.

136. Justice Brennan, who dissented in *Braunfeld*, 366 U.S. at 610, wrote the majority opinion in *Sherbert*, 374 U.S. at 399. Justices Stewart, Harlan and White thought that the *Sherbert* majority opinion required the overruling of the *Braunfeld* decision. Stewart, concurring in the result, *ibid.*, at 417–418 and Harlan and White, dissenting, *ibid* at 421. See Pepper, *Utah Law Review*, p. 332, n. 104; Leo Pfeffer, "The Supremacy of Free Exercise," *Georgetown Law Journal*, vol. 61, no. 5, May 1973, p. 1139.

137. 366 U.S. at 601. See Brennan, concurring and dissenting, *ibid.*, at 610–611.

138. See Stewart, concurring in result, 374 U.S. at 417–418 and Harlan, dissenting, *ibid.*, at 421.

139. 366 U.S. at 607.

140. 374 U.S. at 407. Justice Brennan attempted to distinguish the interests in *Sherbert*, *ibid.*, at 408–409. However, Justice Brennan had called the state interest in *Braunfeld* the "mere convenience of having everyone rest on the same day," and an "administrative convenience." 366 U.S. at 614, 615.

The *Sherbert* decision does raise the question of which governmental interests are compelling for free exercise purposes. See Giannella, *Harvard Law Review*, pp. 1393–1416. At least one commentator has suggested that a balancing process should be used even if the governmental interest is found to be compelling. See Marcus, *Duke Law Journal*, pp. 1245–1247. Several lower courts have followed this approach. See *Church of God v. Amarillo Independent School District*, 511 F.Supp. 613, 618 (N.D. Tex. 1981), *aff'd without further opinion*, 670 F.2d 46 (5th Cir. 1982); *Frank v. State*, 604 P.2d 1068, 1073–1074 (Alaska Sup. Ct. 1979); *Quaring v. Peterson*, 728 F.2 1121, 1126 (8th Cir. 1984), *cert granted sub nom.*, *Jensen v. Quaring*, 53 U.S.L.W. 3235 (10/1/84) (oral argument heard, 1/7/85, 53 U.S.L.W. 3500).

141. See Pfeffer, *Georgetown Law Journal*, p. 1139; Note, *The Yale Law Journal*, p. 354; Note, "General Laws, Neutral Principles and the Free Exercise Clause," *Vanderbilt Law Review*, vol. 33, no. 1, January 1980, pp.

155–157; Galanter, *Wisconsin Law Review*, p. 241; Pepper, *Utah Law Review*, pp. 331–332.

142. 406 U.S. 205 (1972).

143. *Ibid.*, at 214–215.

144. See Note, *Vanderbilt Law Review*, pp. 158–159; Note, *The Yale Law Journal*, pp. 354–355, n. 31.

145. One commentator has suggested that the closer examination of the religious interest was provoked by the historical context of the 1972 *Yoder* decision, when countercultural forms of religion seemed to proliferate. See Pepper, *Utah Law Review*, pp. 335–336. See also Pepper, *Northern Kentucky Law Review*, pp. 274–276.

146. 406 U.S. at 221. See Note, "Sincere Religious Belief, Though Not a Tenet of One's Church or Sect, Still Protected by First Amendment," *Seton Hall Law Review*, vol. 11, no. 2, 1980, p. 226, n.54

147. 406 U.S. at 210, 235–236.

148. 406 U.S. at 215. The definition of religion under the First Amendment has been the subject of extensive commentary. See, e.g., Note, "Toward a Constitutional Definition of Religion," *Harvard Law Review*, vol. 19, no. 5, March 1978, pp. 1056–1089; Jesse H. Choper, "Defining 'Religion' in the First Amendment," *University of Illinois Law Review*, vol. 1982, no. 3, pp. 579–613; George C. Freeman, "The Misguided Search for the Constitutional Definition of 'Religion,' " *Georgetown Law Journal*, vol. 71, no. 6, August 1983, pp. 1519–1565; Kent Greenawalt, "Religion as a Concept in Constitutional Law," *California Law Review*, vol. 72, no. 5, September 1984, pp. 753–816; Note, "The Sacred and the Profane: A First Amendment Definition of Religion," *Texas Law Review*, vol. 61, no. 1, August 1982, pp. 139–173; J. Morris Clark, "Guidelines for the Free Exercise Clause," *Harvard Law Review*, vol. 83, no. 2, December 1969, pp. 336–364; Gail Merel, "The Protection of Individual Choice: A Consistent Understanding of Religion Under the First Amendment," *University of Chicago Law Review*, vol. 45, no. 3, Spring 1978, pp. 805–843.

Compare the definition of religion under the Universal Military Training and Service Act for determining conscientious objector status. See, e.g., *United States v. Seeger*, 380 U.S. 163, 165–166 (1965); *Welsh v. United States*, 398 U.S. 333, 339 (1970).

149. 406 U.S. at 209–213, 216–219.

150. *Ibid.*, at 235.

151. *Ibid.*, at 216.

152. See Pepper, *Utah Law Review*, p. 339, n. 132. Compare note 134 above.

153. *Ibid.*, at 212. The Court's analysis is irreconcilable with the *Reynolds* case. Certainly polygamy was as essential to the Mormons (failure to

engage in plural marriage would mean "damnation in the life to come," 98 U.S. at 161) as the avoidance of higher education was to the Amish. See Pepper, *Utah Law Review*, p. 337, n. 127 and p. 345, n. 165; Linford, *Utah Law Review*, p. 310. See also *Prince v. Massachusetts*, 321 U.S. 158, 163 (1944) (failure of Jehovah's Witness to sell religious literature meant damnation) and Shetreet, *Kentucky Law Journal*, p. 417, n. 232 (no religious exemption for members of the Holiness Church who believed that snakehandling was essential).

154. See Pepper, *Utah Law Review*, p. 338, n. 130.

155. 61 Cal.2d 716 (1964).

156. *Ibid.*, at 718.

157. *Ibid.*, at 722.

158. *Ibid.*, at 725. But see note 153, above, on the comparison with the polygamy case.

159. *Ibid.*, at 727. Several other courts have followed the analysis in *Woody* to grant similar exemptions for religious peyote users. See *State v. Whittingham*, 19 Ariz. App. 27, 29, 504 P.2d 950, 951–952 (1973), *cert. denied*, 417 U.S. 946 (1974); *Whitehorn v. State*, 561 P.2d 539, 544–545 (Okl. Ct. Crim. App. 1977); *Peyote Way Church of God v. Smith*, 742 F.2d 193, 200–201 (5th Cir. 1984). But see *In re Grady*, 61 Cal.2d 887 (1964) (centrality not mentioned; only required that defendant "actually engaged in good faith in the practice of a religion").

160. 377 So.2d 648 (Fla. 1979).

161. *Ibid.*, at 649.

162. *Ibid.*, at 650.

163. *Ibid.*, at 651.

164. 383 F.2d 851 (5th Cir. 1967), *rev'd on other grounds*, 395 U.S. 6 (1969). Several other courts have followed the reasoning of the *Leary* decision. See *United States v. Kuch*, 288 F.Supp. 439 (D.D.C.1968) (no exemption for member of Neo-American Church for sale of marijuana and LSD); *United States v. Middleton*, 690 F.2d 820, 824–826 (11th Cir. 1982) (no exemption for member of Ethiopian Zion Coptic Church for importation and possession of marijuana); *United States v. Hudson*, 431 F.2d 468 (5th Cir. 1970), *cert. denied*, 400 U.S. 1011 (1971) (no exemption for member of Black Muslims for smuggling heroin, marijuana and peyote); *United States v. Spears*, 443 F.2d 895 (5th Cir. 1971), *cert. denied*, 404 U.S. 1020 (1972) (no exemption for member of Moslem religion for smuggling heroin and marijuana); *Randall v. Wyrick*, 441 F.Supp. 312 (W.D.Mo. 1977) (no exemption for leader of Aquarian Brotherhood Church for possession and sale of marijuana and LSD).

One commentator notes that the religious exemption has only been granted to members of the Native American religious traditions for the use of peyote while being consistently denied to religious users of marijuana. See Note, "Soul Rebels: The Rastafarians and the Free Exercise Clause," *Georgetown Law Journal*, vol. 72, no. 5, June 1984, pp. 1620–1626, 1629–1635.

165. 383 F.2d at 860–861.

166. *Ibid.*, at 860.

167. *Ibid.*, at 861.

168. See *Frank v. State*, 604 P.2d 1068 (Alaska Sup. Ct. 1979) (exemption for Central Alaskan Athabascan Indian who unlawfully hunted and transported moose hunted for a funeral ritual feast); *Church of God v. Amarillo Independent School District*, 511 F.Supp. 613, 614 (N.D. Tex 1981), *aff'd without further opinion*, 670 F.2d 46 (5th Cir. 1982) (exemption for Church of God children from limit on school absences for religious purposes in order to attend mandatory religious celebrations); *Quaring v. Peterson*, 728 F.2d 1121, 1125 (8th Cir. 1984), *cert. granted sum nom.*, *Jensen v. Quaring*, 53 U.S.L.W. 3235 (10/1/84) (exemption for woman who believed that picture on driver's license would violate religious belief against idolatry).

169. See Note, "Indian Worship v. Government Development: A New Breed of Religion Cases," *Utah Law Review*, vol. 1984, no. 2, pp. 322–324, 328–330. Courts have required the Native American claimants to plead and prove the centrality of their belief about the sacred sites but have rejected the affidavits of the Indians themselves and of anthropologists as insufficient evidence of centrality. *Sequoyah v. TVA*, 620 F.2d 1159, 1164 (6th Cir.), *cert. denied*, 449 U.S. 953 (1980); *Crow v. Gullet*, 541 F.Supp. 785, 792 (D.S.D. 1982), *aff'd per curiam*, 706 F.2d 856 (8th Cir. 1983); *Wilson v. Block*, 708 F.2d 735, 743–744 (D.C.Cir. 1983). See also, *State v. Bullard*, 267 N.C. 599, 148 S.E.2d 565, 568 (1966) (no exemption for use of peyote and marijuana even though necessary to the practice of the religion of the Neo-American Church).

170. Some commentators argue that the centrality test requires an excessive intrusion into religion because part of the Free Exercise protection is the right to interpret or even change interpretations of one's religious doctrine and belief. See Note, *The Yale Law Journal*, pp. 359–361. Others point out that the centrality test will limit the free exercise rights of new or unorthodox religions because courts will be ill-equipped to evaluate their beliefs and practices. See Note, "Toward a Constitutional Definition of Religion," *Harvard Law Review*, pp.. 1080–1082; Pepper, *Northern Kentucky Law Review*, pp. 283–285. However, other commentators argue that the centrality test is useful if it is limited to testing the subjective centrality of the beliefs of the religious claimant, and any objective evaluation of the centrality of the belief is limited to an inquiry into the credibility of the

claimant. See Note, *Harvard Law Review*, p. 1076, n. 110. Such a centrality test seems to merge with the sincerity test developed after the *Thomas* case. See note 178, below.

171. There were three other Supreme Court decisions between *Yoder* and *Thomas* that did not substantively affect free exercise clause doctrine: *Johnson v. Robinson*, 415 U.S. 361 (1973) (upholding the denial of veterans' educational benefits to a conscientious objector as an incidental burden on religion justified by the compelling governmental interest in raising and supporting an army); *McDaniel v. Paty*, 435 U.S. 618 (1978) (holding unconstitutional a Tennessee law which prohibited priests and ministers from serving as delegates to the state's limited constitutional convention); *NLRB v. Catholic Bishop of Chicago*, 440 U.S. 490 (1979) (affirming that the NLRB had no jurisdiction over the unionization of Catholic schools, without reaching the free exercise issue).

172. 450 U.S. 707 (1981).

173. *Ibid.*, at 717, quoting 406 U.S. at 220.

174. *Ibid.*, quoting 374 U.S. at 403–404.

175. *Ibid.*, at 718–719.

176. *Ibid.*, at 715–716.

177. *Ibid.*

178. Courts have not applied the sincerity test consistently. Compare cases where sincerity was found but the religious exemption was still denied because of the absence of centrality: *Wilson v. Block*, 708 F.2d 735, 740 (D.C.Cir.1983); *Crow v. Gullet*, 541 F.Supp. 785, 790 (D.S.D.1982), *aff'd per curiam*, 706 F.2d 856 (8th Cir. 1983); *Sequoyah v. TVA*, 620 F.2d 1159, 1163 (6th Cir.) *cert. denied*, 449 U.S. 953 (1980); *Leary v. United States*, 383 F.2d 851, 860 (5th Cir. 1967), *rev'd on other grounds*, 395 U.S. 6 (1969); with cases where a religious exemption was granted because the court found both centrality and sincerity: *Frank v. State*, 604 P.2d 1068, 1073 (Alaska Sup. Ct. 1979); *Church of God v. Amarillo Independent School District*, 511 F.Supp. 613, 616 (N.D.Tex.1981), *aff'd without further opinion*, 670 F.2d 46 (5th Cir.1982); *State v. Whittingham*, 19 Ariz. App.27, 504 P.2d 950, 954 (1973) *cert. denied*, 417 U.S. 946 (1974); *Whitehorn v. State*, 561 P.2d 539, 546 (Okla. Ct. Crim. App.1977); and with a case where both sincerity and centrality were insufficient for a religious exemption: *Town v. State ex rel. Reno*, 377 So.2d 648 (Fla. 1979).

179. See Note, "Religious Belief Protected Under Free Exercise Clause Though Not Shown to be Derived from Cardinal Tenets of Common Faith," *Santa Clara Law Review*, vol. 22, no. 1, 1982, pp. 242–243; Note, *Seton Hall Law Review*, pp. 220–229; Pepper, *Utah Law Review*, p. 338, n. 131; Pepper, *Northern Kentucky Law Review*, p. 285.

180. 450 U.S. at 714. However, the *Thomas* court also noted that

claims "so bizarre, so clearly non-religious in motivation" would be rejected as insincere. *Ibid.*, at 715. Insincerity has been found in two cases involving the Neo-American Church: *United States v. Kuch*, 228 F.Supp. 439, 455 (D.D.C. 1968) and *State v. Bullard*, 267 N.C.599, 148 S.E.2d 565, 568 (1966). One commentator points out that the sincerity test helps to ensure the protection of the unorthodox religious beliefs and practices that are the most in need of First Amendment protection. See Note, *Harvard Law Review*, p. 1079. See also *United States v. Ballard*, 322 U.S. 78, 86–87 (1944) (only honest and good faith belief required); *In re Jenison*, 267 Minn. 136, 125 N.W.2d 588, 599 (Minn. Sup. Ct. 1963) (any non-spurious claim); *Stevens v. Berger*, 428 F.Supp.896, 899–901 (E.D.N.Y.1977)

181. See Tribe, *American Constitutional Law*, pp. 863–865. The United States Supreme Court may continue to develop the sincerity test in a case argued during the 1985 term. In *Jensen v. Quaring*, the Court will review the free exercise claim of a woman who is not a member of an organized church, whose belief stems principally from her own study of the Bible and whose belief is not shared by those she is religiously associated with. *Quaring v. Peterson*, 728 F.2d 1121, 1123, and 1124–1125 (8th Cir. 1984), *cert. granted sub nom., Jensen v. Quaring*, 53 U.S.L.W., 3235 (10/1/ 84) (oral argument heard 1/7/85, 53 U.S.L.W. 3500).

182. 450 U.S. at 720–727, Rehnquist, dissenting.

183. See Jesse H. Choper, "The Religion Clauses of the First Amendment: Reconciling the Conflict," *University of Pittsburgh Law Review*, vol. 41, no. 4, 1980, pp. 673–701; Galanter, *Wisconsin Law Review*, pp. 288–295; Pepper, *Utah Law Review*, pp. 346–352; Tribe, *American Constitutional Law*, pp. 819–823, 832–834; Shetreet, *Kentucky Law Review*, pp. 391, 393; Kurland, *Villanova Law Review*, p. 24; Leo Pfeffer, "Freedom and/or Separation: The Constitutional Dilemma of the First Amendment," *Minnesota Law Review*, vol. 64; no. 3, March 1980, pp. 561–584; Mansfield, *California Law Review*, pp. 849–850; Note, "*Thomas v. Review Board:* How Far is the Supreme Court Willing To Go?" *Ohio Northern University Law Review*, vol. 10, no. 1, Winter 1983, pp. 193–201.

Some commentators have noted that the characterization of a case as a free exercise or establishment case can affect the outcome of the case. See Note, *Vanderbilt Law Review*, p. 164, n. 87; Note, *Utah Law Review*, pp. 327–328, 331–332; Phillip E. Johnson, "Concepts and Compromise in First Amendment Religious Doctrine," *California Law Review*, vol. 72, no. 5, September 1984, pp. 821–825; Kurland, *Villanova Law Review*, p. 15; Pepper, *Northern Kentucky Law Review*, pp. 293–295.

184. See *Walz v. Tax Commission*, 397 U.S. 664, 668–669 (1970). On the one hand, the allowance of a broad religious exemption could be interpreted as a government "establishment" of that particular religious view-

point. On the other hand, the denial of religious exemptions because of the establishment clause would effectively nullify the free exercise clause.

185. 450 U.S. at 719–720. See *Sherbert v. Verner*, 374 U.S. at 409; *Wisconsin v. Yoder*, 406 U.S. at 220–221 and 234, n.22; *Frank v. State*, 604 P.2d 1068, 1074–1075 (Alaska Sup. Ct. 1979); *Quaring v. Peterson*, 728 F.2d 1121, 1127–1128 (8th Cir.1984), *cert. granted sub nom.*, *Jensen v. Quaring*, 53 U.S.L.W. 3235 (10/1/84).

186. 455 U.S. 252 (1982).

187. *Ibid.*, at 256. The statutory exemption was created specifically for the Amish. Lee had been self-employed (and qualified for the statutory exemption) but had recently hired several other Amish to help him on his farm and in his carpentry shop. See Note, "Freedom of Religion—Free Exercise Clause—Imposition of Social Security Taxes on Members of Amish Religion," *Northern Kentucky Law Review*, vol. 9, no. 2, 1982, p. 371. However, the Court chose to focus on the fact that the religious claimant had engaged in commercial activity "as a matter of choice," 455 U.S. at 252, and therefore could not now complain about his obligations as an employer. Several commentators have noted that this distinction based on the voluntariness of the religious claimant is inconsistent with the *Sherbert* and *Thomas* decisions. See Note, *United States v. Lee:* An Insensitive Approach to the Free Exercise of Religion," *Tulsa Law Journal*, vol. 18, no. 2, Winter 1982, pp. 326–368; Note, "*United States v. Lee:* Limitations on the Free Exercise of Religion," *Loyola Law Review*, vol. 28, no. 4, Fall 1982, p. 1225, n.65.

188. 455 U.S. at 257. In fact, the Amish viewed participation in the social security system as a sin because it would indicate a lack of responsibility for the aged, disabled and unemployed. See Note, *Northern Kentucky Law Review*, p. 369.

The test of centrality was not mentioned in the decision. See Note, *Tulsa Law Journal*, p. 334.

189. 455 U.S. at 257–258. The shift in tests was noted by Justice Stevens in his concurring opinion, *ibid.*, at 263, n. 3. Commentators called the shift a retreat: Note, *Tulsa Law Journal*, p. 336; Note, *Loyola Law Review*, pp. 1223–1224; Note, "*United States v. Lee:* Has the Retreat Been Sounded for Free Exercise?" *Stetson Law Review*, vol. 12, no. 3, Spring 1983, p. 864; Mansfield, *California Law Review*, p. 901.

190. 455 U.S. at 259.

191. *Ibid.*

192. See Note, *Loyola Law Review*, p. 1223; Note, *Stetson Law Review*, p. 862.

193. 455 U.S. at 258. See Note, *Tulsa Law Journal*, p. 331; Pepper,

Northern Kentucky Law Review, p. 300; Note, *Northern Kentucky Law Review*, p. 377.

194. 455 U.S. at 260.

195. *Ibid.*, at 262. Justice Stevens and several commentators have also pointed out that the majority opinion did not carefully examine the facts of the case: since the Amish employees would never accept the social security benefits anyway, there would be no net loss to the system and perhaps even a net gain since more benefits are generally paid out than contributions received by the federal government. *Ibid.*, and Note, *Tulsa Law Journal*, pp. 331–332; Note, *Stetson Law Review*, p. 863; Note, *Northern Kentucky Law Review*, pp. 377–378.

196. 455 U.S. at 260. The Supreme Court's reluctance to establish a precedent for a tax exemption may help to explain the decision. See Note, *Stetson Law Review*, pp. 863–864; Note, *Tulsa Law Journal*, pp. 325–326; Note, *Loyola Law Review*, p. 1224; Pepper, *Northern Kentucky Law Review*, p. 301.

197. See Note, *Tulsa Law Journal*, p. 327; Pepper, *Northern Kentucky Law Review*, p. 302; Note, *Stetson Law Review*, p. 864. Although Justice Stevens alluded to it, 455 U.S. at 263, n.2, the majority opinion expressly did not reach the establishment Clause issue, *ibid.*, at 260, n.11. See Note, *Tulsa Law Journal*, p. 328.

198. 461 U.S. 574, 103 S.Ct. 2017 (1983).

199. 103 S.Ct. at 2034, n.28. One commentator argues that sincerity should have been the key issue in the free exercise analysis. See Mayer G. Freed and Daniel O. Polsby, "Race, Religion, and Public Policy: *Bob Jones University v. United States*," 1983 Supreme Court Review, p. 29.

200. 103 S.Ct. at 2026–2031. The issue of tax-exempt status for private schools that practice racial discrimination has been the subject of much commentary. See, e.g., Note, "The Internal Revenue Service Has the Power To Revoke the Tax-Exempt Status of Private Schools Which Practice Racial Discrimination Due to Religious Belief, Since These Schools Are Not Charitable, and Revocation Does Not Violate the Free Exercise or the Establishment Clauses of the First Amendment," *Villanova Law Review*, vol. 29, no. 1, February 1984, pp. 253–280; Note, "Conflicts Between the First Amendment Religion Clauses and the Internal Revenue Code: Politially Active Religious Organizations and Racially Discriminatory Private Schools," *Washington University Law Quarterly*, vol. 61, no. 2, Summer 1983, pp. 503–560; Note, "Applying a Public Benefit Requirement to Tax-Exempt Organizations," *Missouri Law Review*, vol. 49, no. 2, Spring 1984, pp. 353–371; Note, "Constitutional Law-Religious Schools, Public Policy, and the Constitution: *Bob Jones University v. United States*,"

North Carolina Law Review, vol. 62, no. 5, June 1984, pp. 1051–1067; Paul B. Stephan, *"Bob Jones University v. United States:* Public Policy in Search of Tax Policy," 1983 Supreme Court Review, pp. 33–82.

201. 103 S.Ct. at 2035.

202. *Ibid.*

203. *Ibid.*

204. *Ibid.*

205. However, the centrality test was again not mentioned. See Note, *North Carolina Law Review*, p. 1060.

206. 103 S.Ct. at 2035, n.30.

207. Neither Justice Powell's concurring opinion, *ibid.*, at 2036–2039, nor Justice Rehnquist's dissenting opinion, *ibid.*, at 2039–2045, discussed the free exercise issue.

208. The United States Supreme Court will decide free exercise issues in at least two cases during its 1985 term. See *Tony and Susan Alamo Foundation v. Donovan*, No. 83–1935, from 722 F.2d 397 (8th Cir.1984) (oral argument heard, 3/25/85, 53 U.S.L.W. 3713) (whether religious foundation that rehabilitates drug addicts and criminals by employing them in commercial businesses owned and operated by the foundation entitled to an exemption to the Fair Labor Standards Act); *Jensen v. Quaring*, No.83–1944, from 728 F.2d 1121 (8th Cir.1984) (oral argument heard, 1/7/85, 53 U.S.L.W.3500) (whether a woman who believes a picture on driver's license would violate religious belief against idolatry entitled to an exemption).

209. *United States v. Elder*, 601 F.Supp. 1574 (S.D.Tex.1985)

210. *Ibid.*, at 1577.

211. *Ibid.*

212. *Ibid.* See also *ibid.*, at 1578 (". . . Elder acted in accordance with his personal view of Christianity").

213. *Ibid.*

214. *Ibid.*, at 1577.

215. *Ibid.*, at 1578.

216. *Ibid.*, at 1579.

217. *Ibid.*, at 1580.

218. Only one commentator has noted a hypothetical case of a humanitarian act done for the benefit of others that is prohibited by statute. See Giannella, *Harvard Law Review*, pp. 1420–1421, 1428–1430. However, several commentators have argued that there should be a distinction in religious exemptions for acts of nonfeasance (when the state requires the performance of a positive act that would violate religious belief) and malfeasance (when the state makes criminal or otherwise prohibits a positive act which the claimant believes to be a religious duty to perform). See

Clark, *Harvard Law Review*, pp. 345–364; Shetreet, *Kentucky Law Journal*, p. 419. Other commentators have argued that the religious exemptions for acts of malfeasance should be limited to those acts involving only the claimant and consenting others. See Galanter, *Wisconsin Law Review*, pp. 282–283; Clark, *Harvard Law Review*, p. 345. Certainly sanctuary activity involves conduct that is only *malum prohibitum*, or made criminal only by statute rather than by society's communal sense of ethics and morality. See LaFave and Scott, *Handbook on Criminal Law*, §6, pp. 29–31; Giannella, *Harvard Law Review*, p. 1403. Such conduct seems most appropriate for a First Amendment exemption.

219. It simply may be that the free exercise clause is outdated in a modern world that has different values and assumptions than the post-Enlightenment world from which it emerged. See Pepper, *Utah Law Review*, pp. 377–378. On the other hand, the freedom of conscience remains a core value in the present system of criminal justice. One commentator notes:

> Criminal responsibility is imposed on the basis that the individual knows the difference between right and wrong. . . . How, then, can you depend on conscience to put morality into your criminal law if you are going to make criminals out of those who most actively follow conscience? (Kurland, *Villanova Law Review*, pp. 828–829).

5. The Ancient Tradition of Sanctuary

1. It is interesting to note the existence of sanctuary practices among the Ashantis in Africa, the Oman in the French Congo, the aborigines of Australia and New Guinea, the Samoans, the Hawaiians and the American Indians (of Florida, Georgia, Virginia, and North and South Carolina). See Carlos Urrutia-Aparicio, *Diplomatic Asylum in Latin America* (Washington, D.C.: American University, 1978) pp. 4, 20–21.

2. Some trace the notion of blood feud to Cain's murder of Abel, when Abel's blood "cried out" from the ground (Genesis 4:10–11). See also Genesis 9:6.

3. W. Gunther Plaut, Bernard J. Bamberger and William W. Hallo, *The Torah: A Modern Commentary* (New York: Union of American Hebrew Congregations, 1981) p. 1249; "City of Refuge," *Interpreter's Dictionary of the Bible* (Nashville: Abingdon Press, 1962), p. 639; Moshe Greenberg, "The Biblical Concept of Asylum," *Journal of Biblical Literature*, June 1959, p. 130.

4. Greenberg, pp. 125, 131.

5. For example, one rabbinic tradition attributes the number of the cities to the six Hebrew words in the Shema (Deuteronomy 6:4–9). See *The Torah*, p. 1250. The Talmudic scholars were reconstructing and elaborating upon the procedures in the post-Exile era. "City of Refuge," *Encyclopedia Judaica*, vol. 5 (Jerusalem: The Macmillan Company, 1971), p. 592. Much rabbinic discourse developed a distinction between the more culpable act of negligence which resulted when an object fell downward upon a victim and the less culpable accident of an object being thrust upward and injuring a victim. The distinction was premised on the duty of the one liable to notice a victim passing below while no such duty to those above existed. Makkot 7b,8a; Mishnah Makkot 2:1.

6. Makkot 10a; "City of Refuge," *Encyclopedia Judaica*, p. 592.

7. Mishnah Makkot 2:5; Makkot 9b; "City of Refuge," *Encyclopedia Judaica*, p. 593.

8. Mishnah Makkot 2:7.

9. For example, fugitives were not to be denied social honor, Mishnah Makkot 2:8; and disciples were to follow their teachers to the city to continue their studies. Makkot 10a.

10. Makkot 10a; Mishnah Makkot 3:9; "City of Refuge," *Encyclopedia Judaica*, p. 592.

10a. Makkot 13a; Maimonides, *Mishneh Torah*, Sefer Nezikin, Rozeah 8:9–10.

10b. The Torah, p. 1470; Dru Gladney in "Basta! Sanctuary Organizers' Nuts and Bolts Supplement No. 1" (Chicago: Chicago Religious Task Force on Central America, undated [Fall 1983] p. 46; Rev. Donovan Cook, "Basta!", p. 43.

11. Charles M. Laymon, ed., *Interpreter's One-Volume Commentary on the Bible* (Nashville: Abingdon Press, 1971), "Exodus," p. 56.

12. *The Torah*, pp. 1242, 1470; and "Sanctuary," *Collier's Encyclopaedia*, vol. 20 (New York: MacMillan Educational Company, 1981), p. 390.

13. "City of Refuge," *Interpreter's Dictionary of the Bible*, p. 639 and Greenberg, pp. 126, 130.

14. "City of Refuge," *Interpreter's Dictionary of the Bible*, p. 639 and Greenberg, p. 130.

15. See Exodus 27:2 regarding the horns of the altar.

16. See, e.g., *Interpreter's Dictionary of the Bible*, "1 Kings," p. 184.

17. Norman M. Trenholme, "The Right of Sanctuary in England," *University of Missouri Studies*, vol. 1, no. 5, February 1903, pp. 2–3.

18. Urrutia-Aparicio, pp. 15–16 and Trenholme, p. 4.

19. Trenholme, pp. 4–5 and Thomas John Mazzinghi, *Sanctuaries* (Stafford: Halden and Son, 1887), p. 108.

20. Urrutia-Aparicio, p. 16 and Trenholme, p. 5.

21. Urrutia-Aparicio, p. 16.

22. J. Charles Cox, *The Sanctuaries and Sanctuary Seekers of Medieval England* (London: George Allen and Sons, 1911), p. 2.

23. Mazzinghi, p. 110 and Trenholme, pp. 5–7.

24. Urrutia-Aparicio, pp. 17–18, and Attorney General's Survey of Release Procedures, vol. III: *Pardon* (Washington, D.C.: U.S. Government Printing Office, 1939) p. 13.

25. Mazzinghi, p. 110.

26. Trenholme, p. 7 and Cox, p. 2.

27. Mazzinghi, p. 77; Trenholme, pp. 7–9; Cox, pp. 3–4; Urrutia-Aparicio, p. 19. This, too, was a departure from the Mosaic law which allowed sanctuary for strangers and sojourners. Mazzinghi, p. 96.

28. Cox, p. 5.

29. Mazzinghi, p. 23. The cross is a Christian image filled with paradox: a holy and sinless Son of God crucified as a common criminal. In the sense that Jesus bore the sins of the world upon the cross, the church could be viewed as bearing the sins or crimes of the sanctuary seekers within its geographical and theological "body." See the discussion of the theological images of sanctuary in Chapter 8.

30. One recurring problem with using secondary sources is the inconsistency among authors, especially with dates. The decree here is variously dated 431 (Urrutia-Aparicio, p. 19), 442 (Trenholme, p. 7) and 450 A.D. (Cox, p. 3).

31. Trenholme, p. 8 and Cox, p. 3. The synod of Orleans in 511 decreed that sanctuary should extend to the bishop's residence and thirty-five paces beyond the church walls. Trenholme, p. 9 and Cox, p. 4.

32. See relevant extracts from Gratian's *Decretum*, dating from a letter of St. Augustine (c. 400) to a pronouncement by Pope Nicholas II in 1059, translated to the French in Pierre Timbal Duclaux de Martin, *Le droit d'asile* (Paris: Librairie du Recueil Sirey, 1939). The general rule was pronounced by Pope Gelasius (492–496) (C. XVIII, qu. 4, c. 32): "After their security has been guaranteed slaves who have fled to the church shall be restored to their master." See also the decree of the Council of Toledo in 681 (C. XVII, qu. 4, c. 35): "A fugitive slave shall not be taken from the courtyard of a church which is enclosed by thirty paces—unless security is first given." English translation of Timbal extracts is in Charles H. Riggs, "Criminal Asylum in Anglo-Saxon Law," *University of Florida Monographs, Social Sciences*, No. 18 (Gainesville: University of Florida Press, Spring 1963), p. 23, n. 56.

33. Riggs, p. 22.

34. Mazzinghi, p. 90.

35. *Decretum* (C. XVII, qu. 4, c. 9), translated in Riggs, p. 37, n. 23.

The *Decretum* also contains references to the exclusion of robbers, highway robbers, and those guilty of grave crimes in churches from the sanctuary privilege. Cox, pp. 4–5. Justinian's Code (528) and Digest (533) also refer to the sanctuary privilege, Urrutia-Aparicio, p. 19 and the exclusion of murderers, adulterers, and rapists. Trenholme, pp. 8–9 and Cox, p. 4.

36. Riggs, p. 22, n. 54; Urrutia-Aparicio, pp. 18–19; Mazzinghi, pp. 110–111; and "Asylum, Right of," *New Catholic Encyclopedia*, vol. 1 (New York: McGraw Hill Book Company, 1967) p. 994.

6. The Law of Sanctuary in England

1. Norman M. Trenholme, "The Right of Sanctuary in England," *University of Missouri Studies*, vol. 1, no. 5, February 1903, p. 98.

1a. For excellent bibliographies of some non-English sources which trace the development of the practice of sanctuary on the European continent, see Charles H. Riggs, "Criminal Asylum in Anglo-Saxon Law," *University of Florida Monographs, Social Science*, No. 18 (Gainesville: University of Florida Press, Spring 1963), p. 21, n. 53 and the Bibliography in Thomas John Mazzinghi, *Sanctuaries* (Stafford: Halden and Son, 1887).

Notably, an entire French village provided sanctuary to refugee Jews during World War II. Under the leadership of André Trocmé, the Protestant church of Le Chambon-sur-Lignon hid hundreds of refugees. This historical incident is documented in Philip Hallie, *Lest Innocent Blood Be Shed* (New York: Harper and Row, 1979).

2. G.O. Sayles, *The Medieval Foundations of England* (London: Methuen and Co., Ltd., 1964), pp. 170–171.

3. Mazzinghi, pp. 7–11; Norman M. Trenholme, "The Right of Sanctuary in England," *University of Missouri Studies*, vol. 1, no. 5, February 1903, pp. 10–11; Charles Cox, *The Sanctuaries and Sanctuary Seekers of Medieval England* (London: George Allen and Sons, 1911), p. 6 and Carlos Urrutia-Aparicio, *Diplomatic Asylum in Latin America* (Washington, D.C.: American University, 1978), p. 22.

4. Sir Sidney Low and F. S. Pulling, *et al.*, *The Dictionary of English History*, New Edition (London: Cassell and Co., Ltd., 1928), "Bot," p. 166.

5. Riggs, p. 10; Trenholme, p. 12 and Cox, p. 7.

6. Riggs, p. 6 and Cox p. 7.

7. Riggs, p. 21.

8. Riggs, p. 23.

9. Riggs, pp. 37–38.

10. Riggs, p. 24, n. 59.

11. Riggs, p. 29.

12. Riggs, pp. 35–36, n. 19; Mazzinghi, pp. 31–32; Trenholme, p. 13; Cox, p. 7. *Wergild* was the compensation payment for a murder. Low and Pulling, "Wergild," p. 1102 and S.H. Steinberg, ed. *A New Dictionary of British History* (New York: St. Martin's Press, Inc., 1963) "Wergild," p. 386.

13. Riggs, p. 34.

14. Riggs, p. 38.

15. Riggs, p. 36.

16. Riggs, pp. 33–34 and Mazzinghi, p. 12.

17. Mazzinghi, p. 12.

18. Riggs, p. 33 and Mazzinghi, p. 102. See Chapter 4.

19. Riggs, p. 40.

20. Riggs, pp. 37–38.

21. Riggs, p. 46; Trenholme, p. 14; Cox, pp 7–8; Urrutia-Aparicio, p. 22.

22. Mazzinghi, p. 32; Trenholme, p. 14; Cox, pp. 126–127. Compare the six zones and the respective fines for a violation of the sanctuary at Hexham: (1) outermost (about one mile radius from the town): 16 pounds; (2) within the town: 32 pounds; (3) within the walls of the church precincts: 48 pounds; (4) within the church: 96 pounds; (5) within the gates of the quire: 144 pounds; (6) around the altar and *frithstol: botless.* Mazzinghi, pp. 26–27 and Cox, p. 155.

23. Isobel D. Thornley, "The Destruction of Sanctuary," in Robert W. Seton-Watson, ed., *Tudor Studies Presented to the Board of Studies in History in the University of London (to Albert Fredrick Pollard)* (London: Longmans, Green and Co., 1924), p. 182. See also John G. Bellamy, *Crime and Public Order in the Latter Middle Ages* (London: Routledge and Kegan Paul and Toronto: University of Toronto Press, 1973), p. 106 and Sir Frederick Pollock and Frederick William Maitland, *The History of English Law Before the Time of Edward I*, 2nd ed. vol. II (Cambridge: C.J. Clay and Sons, 1898), p. 590.

24. Cox, p. 6 and Bellamy, p. 106.

25. Mazzinghi, p. 13.

26. Thornley, p. 183.

27. Bellamy, p. 106 and Thornley, p. 183. These areas included the county palatine of Durham in the north, the lay franchises of Tynedale and Redesdale, and the western counties palatine of Lancashire and Cheshire and the lordships Marcher of Wales.

28. Thornley, p. 183. The locals lords received fines from the sanctuary seekers as a type of admission fee and also claimed their goods and chattels if the fugitives died without heirs. Mazzinghi, p. 16.

29. Thornley, p. 202.

30. For example, King Edgar granted a charter to the Abbey of Ramsey as early as 974. Trenholme, p. 14 and Cox, pp. 199–201.

31. Riggs, pp. 58–59, n. 43; Trenholme, p. 15; Cox, p. 8. The same laws are found repeated in I Canute 3a.1 and I Canute 3a.2. Trenholme, p. 16; Mazzinghi, p. 12; Cox, p. 8.

32. Riggs, pp. 58–59. Another law of Canute confiscated the "land and life" of violators of sanctuary. Riggs, p. 57, n. 40. Murder within the church walls was *botless* in Anglo-Saxon law. Trenholme, p. 15 and Cox, p. 8.

Also see an earlier law of Ethelred which required a fugitive who committed a capital offense to either give the proper *wergild* (compensation for the life of the victim) or go into perpetual *thraldom* or imprisonment. If compensation were paid, the fugitive also had to furnish a surety or bondsman for his future good conduct or take a solemn oath to keep the peace and live an honest life before he was free to leave the sanctuary. If the latter oath were broken, there would be no further sanctuary protection. Trenholme, p. 15 and Cox, p. 8.

33. Riggs, p. 60.

34. Bellamy, pp. 104–105.

35. Cox, p. 11.

36. Trenholme, p. 18 and Cox, p. 9.

37. These laws are attributed to William but are probably of twelfth century origin. Trenholme, p. 18. The fines decreased: 100 shillings for violating the sanctuary of an abbey or great church, 20 shillings for a parish church and 10 shillings for a chapel.

38. Riggs, p. 48, n. 22; Trenholme, pp. 16, 19–20; Cox, p. 10.

39. *Ibid.*

40. Riggs, p. 48, n. 23. However, this early abjuration is only of the local province and pardon may be obtained from the royal justices. The latter abjuration was equivalent to a permanent exile which could only be pardoned by the king. There is no other evidence of any abjurations of the realm before the late eleventh century.

41. Trenholme, pp. 20–21.

42. Thornley, p. 184 and Cox, p. 35.

43. For example, the chattels of sanctuary seekers were forfeited to the king (and thus, forbidden in the churchyard) under Henry II, Trenholme, p. 21, and clergy were given special immunities when they themselves sought sanctuary under Edward I, Cox, pp. 20–21. The period also reveals the first regulations regarding sanctuary privileges in the city of London (a 100 shilling fine for allowing the escape of fugitives from the city sanctuaries, and subjecting the goods and property of fraudulent debt-

ors in sanctuary to seizure by their creditors), Trenholme, p. 26 and Bellamy, p. 107. The London sanctuaries and their abuses are discussed below.

44. 9 (or 10?) Edward II, c. 7, s. 10. Trenholme, p. 33; Cox, p. 18; Bellamy, p. 108.

45. Unfortunately, much of the secondary source material is inconsistent or even contradictory. Without access to the primary source materials, the following description presumes that any inconsistencies are the result of different practices at different times or the incompleteness or inaccuracy of any one given secondary source (the inconsistencies will be noted in the footnotes). Finally, most of the information available is derived from the practice of abjuring the realm at chartered sanctuaries. Thus, while it may be presumed that the royal officers and procedures, such as the role of the coroner, would be the same for the abjurations by those fugitives in the general sanctuaries, there are doubtless differences in the two abjuration practices, which cannot be examined here.

46. St. Cuthbert was the bishop of Lindisfarne who died in 687. When he was dying, he requested to be buried on the island of Farne so that his monks would not have the burden of providing sanctuary to those he knew would flee to his grave. His monks disobeyed their founder and preserved his relics through the Danish invasions, finally establishing a permanent shrine at Durham. Trenholme, pp. 11–12 and Cox, pp. 95–97. There are also curious legends surrounding this sanctuary at Durham, including one where hunted stags would leap over the churchyard walls and be protected from hunters and bloodhounds. Cox, pp. 102–105.

47. Certain fugitives were prohibited from entry: common or notorious offenders, those suspected of or indicted for treason, heretics, sorcerers, witches, church clerks, those who committed felonies in a church and those caught in the act of the crime. Bellamy, p. 107 and Cox, p. 59. *The Mirrour of Justices*, attributed to Andrew Horne (Washington, D.C.: John Byrne and Company, 1903), also records that debtors, those who had already confessed to their crimes and those who had been exiled, banished or outlawed could not be protected by sanctuary (p. 59).

48. Mazzinghi, pp. 25, 28 and Cox, pp. 110–120. One author also dispels the legends surrounding the so-called "sanctuary knockers," large, ornately carved metal rings on church doors. Some contemporary art depicted sanctuary seekers clinging to these rings but it is clear that sanctuary protection began once the fugitive set foot on the church grounds. While some fugitives may have indeed grasped the rings as a sign of their need for sanctuary, the rings were probably a functional tool for opening and closing the heavy church doors. Cox, pp. 120–125.

49. Mazzinghi, pp. 32–33; Cox, pp. 139–140; Bellamy, p. 108. Compare the oath used at the Abbey of St. Peter at Westminster and recorded in a fifteenth century manuscript, in Cox, p. 70.

50. Mazzinghi, p. 33 and Cox, p. 140.

51. Bellamy, p. 108.

52. Mazzinghi, p. 26 and Cox, p. 134.

53. Mazzinghi, p. 27.

54. Mazzinghi, p. 24.

55. Bellamy, p. 108.

56. Thornley, p. 182.

57. Trenholme, p. 24 and Thornley, p. 182.

58. Bellamy, p. 108; Cox, p. 17; *Britton*, Francis Morgan Nichols, rev. and trans. (Oxford: Carledon Press, 1865), p. 63.

59. Pollack and Maitland, p. 590. The office of the coroner existed at least since the time of Henry II. The coroner was a local administrative official who took cognizance of all crimes in his district and held inquests on the bodies of murder victims. Trenholme, p. 23.

60. Trenholme, p. 24, Bellamy, p. 108; Briton, p. 62. At Beverly, unlike other sanctuaries, no coroner, sheriff, or any other royal official was allowed within the sanctuary area. Thus, the fugitive was escorted to the border of the sanctuary if he or she wished to abjure the realm. Cox, pp. 118, 135.

61. Trenholme, p. 24; Bellamy, p. 108; Thornley, p. 182; Bracton, *On the Laws and Custom of England*, G.E. Woodbine, ed., S.E. Thorne, trans. and rev., vol. II (Cambridge: Harvard University Press, 1968), p. 383. Britton, p. 63, writes that the forty days did not begin until the coroner came and recorded the confession.

62. Trenholme, p. 24; Thornley, p. 183; Pollock and Maitland, p. 591; *Mirrour of Justices*, p. 60; Bracton, p. 383. Both Britton, p. 65, and Bracton, p. 383, imply that at the end of the forty days, the fugitive was considered convicted of the crime.

63. Bracton, p. 383.

64. Trenholme, p. 24; Mazzinghi, p. 71; Bellamy, pp. 108–109. For specific violations of sanctuary, see Mazzinghi, pp. 71–84 and Trenholme, pp. 72–84.

65. Bellamy, p. 112.

66. Mazzinghi, p. 32.

67. Cox, pp. 114–115.

68. Mazzinghi, p. 31. Compare the shorter, more generic oaths in Britton, p. 64: "Hear this, you coroner and other good people, that I for such an act which I feloniously did, or assented to the doing thereof, will depart from the realm of England and will never return thereto unless by

leave of the king of England or his heirs, so help me God and the Saints," and in Bracton, p. 382: "Hear this, ye justices (or O ye coroners), that I will go forth from the realm of England and hither I will not return save by leave of the lord King or his heirs, so help me God etc." However, it seems that the abjurer could stay in the sanctuary for up to the allotted forty days before departing. Bellamy, p. 112.

69. Mazzinghi, pp. 33–34 and Cox, pp. 32, 113–114. See also Mazzinghi, pp. 112–133.

70. Bellamy, p. 112 and Pollock and Maitland, p. 590. Britton, p. 62, says that the land and chattels were forfeited upon taking sanctuary.

71. Trenholme, p. 24.

72. Cox, p. 32; Trenholme, p. 35 and *Mirrour of Justices*, p. 59.

73. Bellamy, p. 112.

74. Cox, p. 32.

75. Bellamy, p. 112; Cox, p. 32; Britton, p. 64.

76. Again, the historians disagree: was it a white cross (Mazzinghi, p. 34 and Cox, p. 114), a wooden cross (Bellamy, p. 112 and Britton, p. 64), perhaps a white wooden cross (Cox, p. 118) or a crucifix (Mazzinghi, p. 113)?

77. Cox, p. 27; Bellamy, p. 112; Britton, p. 64; Bracton, p. 382.

78. Trenholme, p. 24 and *Mirrour of Justices*, quoted in Cox, pp. 24–25.

79. Bellamy, p. 113 and Cox, p. 28. It is possible that some of the variation in time was the result of scribal errors. However, it is also possible that an extra long journey was a method of extra punishment. Cox, p. 28. In at least one case, the crafty coroner sent three conspiring highwaymen who had sought sanctuary together off in three separate directions. Cox, p. 31.

80. Cox, p. 26 and Pollock and Maitland, p. 591. The Coroners' Rolls also record the following other points of departure: Rochester, Orwell, Sandwich, Lancaster, Boston, Tynemouth, Portsmouth, Padstow, Looe, Ilfracombe (to Wales), Lynn, Newcastle-on-Tyne, Yarmouth, Ipswich, Southampton, Wichelsea, Plymouth, Lostwithiel for Fowey, Bristol, Chester, and Hull and Berwick (to Scotland). Bellamy, p. 113 and Cox, p. 26. Thus, bordertowns were also sometimes chosen for exile to Ireland or Scotland. Bellamy, p. 113 and Cox, p. 26.

81. Cox, p. 29.

82. Trenholme, p. 24; *Mirrour of Justices*, p. 59; Bracton, p. 382.

83. Bellamy, p. 112 and *Mirrour of Justices* in Cox, p. 25.

84. Bellamy, p. 112.

85. Mazzinghi, p. 34; Thornley, p. 182; Cox, p. 114.

86. Cox, pp. 274–277, describes several examples.

87. Mazzinghi, p. 32 and Bellamy, p. 113. One historian notes that the abjurers were to go into the sea up to their throat and ask for passage three times each day. In Mazzinghi, pp. 112–113.

88. Mazzinghi, p. 31 and Bellamy, p. 113.

89. Cox, p. 31. However, it is unlikely that the ships willingly accepted such passengers. The fate of the abjurers remains a fascinating subject for further research.

90. Cox, p. 25.

91. Cox, p. 16.

92. Bellamy, p. 114 and Cox, p. 31.

93. Mazzinghi, p. 52; Cox, pp. 107–109; Bellamy, p. 110. It is ironical that one of the crimes included harboring a thief, precisely the purpose of the sanctuary itself. Thus, it is clear that the sanctuaries were exempt from the common law prohibiting the harboring of criminals. Cox, p. 109.

94. Cox, pp. 117–118.

95. Mazzinghi, p. 54; Cox, pp. 135–142; Bellamy, p. 110. One historian doubts the completeness of the records because pardons and instant abjurations were not included. Cox, p. 135.

96. Mazzinghi, pp. 35–40 and Cox, pp. 282–283.

97. Compare Bellamy, p. 111 and Cox, p. 33. For greater details about the specific southern sanctuaries at the Cistercian Abbey at Beaulieu, the Abbey at Colchester, the Benedictine Abbey of Abingdon at Culham, the Benedictine Abbey at Bury St. Edmunds at Gloucester, see Thornley, p. 184 and Cox, pp. 183–205. For details about the northern sanctuaries at St. Peter's in York, the colleagiate at St. Wilfrid's at Ripon, St. Andrew's at Hexham, St. Oswin's at Tynemouth, the Cumberland Priory at Wetherhal and the great chartered sanctuaries at Beverly and Durham, see Thornley, p. 184 and Cox, pp. 150–176.

98. See the complaint of London creditors in 1347 in Mazzinghi, p. 44 and by the Commons of Essex in 1394 that the Abbey of St. John of Colchester and the Abbey of Abingdon in Culham were exercising the same privilege as Westminster in hiding debtors without any charter privilege to do so. 3 Par. Roll, 320, 17 Richard II. Mazzinghi, p. 45; Thornley, p. 187 and Cox, pp. 206–207.

99. Mazzinghi, p. 82 and Thornley, pp. 186–188. One historian has noted that "medieval legislation was always in the nature of a manifesto of policy, or the enunciation of a wholesome principle, to which practice should but frequently did not conform." Thornley, p. 187.

100. Mazzinghi, p. 80.

101. Mazzinghi, pp. 49–50, Trenholme, p. 26; Thornley, p. 186.

102. Cox, p. 21–22, 85 and Bellamy, p. 107.

103. 2 Henry V, Par. Roll, vol. 4, p. 39. Mazzinghi, p. 45.

104. Parl. Roll, 503b, 4 Henry IV. Mazzinghi, p. 45; Bellamy, p. 104 and Thornley, p. 188.

105. Thornley, p. 187.

106. Thornley, p. 188.

107. There were notorious criminal raids from St. Martin's again in 1455 and 1456. Trenholme, p. 55; Cox, p. 89; Bellamy, p. 110; Thornley, p. 186. Again an order to produce proof of the privileges was made but again the abuses continued. Cox, pp. 89–90.

108. Cox, p. 91 and Thornley, p. 193.

109. Thornley, pp. 193–195 and Cox, pp. 83–86.

110. Mazzinghi, p. 15; Trenholme, p. 28; Thornley, p. 200; Cox, p. 319. The date of this bull given by each historian is different: 1486, 1467, 1487 and 1482. The bull was confirmed by Pope Alexander VI in 1493 and again by Pope Julius II in 1502. Trenholme, p. 28 and Cox, p. 93.

111. See also papal bulls listed in Urrutia-Aparicio, p. 24.

112. Thornley, p. 197.

113. Thornley, p. 199.

114. Thornley, p. 198.

115. *Ibid.*

116. 21 Henry VIII, c. 2. Mazzinghi, p. 32; Trenholme, p. 29; Cox, p. 321 and Thornley, p. 201.

117. 27 Henry VIII, c. 19. Mazzinghi, p. 15 and Cox, p. 324.

118. 4 Henry VII, c. 2. Thornley, p. 200 and Cox, p. 320. The privilege of benefit of clergy originally was an immunity from prosecution reserved for the clergy. However, since the test for the privilege was a literacy test, many non-clergy claimed the privilege, leading to widespread abuse.

119. Cox, p. 321; Mazzinghi, p. 15; Trenholme, p. 29; Thornley, p. 201.

120. The 1536 protest by clerics known as the Pilgrimage of Grace included an objection to Henry VIII's regulation of the sanctuary privilege. Cox, pp. 323–324.

121. 32 Henry VIII, c. 12, s. 5. Mazzinghi, pp. 16, 19 and 84; Trenholme, pp. 30–31; Thornley,, pp. 203–204; Cox, p. 326. In 1542 the city of Manchester protested that it was simply a linen and cloth manufacturing town, without a mayor, sheriff or bailiff, and without any city walls or a jail, and thus unsuited as a sanctuary. Henry answered the protest by naming Chester as a replacement city for Manchester, reserving the power to appoint another town if Chester was also unsuitable. 33 Henry VIII, c. 15. Mazzinghi, pp. 16, 19–20 and 84; Trenholme, p. 88; Cox, pp. 327–328; Thornley, p. 204. The power of reappointment was exercised when Chester complained (even though it has been a palatine county and therefore a

secular sanctuary); Stafford was chosen to replace Chester as the eighth city of refuge. Trenholme, p. 89; Cox, p. 328; Thornley, p. 204.

122. Mazzinghi, pp. 83–85.

123. For example, in 1540 Henry assumed all the power over the liberties, privileges and franchises of all the dissolved monasteries. 32 Henry VIII, c. 20. Thornley, p. 203. Note that all of the monasteries in or around London had been dissolved by Henry by the mid-1540's. Eliza Jefferies Davis, "The Transformation of London," in Robert W. Seton-Watson, ed., *Tudor Studies Presented to the Board of Studies in History in the University of London (to Albert Frederick Pollard)* (London: Longmans, Green and Co., 1924), p. 298.

124. Thornley, p. 201.

125. 2 Henry V, st. 1, c. 5 and 9 Henry V, st. 1, c. 7. Thornley, pp. 186–187.

126. Thornley, p. 199.

127. Mazzinghi, p. 15; Trenholme, p. 30; Cox, p. 322 and Thornley, pp. 201–203.

128. Thornley, p. 202.

129. Thornley, p. 200.

130. Thornley, p. 182.

131. Thornley, p. 204 and Bellamy, p. 111. There is also some confusing legislation cited by Cox, p. 328, regarding the sanctuary privilege for horse-stealers.

132. Cox, pp. 328, 75–77 and Thornley, p. 204. There are also references to sanctuary at Beverly from 1548 to 1557. Cox, pp. 147–149.

133. Thornley, pp. 204–205.

134. Cox, p. 78 and Thornley, p. 206.

135. 1 James I, c. 25, s. 7. Cox, p. 329; Mazzinghi, p. 16; Trenholme, p. 31; Thornley, p. 206.

136. Thornley, p. 206.

137. 21 James I, c. 28. Cox, p. 329; Mazzinghi, p. 16; Trenholme, p. 31; Thornley, p. 207. The remnants of the privilege apparently still did not disappear for a long time because in 1697, an act of Parliament suppressed "the many notorious and scandalous practices used in many pretended privileged places in and about the cities of London, Westminster, and the Borough of Southwark, co. of Surrey, by obstructing the execution of legal process therein." 8 and 9 William III, c. 27. Mazzinghi, p. 16 and Trenholme, p. 31.

7. Sanctuary in U.S. History

1. Quoted in Ron Young and James S. Best, "The Sanctuary Movement Reaches into the Pacific," *Fellowship*, January, 1969, p. 21. The University of Hawaii became a focal point for sanctuary activity. In October 1971, five sailors jumped their ships and took sanctuary in Wesley Foundation Hall, the Methodist church near the campus. Four of the men—Leo A. Lockard, 20, of Chariton, Iowa; Henry Vanelderen, 21, of Grand Rapids, Michigan; Jim L. Chumbers, 19, of Beckley, West Virginia; Ron Ballard, 21, of Draper, Utah—were from the destroyer *USS Cochrane* and a fifth, David Mills, 19, of Ontario, California, was from the destroyer escort *USS Oulette*. The sailors voluntarily surrendered to military police after several days in the sanctuary. "Five Who Took Sanctuary After Jumping Ship Give Up," *New York Times*, October 18, 1971, p. 40.

There is an interesting federal court case indirectly involving the provision of sanctuary at the Church of the Crossroads and the First Unitarian Church in Honolulu, Hawaii. During August and September of 1969, up to twenty-five AWOL servicemen had entered the sanctuaries. In early September, Armed Services police entered the churches and arrested twelve of the servicemen while thirteen others escaped. The commanding officers of the Naval and Marine bases where the arrested servicemen were held then barred the ministers from the sanctuary churches from further access to the bases on the ground that their presence would be inimical to morale and good order. The ministers and the arrested servicemen filed suit for injunctive and other relief but the action was dismissed. The Ninth Circuit Court of Appeals affirmed the dismissal of the action, upholding the exclusions as time, place and manner regulations reasonably related to a valid public interest. *Bridges v. Davis*, 443 F.2d 970, 973 (9th Cir. 1971), rehearing denied, 445 F.2d 1401 (9th Cir. 1971).

1a. Dennis Willigan, "Sanctuary: A Communitarian Form of Counter-Culture," *Union Seminary Quarterly Review*, vol. 25, Summer 1970, pp. 519–520.

2. See also Chicago Religious Task Force on Central America materials.

3. Rollin G. Osterweis, *Three Centuries of New Haven, 1638–1938* (New Haven: Yale University Press, 1953), pp. 55–57.

4. Horatio T. Strother, *The Underground Railroad in Connecticut* (Middletown, Connecticut: Wesleyan University Press, 1962), p. 182.

5. *Scott v. Sandford*, 60 U.S. (19 How.) 393 (1856).

6. Strother, p. 182.

7. Wilbur H. Siebert, *The Underground Railroad from Slavery to Freedom* (New York: Russell and Russell, 1898, reissued 1967), pp. 272–281.

8. See, e.g., Willigan, pp. 522–531 and Siebert, pp. 93–98.

9. Willigan, p. 532.

10. David R. Weber, ed., *Civil Disobedience in America* (Ithaca, N.Y.: Cornell University Press, 1978), p. 271.

11. Willigan, p. 533.

12. 391 U.S. 907 (1968), from 386 F.2d 811 (1st Cir. 1967).

13. Willigan, p. 533.

14. Willigan, p. 533 and "Evader of Draft Seized in Church," *New York Times*, May 23, 1968, p. 2.

15. "AWOL Soldier in Boston Stays in Church Sanctuary," *New York Times*, May 30, 1968, p. 3.

16. Willigan, pp. 534–535 and "Foe of War Leaves Church Sanctuary," *New York Times*, May 26, 1968, p. 12.

17. Willigan, p. 534.

18. Willigan, p. 534 and "Providence Church Grants Sanctuary to Draft Foes," *New York Times*, June 2, 1968, p. 89. Willigan uses the spelling "Meyer" while the *New York Times* spells the name "Moyer."

19. Willigan, p. 535.

20. Willigan, p. 535 and "2 Draft Resisters Are Dragged From Church by Agents of FBI," *New York Times*, June 4, 1968, p. 12.

21. "Draft Resister Seized in Church as 100 Friends Show Support," *New York Times*, June 14, 1968, p. 49.

22. "Draft Jury Finds L.I. Youth Guilty, " *New York Times*, July 20, 1968, p. 6.

23. "L.I. Draft Resister Is Given Four Years," *New York Times*, September 28, 1968, p. 16.

24. "Soldier Takes Sanctuary," *New York Times*, August 12, 1968, p. 33.

25. "War Critics Give Sanctuary to G.I.," *New York Times*, August 28, 1968, p. 36.

26. Omitted in revised manuscript.

27. Willigan, pp. 536–537.

28. Willigan, pp. 536–537 and "Army Deserter Removed from Boston U. Chapel," *New York Times*, October 7, 1968, p. 29.

29. "Draft Resister Imprisoned," *New York Times*, November 15, 1968, p. 50.

30. "Sanctuary Move Debated at M.I.T.," *New York Times*, November 3, 1968, p. 33.

31. Willigan, pp. 537–538.

32. "Sanctuary Move Debated at M.I.T.," *New York Times*, November 3, 1968, p. 33.

33. "Soldier is Arrested at M.I.T. Sanctuary," *New York Times*, November 11, 1968, p. 17.

34. "G.I. Gets Four Months," *New York Times*, January 6, 1969, p. 48.

35. "AWOL Private Given 'Sanctuary' at City College," *New York Times*, November 1, 1968, p. 14 and Willigan, p. 539 and *Fellowship*, p. 21.

36. "12 War Protestors Seized Here as Youthful Radicals Prepare for More Demonstrations Today," *New York Times*, November 5, 1968, p. 15.

37. "Police Seize 125 on C.C.N.Y. Campus," *New York Times*, November 7, 1968, pp. 1, 4. 18 U.S.C. § 1381 prohibits the harboring of a deserter from the Armed Forces.

38. "175 Hold Protest on C.C.N.Y. Campus," *New York Times*, November 8, 1968, p. 32.

39. "Soldier Convicted of Trespass Here, But Wins Praise," *New York Times*, November 14, 1968, p. 8.

40. "AWOL Soldier Receives Sanctuary at Brandeis U.," *New York Times*, December 5, 1968, p. 2 and "Soldier, Absent From Post, Seized at Base Protest," *New York Times*, December 21, 1968, p. 3.

41. "AWOL Soldier, Protesting War, Awaits Arrest," *New York Times*, October 18, 1969, p. 10 and "Soldier Leaves 'Sanctuary' Here," *New York Times*, October 20, 1969, p. 16.

42. "6 Soldiers Take Sanctuary In Church," *Sacramento Bee*, September 30, 1971, p. D4 and "6 Antiwar Sailors Given Refuge in Catholic Church," *New York Times*, October 1, 1971, p. 7.

43. "Sanctuary-Seeking Sailors Are Arrested, Flown To Ship," *Sacramento Bee*, October 3, 1971, p. A6 and "9 Constellation Sailors Seized, Flown To Ship," *San Diego Union*, October 3, 1971, pp. B1, B7.

44. *San Diego Union*, October 3, 1971, p. B1.

45. *Sacramento Bee*, September 30, 1971, p. D4.

46. *San Diego Union*, October 3, 1971, pp. B1, B7 and "Sanctuary-Seeking Sailors Are Arrested, Flown To Ship," *Sacramento Bee*, October 3, 1971, p. A6.

47. *Sacramento Bee*, October 3, 1971, p. A6; *San Diego Union*, October 3, 1971, p. B1; "Carrier Departs Amid Protestors," *New York Times*, October 3, 1971, p. 5.

48. "1000 Sailors Said to Ask Ban on Carrier's Sailing," *New York Times*, October 12, 1971, p. 17.

49. "Sailors Given Discharges," *Los Angeles Times*, December 7,

1971, p. A24; "Discharged Sailors Speak Up," *San Francisco Examiner*, December 8, 1971, p. 64; "General Discharge Given to 8 Sailors Who Avoided War," *New York Times*, December 7, 1971, p. 10.

50. "Sanctuary Offer to Anti-War GI's," *San Francisco Chronicle*, November 10, 1971, p. 16.

51. *Ibid.*

52. "Berkeley Council Offers Facilities to Military Deserters," *Los Angeles Times*, November 12, 1971, p. A3 and "Berkeley Backs Dissenters," *Sacramento Bee*, November 11, 1971, p. A14.

53. "No 'Sanctuary' for Berkeley Council," *San Francisco Chronicle*, November 12, 1971, p. 11.

54. "Coral Sea Sails to War; 17 Protesters Held," *San Francisco Examiner*, November 12, 1971, p. 4 and "Coral Sea Sails as Protest Founders," *San Francisco Chronicle*, November 13, 1971, pp. 1, 18.

55. "Church Sanctuary Taken By Sailor," *San Diego Union*, January 7, 1971, p. B2.

56. W. Evan Golder, "War Resister's Sanctuary," *U.S. Catholic*, November 1971, pp. 34–36; "Sanctuary sailor gets discharge," *National Catholic Reporter*, vol. 8, March 3, 1972, p. 24., W. Evan Golder, "Sailor sentenced after four-day sanctuary," *National Catholic Reporter*, vol. 8, February 4, 1972, p. 16. See also Robert McAfee Brown, *Theology in a New Key: Responding to Liberation Themes* (Philadelphia: Westminster Press, 1978), pp. 183–186. Brown notes that a new community, enriched with new liturgical understanding, grew out of the sanctuary experience. Similar observations about the current sanctuary movement will be developed in Chapter Eight.

57. November 30, 1983 interview with Rev. Gustav Schultz, University Lutheran Chapel, Berkeley, California and "The Sanctuary Coalition," *San Francisco Sunday Examiner and Chronicle*, July 23, 1972, "California Living," pp. 7–8.

8. Application of Sanctuary History to Central American Refugees Today

1. Eric Jorstad, "A Theological Reflection on Sanctuary," *Christianity and Crisis*, vol. 43, October 31, 1983, p. 405.

2. For example, see "Report of the 195th General Assembly Presbyterian Church (U.S.A.)," *Church and Society*, vol. 73, July/August 1983, pp. 82–84; "Report of the 196th General Assembly, Presbyterian Church (U.S.A.)," *Church and Society*, vol. 74, July/August 1984, pp. 50–58; "As-

sistance and Sanctuary for Central American Refugees, Resolution of the 1984 General Conference of the United Methodist Church, *Engage/Social Action*, vol. 12, June/July 1984, p. 7; "Church of Brethren Endorses 'Sanctuary' for Illegal Aliens," *The Baltimore Sun*, July 3, 1983 (1983 Annual Conference of the Church of the Brethren); "Nuns Offer Refugees 'Sanctuary'," *Wichita Eagle*, April 28, 1983 (Commission on Ministries of the General Conference Mennonite Church); "Government Crackdown on Sanctuary Movement," *Central American Refugee Defense Fund Newsletter*, June 1984, p. 4 (Conservative Rabbinical Council of the United States); "Churches' sanctuary movement: Heeding a 'higher call,' " *Philadelphia Inquirer*, January 28, 1985 (General Board of the American Baptist Churches in the U.S.A.).

While the United States Roman Catholic bishops as a whole have not taken a position on the question of sanctuary, several individual bishops have endorsed the movement. See, e.g., Rob Cogswell, "Refugee Worker Arrested," *The Christian Century*, vol. 101, May 2, 1984, "Events and People," p. 454 (Bishop John Fitzpatrick, of Brownsville, Texas); "A Refuge Outside the Law," *Newsday* (Long Island, New York), July 24, 1983 (Archbishop Raymond Hunthausen of Seattle, Washington and Bishop John R. McGann of Rockville Centre, New York); "Churches Give Sanctuary to Illegal Refugees Who Face Deportation," *New York Times*, April 18, 1983, p. A16 (Archbishop Rembert Weakland of Milwaukee, Wisconsin); "Pastoral Letter on Central America," October 1983 (Archbishop John R. Quinn, San Francisco, California). After the Arizona indictments, three local bishops issued a joint letter of support for the sanctuary movement (Bishops Thomas J. O'Brien of Phoenix, Manuel Moreno of Tucson, and Jerome Hastrich of Gallup, New Mexico).

In addition, the 1984 National Assembly of the Conference of Major Superiors of Men of the Roman Catholic Church passed a resolution endorsing the sanctuary movement. *National Catholic Reporter*, vol. 20, September 7, 1984, p. 3.

Finally, the Rev. Jesse Jackson is the first major national politician to endorse the sanctuary movement. Jackson's Operation PUSH in Chicago has received a refugee family into its care and protection. "Jackson Supports Refugee 'Caravan'," *Oakland Tribune*, October 1, 1984, p. A2; "Basta!" Newsletter of the Chicago Religious Task Force on Central America, January 1985, p.1.

3. The same legislative proposal for sanctions against employers who hire undocumented workers also contained a system for lawfully importing agricultural workers. See final Simpson-Mazzoli bills H.R. 1510 (§§ 211 and 214) and S. 529 (§§ 211 and 214), reprinted in 130 *Congressional*

Record H6176-H6181 and H6160-H6162. See also Michael S. Teitelbaum, "Right Versus Right: Immigration and Refugee Policy in the United States," *Foreign Affairs*, vol. 21, Fall 1980, pp. 1455–1462 and Alan K. Simpson, "Immigration Reform and Control," *Labor Law Journal*, vol. 34, no. 4, April 1983, pp. 195–200.

4. The idea of identifying with the poor emerged at the 2nd General Conference of Latin American Bishops, held in 1968 at Medellín, Colombia. See *The Church in the Present-Day Transformation of Latin America in Light of the Council*, English translation (Washington, D.C.: National Conference of Catholic Bishops, 1979), sections on "Peace" (22 and 23) and "Poverty of the Church." The concept of a preferential option for the poor was treated in a full chapter in the final document of the 3rd General Conference of Latin American Bishops, held in early 1979 at Puebla de Los Angeles, Mexico. See *Evangelization in Latin America's Present and Future*, English translation (Washington, D.C.: National Conference of Catholic Bishops, 1979), 1134–1165.

5. Jim Corbett, "Sanctuary and the Covenant Community," June 1984, unpublished paper.

6. "Refugee Underground Leads to Chicago Area," *Chicago Tribune*, May 30, 1983.

7. Michael McConnell and Renny Golden, "A Theology of Sanctuary," *Engage/Social Action*, vol. 12, February 1984, p. 6 and Christine K. Thompson, "The Liberating Quality of Truth: Churches and the Sanctuary Movement," *Engage/Social Action*, vol. 12, February 1984, p. 45 (quote from Richard Adams, sanctuary coordinator for St. Francis House, Madison, Wisconsin).

8. Eric Jorstad, "Sanctuary for Refugees: A Statement on Public Policy," *The Christian Century*, vol. 101, March 14, 1984, p. 276 and Fred Krueger, "Land of the free, home of the eligible," *Christianity and Crisis*, vol. 44, July 9, 1984, p. 275 (quote from Sr. Kay Hauer from Boston).

9. McConnell and Golden, *Engage/Social Action*, pp. 7–8. Jim Corbett shares how the exile church of refugees has taught him liberation theology: "What we have experienced as an effort to save undocumented Salvadoran and Guatemalan refugees may prove, in retrospect, to have been the belated arrival in Anglo-America of the radical reformation that has been taking place in the Latin America church." Quoted in Renny Golden, " 'Coyote'," *Witness*, vol. 67, January 1984, p. 9.

9a. Quoted in Statement of Faith of the Chicago Religious Task Force on Central America, "Basta!" (Tucson edition), January 1985, p. IV.

10. W. Gunther Plaut, Bernard J. Bamberger and William W.

Hallo, *The Torah: A Modern Commentary* (New York: Union of American Hebrew Congregations, 1981), p. 1409. The biblical injunction to love the stranger is repeated thirty-six times. *Ibid.*

11. There are several Hebrew words used for the English words stranger or alien that have also been translated as sojourner or foreigner. *Nochri* or *zar* is used for the foreigner residing temporarily in Israel while *ger* (especially its later form, *ger toshav*) means a resident alien. These words are to be distinguished from *ger tzedek*, a full proselyte who became a member of the Israelite community. *Ibid.*

12. Several contemporary Christian writers have focused on the redemptive Jubilee as the foundation of Jesus' social justice ministry (cf. Luke 4:16–21). See, e.g., John Howard Yoder, *The Politics of Jesus* (Grand Rapids, Michigan: William B. Eerdmans Publishing Company, 1972).

13. See also Ruth 2:1–8 for an account of a foreigner (Ruth) allowed to glean in the fields of Boaz.

14. Jesus was also a refugee, fleeing to Egypt to escape Herod (Matthew 2:13–15; cf Hosea 11:1). See Stephen T. DeMott, "Jesus the refugee" (editorial), and Enrique Dussel ". . . to be a stranger" in *Maryknoll*, vol. 78, June 1984, pp. 34–39; John R. Quinn, "When I Was A Stranger," (Pastoral Statement on our National Response to the Refugees of Central America), unpublished, March 12, 1985, pp. 1–2.

14a. In the New Testament, this universality is expressed in the reconciliation of all nations in one heavenly citizenship. See Ephesians 2:12–19, Galatians 3:28 and Colossians 3:11.

15. See, e.g., Psalm 9:9 ("The Lord is a stronghold for the oppressed, a stronghold in times of trouble"); Psalm 46:1 ("God our refuge and strength, a very present help in trouble"); Psalm 62:6–8.

16. See, e.g., Psalm 59:16–17 (and 2 Samuel 22:1–3), composed by David as he was fleeing Saul (1 Samuel 19:11) and Psalm 142:5–7, again composed by David while he was hiding in the cave (1 Samuel 22:1 and 24:3).

17. Jesus also declared himself to be the new temple (John 2:18–21 and Revelation 21), and one who rescues and saves.

18. See, e.g., Danny Collum, "Trespassing in the Basin," *Crucible of Hope* (Washington, D.C.: Sojourners, 1984), pp. 6–9; Walter LeFeber, *Inevitable Revolutions: The United States in Central America* (New York: W.W. Norton, 1983); Roger Burback and Patricia Flynn, eds., *The Politics of Intervention: The United States in Central America* (New York: Monthly Review Press, 1984).

19. See "Scores of U.S. Churches Take in Illegal Aliens Fleeing Latin America," *Wall Street Journal*, June 21, 1984, pp. 1, 27.

20. Mark Gibney, "Seeking Sanctuary: A Special Duty for the U.S.?" *Commonweal*, vol. 111, May 18, 1984, p. 295.

21. Peter H. Schuck, "The Transformation of Immigration Law," *Columbia Law Review*, vol. 84, no. 1, January 1984, p. 81.

22. Religious Leaders' Affirmation of Sanctuary Ministry, unpublished, January 23, 1985.

BIBLIOGRAPHY

Books

Bedau, Hugo Adam, ed. *Civil Disobedience: Theory and Practice*. (Indianapolis: Bobbs-Mcrrill Educational Publishing, 1969)

Bellamy, John G. *Crime and Public Order in England in the Latter Middle Ages*. (London: Routledge and Kegan Paul and Toronto: University of Toronto Press, 1973)

Bouscaren, T. Lincoln, Adam C. Ellis and Francis N. Korth. *Canon Law: A Text and Commentary*, 4th ed. (Milwaukee: The Bruce Publishing Company, 1963)

Bracton's Note Book, F.W. Maitland, ed., vol. III. (London: C.J. Clay and Sons, 1887)

Bracton, *On the Laws and Customs of England*, G.E. Woodbine, ed., S.E. Thorne, trans. and rev., vol. II. (Cambridge: Harvard University Press, 1968)

Britton, Francis Morgan Nichols, rev. and trans., vol. I. (Oxford: Clarendon Press, 1865)

Brown, Robert McAfee. *Theology in a New Key: Responding to Liberation Themes* (Philadelphia: Westminster Press, 1978)

Buckmaster, Henrietta. *Let My People Go*. (Boston: Beacon Press, 1941)

Childress, James F. *Civil Disobedience and Political Obligation: A Study in Christian Social Ethics*. (New Haven: Yale University Press, 1971)

Coriden, James A., Thomas J. Green and Donald E. Heintschel, eds. *The Code of Canon Law: A Text and Commentary*. (Ramsey, N.J.: Paulist Press, 1984)

Cox, J. Charles. *The Sanctuaries and Sanctuary Seekers of Medieval England*. (London: George Allen and Sons, 1911)

Craig, Richard B. *The Bracero Program: Interest Groups and Foreign Policy*. (Austin: University of Texas Press, 1971)

Daube, David. *Civil Disobedience in Antiquity*. (Edinburgh: Edinburgh University Press, 1972)

Davis, Eliza Jefferies. "The Transformation of London," in Robert W. Seton-Watson, ed., *Tudor Studies Presented to the Board of Studies in History in the University of London (to Albert Frederick Pollard).* (London: Longmans, Green and Co., 1924) pp. 182–207

Dorr, Donal. *Option For the Poor: A Hundred Years of Vatican Social Teaching.* (Maryknoll: Orbis Books, 1984)

Dunbar, Tony and Linda Kravitz, *Hard Traveling: Migrant Farm Workers in America.* (Cambridge, MA: Ballinger Publishing Co., 1976)

Eliot, T.S. *Murder in the Cathedral.* (New York: Harcourt, Brace and Company, 1935)

Galarza, Ernesto. *Farmworkers and Agribusiness in California, 1947–1960.* (Notre Dame: University of Notre Dame Press, 1977)

Galarza, Ernesto, *Merchants of Labor: The Mexican Bracero Story.* (Santa Barbara, CA: McNally and Loftin, 1964)

Gara, Larry. *The Liberty Line.* (Lexington: University of Kentucky Press, 1961)

Goldfarb, Ronald L. *Migrant Farmworkers: A Caste of Despair.* (Ames: Iowa State University Press, 1981)

Grahl-Madsen, Atle. *Territorial Asylum.* (Stockholm: Almquist and Wiksell International, 1980)

Gutierrez, Gustavo. *A Theology of Liberation.* (Maryknoll: Orbis Books, 1973)

Hallie, Philip P. *Lest Innocent Blood Be Shed: The Story of the Village of Le Chambon and How Goodness Happened There.* (New York: Harper and Row, 1979)

Haughey, John C., ed. *The Faith That Does Justice: Examining the Christian Sources for Social Change* (New York: Paulist Press, 1977)

Mazzinghi, Thomas John. *Sanctuaries.* (Stafford: Halden and Son, 1887)

Miguez-Bonino, Jose. *Doing Theology in a Revolutionary Situation* (Philadelphia: Fortress Press, 1975)

Mirrour of Justices (Andre Horne). (Washington, D.C.: John Byne and Company, 1903)

Osterweis, Rollin G. *Three Centuries of New Haven, 1638–1938.* (New Haven: Yale University Press, 1953) pp. 54–57

Pollock, Sir Frederick and Frederick William Maitland, *The History of English Law Before the Time of Edward I,* 2nd ed., vol. II. (Cambridge: C. J. Clay and Sons, 1898) pp. 590–591

Riggs, Charles H. "Criminal Asylum in Anglo-Saxon Law," *University of Florida Monographs, Social Sciences,* No. 18. (Gainesville: University of Florida Press, Spring 1963)

Samora, Julian. *Los Mojados: The Wetback Story.* (Notre Dame, IN: University of Notre Dame Press, 1971)

Sayles, G.O. *The Medieval Foundations of England.* (London: Methuen and Co., Ltd., 1964)

Scott, Waldron. *Bring Forth Justice* (Grand Rapids: Wm. B. Eerdmans Publishing Co., 1980)

Segundo, Juan Luis. *The Liberation of Theology* (Maryknoll: Orbis Books, 1976)

Seibert, Wilbur H. *The Underground Railroad from Slavery to Freedom*. (New York: Russell and Russell, 1898, reissued 1967)

Seibert, Wilbur, H. *Vermont's Anti-Slavery and Underground Railroad Record*. (Columbus, Ohio: The Spahr and Glenn Co., 1937)

Sider, Ronald J., ed. *Cry Justice* (New York: Paulist Press, and Downers Grove: InterVarsity Press, 1980)

Stevick, Daniel B. *Civil Disobedience and the Christian*. (New York: Seabury Press, 1969)

Strother, Horatio T. *The Underground Railroad in Connecticut*. (Middletown, Connecticut: Wesleyan University Press, 1962)

Thornley, Isobel D. "The Destruction of Sanctuary," in Robert W. Seton-Watson, ed., *Tudor Studies Presented to the Board of Studies in History in the University of London (to Albert Frederick Pollard)*. (London: Longmans, Green and Co., 1924), pp. 182–207

Timbal Duclaux de Martin, Pierre. *Le droit d' asile*. (Paris: Librairie du Recueil Sirey, 1939)

Trenholme, Norman M. "The Right of Sanctuary in England," *University of Missouri Studies*, vol. 1, no. 5, February 1903

Urrutia-Aparicio, Carlos. *Diplomatic Asylum in Latin America*. (Washington, D.C.: American University, 1959)

United States Department of Justice, *Attorney General's Survey of Release Procedures*, Volume III: Pardon. (Washington, D.C.: U.S. Government Printing Office, 1939) pp. 6–7, 37–39

Vaux, Roland de. *Ancient Israel: Its Life and Institutions*, John McHugh, trans. (New York: McGraw-Hill Book Co., Inc., 1961)

Wallis, Jim. *The Call to Conversion*. (San Francisco: Harper and Row, 1981)

Weber, David R., ed. *Civil Disobedience in America*. (Ithaca, N.Y.: Cornell University Press, 1978)

Wolf, Hazel Catherine. *On Freedom's Altar*. (Madison, WI: University of Wisconsin Press, 1952)

Legal Periodicals

Aleinkoff, T. Alexander, "Aliens, Due Process and 'Community Ties': A Response to Martin," *University of Pittsburgh Law Review*, vol. 44, no. 2, Winter 1983, pp. 237–260

Aleinkoff, T. Alexander, "Political Asylum in the Federal Republic of

Germany and the Republic of France: Lessons for the United States," *University of Michigan Journal of Law Reform*, vol. 17, no. 2, Winter 1984, pp. 183–241

Anker, Deborah E. and Michael H. Posner, "The Forty Year Crisis: A Legislative History of the Refugee Act of 1980," *San Diego Law Review*, vol. 19, no. 1, December 1981, pp. 9–89

Blum, Carolyn Patty, "The Half Open Door: U.S. Refugee Law and the *Stevic* Case," *Federal Bar News and Journal*, vol. 31, no. 5, May 1984, pp. 198–201

Blum, Jeffrey M. and Ralph G. Steinhardt, "Federal Jurisdiction over International Human Rights Claims: The Alien Tort Claims Act after *Filartiga v. Pena-Irala*," *Harvard International Law Journal*, vol. 22, no. 1, Winter 1981, pp. 53–113

Brom, Thomas, "Church sanctuary for Salvadorans," *California Lawyer*, vol. 3, no. 7, July 1983, pp. 42–43

Burke, Kathryn, Sandra Coliver, Connie de la Vega and Stephen Rosenbaum, "Application of International Human Rights Law in State and Federal Courts," *Texas International Law Journal*, vol. 18, no. 2, Spring 1983, pp. 291–328

Choper, Jesse H., "Defining 'Religion' in the First Amendment," *University of Illinois Law Review*, vol. 1982, no. 3, pp. 579–613

Choper, Jesse H., "The Religion Clauses of the First Amendment: Reconciling the Conflict," *University of Pittsburgh Law Review*, vol. 41, no. 4, 1980, pp. 673–701

Clark, J. Morris, "Comments on Some Policies Underlying the Constitutional Law of Religious Freedom," *Minnesota Law Review*, vol. 64, no. 3, March 1980, pp. 453–466

Clark, J. Morris, "Guidelines for the Free Exercise Clause," *Harvard Law Review*, vol. 83, no. 2, December 1982, pp. 327–365

Comment, "Harboring of Illegal Aliens: New Meaning to the Concept of Shielding From Detection," *Suffolk Transnational Law Journal*, vol. 7, no. 1, Spring 1983, pp. 255–266

Comment, "Political Asylum and Withholding of Deportation: Defining the Appropriate Standard of Proof Under the Refugee Act of 1980," *San Diego Law Review*, vol. 21, no. 1, December 1983, pp. 171–194

Esbeck, Carl. H. "State Regulation of Social Services Ministries of Religious Organizations," *Valparaiso University Law Review*, vol. 16, no. 1, Fall 1981, pp. 1–56

Freed, Mayer G. and Daniel O. Polsby, "Race, Religion, and Public Policy: *Bob Jones University v. United States*," 1983 *Supreme Court Review*, pp. 1–31

Freeman, George C., "The Misguided Search for the Constitutional Definition of 'Religion,' " *Georgetown Law Journal*, vol. 71, no. 6, August 1983, pp. 1519–1565

Freeman, Harrop A., "A Remonstrance for Conscience," *University of Pennsylvania Law Review*, vol. 106, no. 5, March 1958, pp. 806–830

Galanter, Marc, "Religious Freedoms in the United States: A Turning Point?" *Wisconsin Law Review*, vol. 1966, no. 2, Spring 1966, pp. 217–296

Georgetown University Institute for Public Representation, "The State Department Advisory Opinion: A Due Process Critique," *Immigration Law Reporter*, Spring 1984, pp. 13–21

Giannella, Donald A., "Religious Liberty, Non-Establishment and Doctrinal Development, Part I: The Religious Liberty Guarantee," *Harvard Law Review*, vol. 80, no. 7, May 1967, pp. 1381–1431

Gilbert, Geoffrey S., "Right of Asylum: A Change of Direction," *International and Comparative Law Quarterly*, vol. 32, July 1983, pp. 663–650

Golden, Renny, "Refugee Sanctuary: Churches Break the Law," *Immigration Newsletter* (of the National Immigration Project of the National Lawyers Guild, Inc.) vol. 12, no. 2, July–August, 1983, pp. 3–5

Grahl-Madsen, Atle, "International Refugee Law Today and Tomorrow," *Archiv des Völkerrechts*, vol. 20, 1982, pp. 411–467

Greenawalt, Kent, "Religion as a Concept in Constitutional Law," *California Law Review*, vol. 72, no. 5, September 1984, pp. 753–816

Hanrahan, Eileen M., "Constitutionality of Legislation Denying Tax-Exempt Status to Racially Discriminatory Schools," *The Catholic Lawyer*, vol. 28, no. 2, Spring 1983, pp. 137–143

Helton, Arthur C., "Persecution on Account of Membership in a Social Group as a Basis for Refugee Status," *Columbia Human Rights Law Review*, vol. 15, no. 1, Fall 1983, pp. 39–67

Helton, Arthur C., "Political Asylum Under the 1980 Refugee Act: An Unfulfilled Promise," *University of Michigan Journal of Law Reform*, vol. 17, no. 2, Winter 1984, pp. 243–269

Higham, John, "American Immigration Policy in Historical Perspective," *Law and Contemporary Problems*, vol. 21, Spring 1956, pp. 213–235

Johnson, Phillip E., "Concepts and Compromise on First Amendment Religious Doctrine," *California Law Review*, vol. 72, no. 5, September 1984, pp. 817–846

Katz, Wilber G. "Freedom of Religion and State Neutrality," *University of Chicago Law Review*, vol. 20, no. 3, Spring 1953, pp. 426–440

Krenz, Frank E., "The Refugee as a Subject of International Law," *International and Comparative Law Quarterly*, vol. 15, 1966, pp. 90–116

Kurland, Philip B., "Of Church and State and the Supreme Court," *University of Chicago Law Review*, vol. 29, no. 1, Autumn 1961, pp. 1–96

Kurland, Philip B., "The Irrelevance of the Constitution: The Religion Clauses of the First Amendment and the Supreme Court," *Villanova Law Review*, vol. 24, no. 1, November 1978, pp. 3–27

Kurzban, Ira J., "Restructuring the Asylum Process," *San Diego Law Review*, vol. 19, no. 1, December 1981, pp. 91–117

LeMaster, Roger J. and Barnaby Zall, "Compassion Fatigue: The Expansion of Refugee Admissions to the United States," *Boston College International and Comparative Law Review*, vol. 6, no. 2, Spring 1983, pp. 447–474

Levy, Deborah M., "Detention in the Asylum Context," *University of Pittsburgh Law Review*, vol. 44, no. 2, Winter 1983, pp. 297–328

Linford, Orma, "The Mormons and the Law: The Polygamy Cases, Part I," *Utah Law Review*, vol. 9, no. 2, Winter 1964, pp. 308–370

Lopez, Gerald P., "Undocumented Mexican Migration: In Search of a Just Immigration Law and Policy," *UCLA Law Review*, vol. 28, no. 4, April 1981, pp. 615–714

Mansfield, John H., "The Religion Clauses of the First Amendment and the Philosophy of the Constitution," *California Law Review*, vol. 72, no. 5, September 1984, pp. 847–907

Marcus, Paul, "The Forum of Conscience: Applying Standards Under the Free Exercise Clause," *Duke Law Journal*, vol. 1973, no. 6, January 1973, pp. 1217–1272

Martin, David A., "Due Process and Membership in the National Community: Political Asylum and Beyond," *University of Pittsburgh Law Review*, vol. 44, no. 2, Winter 1983, pp. 165–235

Martin, David A., "Large-Scale Migrations of Asylum Seekers, *American Journal of International Law*, vol. 76, no. 3, July 1982, pp. 598–609

Martin, David A., "The Refugee Act of 1980: Its Past and Future," *1982 Michigan Yearbook of International Legal Studies: Transnational Legal Problems of Refugees*, p. 101

Martin, Scott M., "Non-refoulement of Refugees: United States Compliance with International Obligations," *Harvard International Law Journal*, vol. 23, no. 2, Winter 1983, pp. 357–380

Merel, Gail, "The Protection of Individual Choice: A Consistent Understanding of Religion Under the First Amendment," *University of Chicago Law Review*, vol. 45, no. 3, Spring 1983, pp. 805–843

Note, "Aliens' Rights—The Refugee Act of 1980 as Response to the 1967 Protocol Relating to the Status of Refugees: The First Test," *Vanderbilt Journal of Transnational Law*, vol. 14, Summer 1981, pp. 561–584

Note, "Basing Asylum Claims on a Fear of Persecution Arising From a Prior Asylum Claim," *Notre Dame Lawyer*, vol. 56, no. 4, April 1981, pp. 719–730

Note, "Behind the Paper Curtain: Asylum Policy Versus Asylum Practice," *New York Univeristy Review of Law and Social Change*, vol. 7, no. 1, Winter 1978, pp. 107–141

Note, "General Laws, Neutral Principles and the Free Exercise Clause," *Vanderbilt Law Review*, vol. 33, no. 1, January 1980, pp. 149–174

Note, "*Heffron v. International Society for Krishna Consciousness, Inc.*: Confusing Free Speech with Free Exercise Rights," *California Law Review*, vol. 71, no. 3, May 1983, pp. 1012–1029

Note, "Immigration Law: State Regulation and Equal Protection; Political Asylum Cases; and Exclusion Hearings," *1983 Annual Survey of American Law*, March 1984, issue 4, pp. 837–866

Note, "Immigration Policy and the Rights of Aliens," *Harvard Law Review*, vol. 96, no. 6, April 1983, pp. 1286–1465

Note, "Indian Worship v. Government Development: A New Breed of Religion Cases," *Utah Law Review*, vol. 1984, no. 2, pp. 313–336

Note, "Protecting Aliens From Persecution Without Overloading the INS: Should Illegal Aliens Receive Notice of the Right to Apply for Asylum?" *Virginia Law Review*, vol. 69, no. 5, June 1983, pp. 901–930

Note, "Religious Belief Protected Under Free Exercise Clause Though Not Shown to be Derived from Cardinal Tenets of Common Faith," *Santa Clara Law Review*, vol. 22, no. 1, 1982, pp. 235–245

Note, "Religious Exemptions Under the Free Exercise Clause: A Model of Competing Authorities," *The Yale Law Journal*, vol. 90, no. 2, December 1980, pp. 350–376

Note, "Sincere Religious Belief Though Not a Tenet of One's Church Sect, Still Protected by First Amendment," *Seton Hall Law Review*, vol. 11, no. 2, 1980, pp. 220–229

Note, "Soul Rebels: The Rastafarians and the Free Exercise Clause," *Georgetown Law Journal*, vol. 72, no. 5, June 1984, pp. 1605–1635

Note, "The Domestic Application of International Human Rights Law: Evolving the Species," *Hastings International and Comparative Law Review*, vol. 5, no. 1, Fall 1981, pp. 161–209

Note, "The Endless Debate: Refugee and Law and Policy and the 1980 Refugee Act," *Cleveland State Law Review*, vol. 32, no. 1, 1983–1984, pp. 117–174

Note, "The Right of Asylum Under United States Law," *Columbia Law Review*, vol. 80, no. 5, June 1980, pp. 1125–1148

Note, "The Right to Asylum Under U.S. Immigration Law," *University of Florida Law Review*, vol. 33, no. 4, Summer 1981, pp. 539–564

Note, "The Sacred and the Profane: A First Amendment Definition of Religion," *Texas Law Review*, vol. 61, no. 1, August 1982, pp. 139–173

Note, "*Thomas v. Review Board:* How Far is the Supreme Court Willing to Go?" *Ohio Northern University Law Review*, vol. 10, no. 1, Winter 1983, pp. 193–201

Note, "Toward a Constitutional Definition of Religion," *Harvard Law Review*, vol. 91, no. 5, March 1978, pp. 1056–1089

Note, "U.S. Immigration and Refugee Reform: A Critical Evaluation," *Virginia Journal of International Law*, vol. 22, no. 4, Summer 1982, pp. 805–848

Note, "*United States v. Lee:* An Insensitive Approach to the Free Exercise of Religion," *Tulsa Law Journal*, vol. 18, no. 2, Winter 1982, pp. 305–337

Note, "*United States v. Lee:* Has the Retreat Been Sounded for Free Exercise?" *Stetson Law Review*, vol. 12, no. 3, Spring 1983, pp. 852–864

Note, "*United States v. Lee:* Limitations on the Free Exercise of Religion," *Loyola Law Review*, vol. 28, no. 4, Fall 1982, pp. 1216–1225

Note, "Applying a Public Benefit Requirement to Tax-Exempt Organizations," *Missouri Law Review*, vol. 49, no. 2, Spring 1984, pp. 353–371

Note, "Conflicts Between the First Amendment Religion Clauses and the Internal Revenue Code: Politically Active Religious Organizations and Racially Discriminatory Private Schools," *Washington University Law Quarterly*, vol. 61, no. 2, Summer 1983, pp. 503–560

Note, "Constitutional Law—Religious Schools, Public Policy, and the Constitution: *Bob Jones University v. United States*," *North Carolina Law Review*, vol. 62, no. 5, June 1984, pp. 1051–1067

Note, "First Amendment—Free Exercise—Conflict with 42 U.S.C. § 1981," *Northern Kentucky Law Review*, vol. 9, no. 2, 1982, pp. 381–403

Note, "Freedom of Religion—Free Exercise Clause—Imposition of Social Security Taxes on Members of Amish Religion," *Northern Kentucky Law Review*, vol. 9, no. 2, 1982, pp. 369–380

Note, "The Internal Revenue Service Has the Power to Revoke the Tax-Exempt Status of Private Schools Which Practice Racial Discrimination Due to Religious Belief, Since These Schools Are Not Charitable, and Revocation Does Not Violate the Free Exercise or the Establishment Clause of the First Amendment," *Villanova Law Review*, vol. 29, no. 1, February 1984, pp. 253–280

O'Brien, Maureen, "The Kudirka Affair: Bringing Sanity to the Law of Asylum," *Human Rights*, vol. 8, no. 4, Winter 1980, pp. 38–43

Parker, Karen, "Geneva Convention Protections for Salvadoran Refugees," *Immigration Newsletter* (of the National Immigration Project of the National Lawyers Guild, Inc.), vol. 13, no. 3, May–June 1984, pp. 1, 5–13

Pepper, Stephen, *"Reynolds, Yoder,* and Beyond: Alternatives for the Free Exercise Clause," *Utah Law Review*, 1981, no. 2, pp. 309–378

Pepper, Stephen L., "The Conundrum of the Free Exercise Clause: Some Reflections on Recent Cases," *Northern Kentucky Law Review*, vol. 9, no. 2, 1982, pp. 265–303

Pfeffer, Leo, "Freedom and/or Separation: The Constitutional Dilemma of the First Amendment," *Minnesota Law Review*, vol. 64, no. 3, March 1980, pp. 561–584

Pfeffer, Leo, "The Supremacy of Free Exercise," *Georgetown Law Journal*, vol. 61, no. 5, May 1973, pp. 1115–1142

Pugash, James Z., "The Dilemma of the Sea Refugee: Rescue Without Refuge," *Harvard International Law Journal*, vol. 18, no. 3, Summer 1977, pp. 577–604

Riga, Peter J., "Religion, Sincerity and Free Exercise," *Catholic Lawyer*, vol. 25, no. 3, Summer 1980, pp. 246–262

Scanlan, John A., "Asylum Adjudication: Some Due Process Implications of Proposed Immigration Legislation," *University of Pittsburgh Law Review*, vol. 44, no. 2, Winter 1983, pp. 261–295

Scanlan, John A., "Regulating Refugee Flow: Legal Alternatives and Obligations Under the Refugee Act of 1980," *Notre Dame Lawyer*, vol. 56, no. 4, April 1981, pp. 618–643

Schey, Peter A., "The 'Right' to Apply for Political Asylum in the United States," *Houston Journal of International Law*, vol. 5, no. 2, Spring 1983, pp. 223–241

Schuck, Peter H., "The Transformation of Immigration Law," *Columbia Law Review*, vol. 84, no. 1, January 1984, pp. 1–90

Shetreet, Shimon, "Exemptions and Privileges on Grounds of Religion and Conscience," *Kentucky Law Journal*, vol. 62, no. 2, 1973–1974, pp. 377–420

Simpson, Alan K., Immigration Reform and Control," *Labor Law Journal*, vol. 34, no. 4, April 1983, pp. 195–200

Smith, Michael E., "The Special Place of Religion in the Constitution," *1983 Supreme Court Review*, pp. 83–123

Steinberg, Kip, "The Standard of Proof in Asylum Cases After *INS v. Stevic*," *Immigration Newsletter* (of the National Immigration Project of the National Lawyers Guild, Inc.) vol. 13, no. 4, July–August 1984, pp. 1, 6–8

Stephan, Paul B., *"Bob Jones University v. United States:* Public Policy in Search of Tax Policy," 1983 *Supreme Court Review*, pp. 33–82

Van Der Hout, Marc, "The politics of asylum," *California Lawyer*, vol. 5, April 1985, p. 72

Verkuil, Paul R., "A Study of Immigration Procedures," *UCLA Law Review*, vol. 31, no. 6, 1984, pp. 1141–1207

Vierdag, E. W., " 'Asylum' and Refugee in International Law," *Netherlands International Law Review*, vol. 24, Special Issue 1–2, 1977, pp. 287–303

Vincent-Daviss, Diana, "Human Rights Law: A Research Guide to the Literature. Part I: International Law and the United Nations." *New York University Journal of International Law and Policy*, vol. 14, Fall 1981, pp. 209–319

Vincent-Daviss, Diana, "Human Rights Law: A Research Guide to the Literature. Part II: International Protection of Refugees and Humanitarian Law." *New York University Journal of International Law and Policy*, vol. 14, Winter 1982, pp. 487–573

Weiss, Jonathan, "Privilege, Posture and Protection: 'Religion' in the Law," *The Yale Law Journal*, vol. 73, no. 4, March 1964, pp. 593–623

Weiss, P., "The 1967 Protocol Relating to the Status of Refugees and Some Questions of the Law of Treaties," *The British Year Book of International Law*, 1967, vol. 42, pp. 39–70

Weiss, P., "The United Nations Declaration on Territorial Asylum," *The Canadian Yearbook of International Law*, vol. 7, 1969, pp. 92–149

Other Periodicals

"A Haven for Salvadorans," *Newsweek*, vol. 99, April 5, 1982, p. 32

"A Long Road to Sanctuary," *The Washington Post*, March 25, 1985, pp. B1, B7

"A Refuge Outside the Law," *Newsday*, July 24, 1983 (Long Island, N.Y.)

"An Asylum in Berkeley" (editorial), *San Francisco Chronicle*, February 21, 1985, p. 56

"An Underground Railroad Set Them Free," *Providence Journal*, April 15, 1984

"Acquittal Cheered," *The Christian Century*, vol. 102, February 6–13, 1985, "Events and People," p. 119

"Acquittal in 'Sanctuary' Case Hailed," *San Francisco Chronicle*, January 26, 1985, p. 9

"Activist working with Salvador refugees doesn't regret choosing to live her faith," *Contra Costa Times*, October 21, 1984, "Times-Plus," p. 2

"All Berkeley is 'sanctuary,' " *The Oakland Tribune*, February 20, 1985, p. A1

"Ames Church Votes Against Providing 'Sanctuary,' " *Des Moines Register*, September 12, 1983

"Arkansans Join Illegal Effort to Aid Central Americans," *Arkansas Gazette*, May 19, 1984

"Assistance and Sanctuary for Central American Refugees," Resolution of the 1984 General Conference of the United Methodist Church, *Engage/Social Action*, vol. 12, June/July 1984, p. 7

Atkins, Henry L., "Public sanctuary: call to an option," *Witness*, vol. 67, August 1984, pp. 8–9

"Bay Area sets pace for refugee sanctuary," *The Oakland Tribune*, February 22, 1985, pp. D1, D3

"Berkeley Backs Dissenters," *The Sacramento Bee*, November 11, 1971, p. A14

"Berkeley Becomes a 'Sanctuary'," *San Francisco Chronicle*, February 20, 1985, pp. 1, 14

"Berkeley Council Offers Facilities to Military Deserters," *Los Angeles Times*, November 12, 1971, p. A3

"Berkeley Refuge," *The Christian Century*, vol. 102, March 13, 1985, "Events and People," p. 264

"Berkeley Votes to Be Sanctuary for Refugees," *Los Angeles Times*, February 21, 1985, Part I, p. 23

"Berkeley's 'sanctuary' greeted by praise, yawns," *The Oakland Tribune*, February 21, 1985, p. A1

Bernstein, Dennis and Connie Blitt, "Die or Say Goodbye: Salvadorans on the Run," *Commonweal*, vol. 111, December 14, 1984, pp. 676–677

"Blessed are the Sanctuaries" (editorial), *The Oakland Tribune*, January 21, 1985

Block, Robert, "Sanctuary and the defiant churches," *Maclean's*, vol. 97, January 30, 1984, p. 43

Brown, Robert McAfee, "Community-making as Ministry," *NICM Journal*, vol. 2, Winter 1977, pp. 24–36

Burks, Paul, "The Caravan: Sanctuary Goes Public," *Sequoia*, October-November 1984, pp. 3, 7

Burks, Paul, "This is Sanctuary: A Reformation in Our Time," *Sequoia*, February 1985, pp. A–D

Cahill, Greg, "Convenanting to Provide Sanctuary," *The Christian Century*, vol. 100, August 3–10, 1983, pp. 719–721

"Cambridge Now A Sanctuary For Refugees," *San Francisco Chronicle*, April 9, 1985, p. 13

"Candidates' Views on Religion Remain Big Campaign Issue," *Wall Street Journal*, September 18, 1984, pp. 1, 24

"Caught in the Storm of Sanctuary," *Washington Post*, March 12, 1985, p. C1

"Central American Diaspora Tests Immigration Policies of 3 Nations," *Los Angeles Times*, January 2, 1983

"Central Americans seek sanctuary in vain," *Washington Post*, February 11, 1985

"Church aid for illegal aliens raises legal, moral questions," *Dallas Morning News*, January 20, 1985

"Church balks at giving sanctuary to refugees," *The Oakland Tribune*, March 25, 1985, p. A10

"Church Gives Sanctuary to Refugees," *Miami Herald*, March 29, 1983

"Church-group head indicted in transporting of aliens," *Arizona Republic*, May 17, 1984

"Church of Brethren Endorses 'Sanctuary' for Illegal Aliens," *The Baltimore Sun*, July 3, 1983

"Church-protected refugee says he raped, tortured," *Minneapolis Star and Tribune*, July 8, 1984

"Church Sanctuary—ancient tradition in modern world," *Christian Science Monitor*, August 22, 1983, p. 5

"Church Sanctuary Movement for Refugees Grows in U.S.," *Washington Post*, January 27, 1983, p. A20

"Church Sanctuary Taken by Sailor," *San Diego Union*, January 7, 1972, p. B2

"Churches fear U.S. crackdown on refugees," *San Francisco Sunday Examiner and Chronicle*, June 10, 1984, p. A2

"Churches Ignore Laws to Harbor Illegal Aliens," *Cincinnati Enquirer*, July 10, 1983

"Churches' sanctuary movement: Heeding a 'higher call,' " *Philadelphia Inquirer*, January 28, 1985

"Churches shelter illegal Central American aliens," *The Daily Californian*, March 5, 1984, p. 3

"Churches Stand by Sanctuary Policy," *San Francisco Chronicle*, January 16, 1985, p. 14

"Clerics Indicted For Sheltering Latin Refugees," *San Francisco Chronicle*, January 15, 1985, p. 9

"Coalition Offers Long-Term Aid for Refugees," *Cincinnati Enquirer*, September 18, 1983

Coffin, William Sloane, "Sanctuary for refugees—and ourselves," *Christianity and Crisis*, vol. 45, March 18, 1985, pp. 75–76

Cogswell, Rob, "Bishop Posts Bond," *The Christian Century*, vol. 102, January 2–9, 1985, "Events and People," p. 8

Cogswell, Rob, "Refugee Worker Arrested," *The Christian Century*, vol. 101, May 2, 1984, "Events and People," p. 454

Collum, Danny, "Trespassing in the Basin," *Crucible of Hope* (Washington, D.C.: Sojourners, 1984) pp. 6–9

"Congregation Faces Sanctuary Question," *Burlington Free Press*, April 29, 1984

"Connie Sails Without Disruption," *San Diego Union*, October 2, 1971, p. B1

"Conspiracy of Compassion," *Sojourners*, vol. 14, March 1985, pp. 14–18

"Coral Sea Sails as Protest Founders," *San Francisco Chronicle*, November 13, 1971, pp. 1, 18

"Coral Sea Sails to War; 17 Protestors Held," *San Francisco Examiner*, November 12, 1971, pp. 1, 4

DeMott, Stephen T., "Jesus the refugee" (editorial), *Maryknoll*, vol. 78, June 1984, pp. 34–35

"Deporting of Latin Refugees Is Condemned," *San Francisco Chronicle*, January 24, 1985, p. 15

Dilling, Yvonne, "Opened Hearts and Homes," *Sojourners*, vol. 14, March 1985, pp. 21–22

"Discharged Sailors Speak Up," *San Francisco Examiner*, December 8, 1971, p. 64

"Dissenters' Sanctuary," *San Francisco Sunday Examiner and Chronicle*, November 14, 1971, "This World," p. 6

Dussel, Enrique, ". . . to be a stranger," *Maryknoll*, vol. 78, June 1984, pp. 36–39

Elder, Jack, "Against the Best of Our Traditions," *Sojourners*, vol. 13, September 1984, p. 10

"Faith, Hopes and Votes," *Newsweek*, vol. 104, September 17, 1984, pp. 34–35

Farrell, Michael J., "Sanctuary: part of a bigger picture," *National Catholic Reporter*, vol. 20, September 14, 1984, pp. 9–11, 14

"Foreign, domestic policies tied, Coffin says," *The Arizona Daily Star*, January 24, 1985

Frame, Randy, "Churches Violate Federal Law to Shelter Illegal Aliens," *Christianity Today*, vol. 28, March 16, 1984, pp. 34–36

Frame, Randy, "Sanctuary Workers Indicted for Harboring Illegal Aliens," *Christianity Today*, vol. 29, March 1, 1985, pp. 30–31

"Franciscans Open Door to Latin Refugees," *San Francisco Chronicle*, March 22, 1985, p. 24

Gerlernter, Carey Quan, "Salvadorans' Lives and Seattle Faith Make a Long Journey," *Seattle Times*, January 15, 1983, reprinted in *Church and Society*, vol. 73, March/April 1983, pp. 51–54

Geyer, Georgie Anne, "The sanctuary movement: politically naive church members lured by ideals," *Washington Times*, January 23, 1985

Gibney, Mark, "Seeking Sanctuary: A Special Duty for the U.S.?" *Commonweal*, vol. 111, May 18, 1984, pp. 295–296

Golden, Renny, "Churches Confront INS, Offer Refugees Sanctuary," *Witness*, vol. 65, no. 2, December 1982, pp. 4–7

Golden, Renny, " 'Coyote,' " *Witness*, vol. 11, December 1982, pp. 24–26

Golden, Renny, "Sanctuary," *Sojourners*, vol. 11, December 1982, pp. 24–26, updated and reprinted in *Crucible of Hope* (Washington, D.C.: Sojourners, 1984), pp. 111–114

Golden, Renny and Michael McConnell, "Sanctuary: Choosing Sides," *Christianity and Crisis*, vol. 43, February 21, 1983, pp. 31–36

Golder, W. Evan, "War Resister's Sanctuary," *U.S. Catholic*, November 1972, pp. 34–36

Gollub, Fr. Tim, "Are refugees 'illegal aliens?' " *Texas Catholic*, April 27, 1984

Greenberg, Moshe, "The Biblical Concept of Asylum," *Journal of Biblical Literature*, June 1959, pp. 125–132

Hall-Williams, Steven, "Caught in the Net," *Sojourners*, vol. 13, September 1984, p. 8

Hall-Williams, Steven, "Refugee Workers' Trials Continue," *Sojourners*, vol. 13, August 1984, "For the Record," p. 6

Henriot, Peter J., "Religious roots of political action," *Maryknoll*, vol. 78, October 1984, pp. 43–46

Hollyday, Joyce, "A Spirit of Resolve," *Sojourners*, vol. 14, March 1985, pp. 9–10

Hollyday, Joyce, "Wayfare," *Sojourners*, vol. 14, March 1985, p. 23

"Illegal-alien drive names Minnetonkan," *Minneapolis Star and Tribune*, January 16, 1985

"Immigration Chief Decries 'Anarchy,' of Sanctuary Movement," *Los Angeles Daily Journal*, March 20, 1985, p. 3

"INS Assails Berkeley's Latin Sanctuary," *San Francisco Chronicle*, February 21, 1985, p. 7

"INS Chief Links Sanctuary Move with Anarchy," *San Francisco Chronicle*, March 20, 1985, p. 11

"INS official knocks refugee volunteers," *National Catholic Reporter*, vol. 20, May 25, 1984, p. 21

"Invasion of the Sanctuaries" (editorial), *Los Angeles Times*, January 20, 1985

"Jackson Supports Refugee 'Caravan,' " *The Oakland Tribune*, October 1, 1984, p. A2

Jorstad, Eric, "A Theological Reflection on Sanctuary," *Christianity and Crisis*, vol. 43, October 31, 1983, pp. 404–407

Jorstad, Eric, "Sanctuary for Refugees: A Statement on Public Policy," *The Christian Century*, vol. 101, March 14, 1984, pp. 274–276

"Judge Relents On Sanctuary Worker's Term," *San Francisco Chronicle*, March 29, 1985, p. 14

"Jury in Texas Acquits Sanctuary Worker of Transporting Salvadoran Refugees," *Los Angeles Times*, January 25, 1985, Part I, p. 18

Kahn, Robert, "Interviews support political contention," *National Catholic Reporter*, vol. 21, February 1, 1985, pp. 1, 18

Kellerman, Bill, "The Hospitality of God," *Sojourners*, vol. 12, April 1983, pp. 26–28, also reprinted in *Crucible of Hope* (Washington, D.C.: Sojourners, 1984), pp. 108–110

Kemper, Vicki, "Refugees, Sanctuary Workers Face Charges," *Sojourners*, vol. 14, February 1985, p. 9

Kemper, Vicki, "Sanctuary Opponents Promote 'Civil Obedience,' " *Sojourners*, vol. 14, April 1985, p. 7

Krueger, Fred, "Land of the free, home of the eligible," *Christianity and Crisis*, vol. 44, July 9, 1984, pp. 274–278

"Law vs. a nun's higher order: Aid to refugees," *Chicago Tribune*, January 23, 1985

"Lay off the sanctuary folk" (editorial), *San Francisco Sunday Examiner and Chronicle*. January 20, 1985, p. B8

Lefevere, Patricia Scharber, "Elder acquitted of transporting aliens," *National Catholic Reporter*, vol. 21, February 1, 1985, p. 19

Lefevere, Patricia Scharber, "Elder and Merkt guilty; attorney says he won't heed sanctuary 'setback'," *National Catholic Reporter*, vol. 21, March 1, 1985, p. 7

Lefevere, Patricia Scharber, "Judge allows Elder's religious defense," *National Catholic Reporter*, vol. 21, January 25, 1985, p. 6

Lefevere, Patricia Scharber, "On trial in Texas: is it legal or not to help refugees?" *National Catholic Reporter*, vol. 20, May 18, 1984, pp. 1, 21, 22

Lefevere, Patricia Scharber, "Sanctuary trials, new arrests are electrifying the church, Texan says," *National Catholic Reporter*, vol. 21, January 25, 1985, p. 27

Lefevere, Patricia Scharber, "Sanctuary workers face trial; Texas bishop pays their bonds," *National Catholic Reporter*, vol. 21, December 21, 1984, p. 4

Lefevere, Patricia Scharber, "Texas sanctuary trial moved; local hostility cited," *National Catholic Reporter*, vol. 21, February 15, 1985

"Local Churches to Shield Central Americans," *San Jose Mercury*, March 24, 1983

MacEoin, Gary, "Sanctuary crackdown called federal feint," *National Catholic Reporter*, vol. 21, January 25, 1985, p. 27

MacEoin, Gary, "Stakes high for sanctuary future," *National Catholic Reporter*, vol. 20, May 18, 1984, p. 22

"Man Cleared in Aiding Salvadorans," *Washington Post*, January 25, 1985

Maharidge, Dale, "Escape from El Salvador," reprinted from *The Sacramento Bee*, August 26–30, 1984

Matthews, Karen, "Sanctuary," *The Berkeley Monthly*, vol. 15, no. 3, December 1984, pp. 23–29

Maurovich, Frank, "Helping people take new steps," *Maryknoll*, vol. 78, June 1984, pp. 48–54

McCarthy, Tim, "Crackdown butts church against state," *National Catholic Reporter*, vol. 21, January 25, 1985, pp. 1, 12, 26

McCarthy, Tim, "Sanctuary activists unite, despite tensions," *National Catholic Reporter*, vol. 21, February 8, 1985, p. 6

McCarthy, Tim, "Sanctuary movement: crucible of crisis," *National Catholic Reporter*, vol. 21, February 1, 1985, pp. 1, 20

McClory, Robert J., "Midwest sanctuary leaders say federal crackdown will backfire," *National Catholic Reporter*, vol. 21, January 25, 1985, p. 26

McConnell, Michael, "Claiming Space for God's Justice: How One Church Responded to the Plight of the Central American Refugees," *The Other Side*, vol. 19, February 1983, pp. 15–17

McConnell, Michael, "Sanctuary: No Stopping It Now," *The Other Side*, vol. 21, March 1985, pp. 32–35

McConnell, Michael and Renny Golden, "A Theology of Sanctuary," *Engage/Social Action*, vol. 12, February 1984, pp. 4–8

McConnell, Michael and Renny Golden, "Taking to the Road," *Crucible of Hope* (Washington, D.C.: Sojourners, 1984), pp. 106–107

McMullen, Marianne, "Six Sanctuary Workers Arrested," *Sojourners*, vol. 13, April 1984, "For the Record," p. 6

"Merkt, Elder await jail for doing 'what was legal,' " *National Catholic Reporter*, vol. 21, April 5, 1985, p. 5

Merkt, Stacey, "An Upside-Down World," *Sojourners*, vol. 13, September 1984, p. 9

Miller, Kay, "Church Shelters Salvadoran Refugee," *The Minneapolis Tribune*, December 12, 1982, reprinted in *Church and Society*, vol. 73, March/April 1983, pp. 55–59

"Moral Minorities" (editorial), *The Nation*, vol. 240, January 26, 1985, p. 68

Mosley, Dan, "Waystations on a Journey," *Crucible of Hope* (Washington, D.C.: Sojourners, 1984), pp. 115–117

" 'My head is not bowed': guilty sanctuary worker," *National Catholic Reporter*, vol. 20, May 25, 1984, p. 21

"New Hampshire order offers sanctuary," *National Catholic Reporter*, vol. 21, January 18, 1985, p. 3

"No Hiding Place Here," *Newsweek*, vol. 105, March 4, 1985, pp. 14–15

"No 'Sanctuary' for Berkeley Council," *San Francisco Chronicle*, November 12, 1971, p. 11

"Nuns Offer Refugees 'Sanctuary,' " *Wichita Eagle*, April 28, 1983

"Of refugees and refuge," *One World*, no. 88, July/August 1983, p. 13

"Offering sanctuary to Salvadoran refugees—illegally," *Philadelphia Inquirer*, March 5, 1984

Oliver, Gordon, "Sanctuary? Yes!" *National Catholic Reporter*, vol. 21, March 15, 1985, p. 7

"Political Asylum," *San Francisco Sunday Examiner and Chronicle*, October 7, 1984, "This World," p. 15

"Politics and the Pulpit," *Newsweek*, vol. 104, September 17, 1984, pp. 24–27

"Politics of terror drives refugees to Houston," *Houston Post*, May 20, 1984

"Presbyterians Honor Tucson Congregation," *Arizona Daily Star*, June 3, 1984

"Priests, Nuns Charged With Alien Smuggling," *Los Angeles Times*, January 15, 1985, Part I, pp. 1, 8

"Protest at border crossing supports priest indicted for sanctuary activity," *Arizona Daily Star*, January 27, 1985

"Providing Sanctuary Increases Religious Fervor," *Seattle Times*, November 12, 1983

Rauber, Paul, "Conscientious Protectors," *San Francisco Focus*, vol. 31, September 1984, pp. 50–57

Rauber, Paul, "Deportation to Death," *San Francisco Bay Guardian*, August 15, 1984

"Refugee aid a fitting response" (editorial), *National Catholic Reporter*, vol. 21, February 1, 1985, p. 12

"Refugee Underground Leads to Chicago Area," *Chicago Tribune*, May 30, 1983

"Refugee tells of repression," *Contra Costa Times*, October 21, 1984, p. 7

"Refugee work will continue, activists vow," *Arizona Republic*, January 16, 1985

"Refugees and Sanctuary," *The Christian Century*, vol. 100, no. 7, March 9, 1983, "Events and People," p. 209

"Refugees Travel Openly, Illegally to Find a Haven," *Los Angeles Times*, June 30, 1984, p. 1

"Refusing To Give Sanctuary," *Washington Post*, February 9, 1985, p. B6

"Religious Groups, Prosecutors Clash Over Salvadorans," *Los Angeles Daily Journal*, July 20, 1984, pp. 1, 16

"Religious freedom issue likely to be linchpin of sanctuary trial defense," *Christian Science Monitor*, February 7, 1985, pp. 3–4

"Report of the 195th General Assembly, Presbyterian Church (U.S.A.)," *Church and Society*, vol. 73, July/August 1983, pp. 82–84

"Report of the 196th General Assembly, Presbyterian Church (U.S.A.)," *Church and Society*, vol. 74, July/August 1984, pp. 50–58

Riordan, Dennis P., "No Sanctuary From Government: Prosecution of Those Aiding Refugees Intrudes on Religion," *Los Angeles Times*, January 23, 1985

"Roman Catholics Are Deeply Torn by Debate Over Religion, Politics," *Wall Street Journal*, September 19, 1984, pp. 1, 16

"Sailors Given Discharges," *Los Angeles Times*, December 7, 1971, p. A24

"Sailors Vow to Miss Ship," *San Francisco Examiner*, October 12, 1971, p. 48

"Salvador Refugees' Stories of Torture," *San Francisco Chronicle*, October 15, 1984, p. 9

"Salvadoran Refugees Find Haven," *Sacramento Bee*, March 18, 1984

"Salvadorans Testify in Trial of Two Sanctuary Workers," *Washington Post*, February 20, 1985

Samples, Pat, "The Church as Sanctuary," *The Other Side*, vol. 19, February 1983, pp. 18–19

"Sanctuary," *The Christian Century*, vol. 101, October 17, 1984, "Events and People," pp. 951–952

"Sanctuary: A Refuge in the Bible," *Los Angeles Times*, January 19, 1985

"Sanctuary Backers Protest U.S. Action," *San Francisco Chronicle*, January 17, 1985, p. 6

"Sanctuary churches rally after U.S. crackdown," *Christian Science Monitor*, January 17, 1985, pp. 1, 36

"Sanctuary: Churches' Way to Protest," *U.S. News and World Report*, vol. 97, September 24, 1984, p. 43

"Sanctuary Conviction," *The Christian Century*, vol. 102, March 6, 1985, "Events and People," p. 240

"Sanctuary Developments," *The Christian Century*, vol. 102, January 30, 1985, "Events and People," p. 96

"Sanctuary for Salvadorans," *Newsweek*, vol. 102, July 11, 1983, p. 27

"Sanctuary Illegal? Official Not Sure," *Seattle Times*, June 12, 1983

"Sanctuary Leaders Get Support, Vow to Fight," *Los Angeles Times*, January 16, 1985, Part I, pp. 3, 13

"Sanctuary movement grows more active as US cracks down," *Christian Science Monitor*, January 23, 1985, p. 6

"Sanctuary Movement leaders under surveillance, they think," *The Daily Californian*, March 15, 1985, pp. 1, 4, 19

"Sanctuary movement mixes religion with politics," *San Jose Post-Record*, January 29, 1985, pp. 1, 8

"Sanctuary Movement Workers Get Jail Terms," *San Francisco Chronicle*, March 28, 1985, p. 15

"Sanctuary Offer to Anti-War GI's," *San Francisco Chronicle*, November 10, 1971, p. 16

"Sanctuary: rooted in values that confront American way" (editorial), *National Catholic Reporter*, vol. 21, February 22, 1985, p. 12

"Sanctuary-Seeking Sailors Are Arrested, Flown to Ship," *The Sacramento Bee*, October 3, 1971, p. A6

"Sanctuary Sparks Conflict Between Church and State," *Newsday*, February 27, 1985

"Sanctuary supporters outline legal strategies," *Christian Science Monitor*, January 18, 1985, pp. 3, 7

"Sanctuary targets U.S. injustice" (editorial), *National Catholic Reporter*, vol. 21, January 25, 1985, p. 16

"Sanctuary Without Safety," *Time*, vol. 124, July 23, 1984, p. 68

"Sanctuary Worker Loses Her Probation," *San Francisco Chronicle*, March 27, 1985, p. 3

Scherer, Peggy, "Offering Sanctuary," *The Catholic Worker*, January–February, 1985, pp. 1–3

"Scores of U.S. Churches Take In Illegal Aliens Fleeing Latin America," *Wall Street Journal*, June 21, 1984, pp. 1, 27

"Should Churches Provide Sanctuary?" (editorial), *The Christian Century*, vol. 100, no. 2, April 27, 1983, p. 387

"Shutting down the sanctuaries," *National Catholic Reporter*, February 10, 1985

"Sisters Seen Going Ahead With Sanctuary Plan," *Union Leader*, January 11, 1985

"Small Band of Springs Catholics Aids Salvadorans," *Denver Post*, February 21, 1984

"Smuggling Aliens Into U.S.—Booming Business," *U.S. News and World Report*, vol. 93, September 13, 1982, pp. 57–58

Somlo, Patty, "A Sanctuary for Salvadorans," *America*, vol. 148, March 19, 1983, pp. 211–212

"Students Vow to Expand Campus Sanctuary Efforts," *Los Angeles Times*, February 10, 1985, Part I, p. 27

Taylor, Paul, "The Road to Sanctuary," *The Washington Post* (National Weekly Edition), March 11, 1985, pp. 6–7

Teitelbaum, Michael S., "Right Versus Right: Immigration and Refugee Policy in the United States," *Foreign Affairs*, vol. 59, Fall 1980, pp. 21–59

"The Dilemma of Salvadoran Refugees, *San Francisco Chronicle*, April 11, 1984, p. F-1

"The Roles Religion Plays," *Newsweek*, vol. 104, September 17, 1984, pp. 31–32

"The Sanctuary Coalition," *San Francisco Examiner and Chronicle*, July 23, 1972, "California Living," pp. 7–8

"The Sanctuary Indictments: Shelter Skelter," *Village Voice*, January 29, 1985

"The Sanctuary Movement," *Providence Journal*, January 20, 1985

"This Is a Freedom Train," *Newsweek*, vol. 103, April 2, 1984, pp. 36–37

Thompson, Christine K. "The Liberating Quality of Truth: Churches and the Sanctuary Movement," *Engage/Social Action*, vol. 12, February 1984, pp. 41–45

Thorkelson, Willmar, "Former Salvadoran soldier arrested, says he will die if deported by INS," *National Catholic Reporter*, vol. 21, February 15, 1985

Thorkelson, Willmar, "Roach backs those who offer refuge, but 'it's not for me,' " *National Catholic Reporter*, vol. 21, February 1, 1985, p. 20

Thorkelson, Willmar, "Sanctuary? No!" *National Catholic Reporter*, vol. 21, March 15, 1985, p. 6

"Two Arrested for assisting war refugees," *The Daily Californian*, December 12, 1984, pp. 1, 12

"Two Convicted of Smuggling Salvadorans, Vow to Continue Sanctuary Refugee Work," *Los Angeles Times*, February 22, 1985, Part I, p. 4

"Two Startled Churches Choose," *Seattle Times*, June 12, 1983

"UC Riverside first school to offer sanctuary," *Los Angeles Herald-Examiner*, May 16, 1984

"Underground RR tries to publicize refugees' plight," *The Daily Californian*, July 3, 1984, pp. 1, 9

"Underground Railroad to go public," *Seattle Times*, May 19, 1984

"Up Against the Authorities," *Sojourners*, vol. 13, September 1984, pp. 9–10

"U.S. Churches Defy Law and Harbor El Salvadoran Refugees," *Christian Science Monitor*, August 20, 1982

"U.S. Moves to Curb Defense in Sanctuary Case," *San Francisco Chronicle*, January 28, 1985, p. 12

"U.S. sweeps down on churches accused of smuggling aliens," *The Oakland Tribune*, January 15, 1985

"Urge Refugee Asylum," *The Christian Century*, vol. 100, April 20, 1983, "Events and People," p. 361

"Violating the Sanctuary" (editorial), *America*, vol. 152, February 9, 1985, p. 97

Wall, James M., "Undelivered Gifts: INS v. Sanctuary," *The Christian Century*, vol. 102, February 20, 1985, pp. 171–172

Wallis, Jim, "From Protest to Resistance," *Crucible of Hope* (Washington, D.C.: Sojourners, 1984), pp. 119–120

Wallis, Jim, Marginal Notes, *Sojourners*, vol. 14, March 1985, p. 19

Wallis, Jim, "The Court Prophets," *Sojourners*, vol. 13, September 1984, pp. 3–4

Wallis, Jim, "The President's Pulpit," *Sojourners*, vol. 13, September 1984, pp. 17–21

"When Churches Smuggle Aliens," *U.S. News and World Report*, vol. 98, January 28, 1985, p. 14

"When home becomes a place of terror," *The Daily Californian*, April 1, 1985, p. 9

"Who Are Sanctuary Refugees? The Answer Bothers Washington," (op-ed), *Los Angeles Times*, January 28, 1985

"Why Illegal Aliens Get Sanctuary," *San Francisco Chronicle*, April 11, 1984, p. F-3

"Why Sanctuary?" *Washington Post*, February 3, 1985

"Why U.S. churchgoers take risks to shelter refugees," *San Francisco Examiner*, January 27, 1985, p. A8

Willigan, Dennis, "Sanctuary: A Communitarian Form of Counter-Culture," *Union Seminary Quarterly Review*, vol. 25, Summer 1970, pp. 517–541

Wolterstorff, Nicholas, "Until Justice and Peace Embrace," *The Other Side*, vol. 20, May 1984, pp. 20–23

Young, Ron and James S. Best, "The Sanctuary Movement Reaches into the Pacific," *Fellowship*, January 1969, p. 21

"1 in 50 Salvadorans May Be Dead, Study Shows," *Los Angeles Times*, January 25, 1984

"2 Who Aided Refugees Guilty of Conspiracy," *San Francisco Chronicle*, February 22, 1985, p. 23

"6 Sailors Take Sanctuary In Church," *The Sacramento Bee*, September 30, 1971, p. D4

"8 'Connie' Sailors Face Discharge," *San Diego Union*, December 3, 1971, p. D5

"9 Constellation Sailors Seized, Flown To Ship," *San Diego Union*, October 3, 1971, pp. B1, B7

"13 Leaders of Sanctuary Movement Plead Not Guilty," *Los Angeles Times*, January 24, 1985, Part I, p. 16

"16 Charged with conspiring to bring illegal aliens to US," *Christian Science Monitor*, January 15, 1985

New York Times (in chronological order)

"War Foes Are Promised Churches as Sanctuary," October 3, 1967, p. 5

"All Male Jury Picked for Trial of Spock and 4," May 21, 1968, p. 4

"Evader of Draft Seized in Church," May 23, 1968, p. 2

"AWOL Soldier in Boston Stays in Church Sanctuary," May 26, 1968, p. 3

"Army Acts to Remove G.I. From Sanctuary in Church," May 28, 1968, p. 33

"Foe of War Leaves Church Sanctuary," May 30, 1968, p. 12

"Church in Boston is Hub of Dissent," June 2, 1968, p. 88

"Providence Church Grants Sanctuary to Draft Foes," June 2, 1968, p. 89

"2 Draft Resisters Are Dragged From Church by Agents of F.B.I.," June 4, 1968, p. 12

"Draft Resister Seized in Church as 100 Friends Show Support," June 14, 1968, p. 49

"Draft Jury Finds L.I. Youth Guilty," July 20, 1968, p. 6

"Soldier Takes Sanctuary," August 21, 1968, p. 33

"War Critics Give Sanctuary to G.I.," August 28, 1968, p. 36

"L.I. Draft Resister is Given Four Years," September 28, 1968, p. 16

"Army Deserter Removed From Boston U. Chapel," October 7, 1968, p. 29

"AWOL Private Given 'Sanctuary' at City College," November 1, 1968, p. 14

"Sanctuary Move Debated at M.I.T.," November 3, 1968, p. 33

"AWOL Soldier Set to Lecture at M.I.T.," November 6, 1968, p. 44

"MIT Says Fugitive GI Has No Official Status," November 7, 1968, p. 50

"Police Seize 125 on C.C.N.Y. Campus," November 7, 1968, pp. 1, 4

"175 Hold Protest on C.C.N.Y. Campus," November 8, 1968, p. 32

"12 War Protesters Seized Here as Youthful Radicals Prepare for More Demonstrations Today," November 9, 1968, p. 15

"Soldier is Arrested at M.I.T. Sanctuary," November 11, 1968, p. 17

"Soldier Convicted of Trespass Here, But Wins Praise," November 14, 1968, p. 8

"City College Administration Chided," November 15, 1968, p. 27

"Draft Resister Imprisoned," November 15, 1968, p. 50

"AWOL Soldier Receives Sanctuary at Brandeis U.," December 5, 1968, p. 2

"Soldier, Absent From Post, Seized at Base Protest," December 21, 1968, p. 3

"G.I. Gets Four Months," January 6, 1969, p. 48

"Mock Trial Prepares Students of C.C.N.Y. for Day in Court," January 19, 1969, p. 44

"AWOL Soldier, Protesting War, Awaits Arrest," October 18, 1969, p. 10

"Soldier Leaves 'Sanctuary' Here," October 20, 1969, p. 16

"Hawaii Campus Church Bridges the Generation Gap," April 19, 1971, p. 26

"6 Antiwar Sailors Given Refuge in Catholic Church," October 1, 1971, p. 7

"9 Ashore as Carrier Sails: Navy Calls Them Deserters," October 2, 1971, p. 62

"Carrier Departs Amid Protests," October 3, 1971, p. 5

"1000 Sailors Said to Ask Ban on Carrier's Sailing," October 12, 1971, p. 17

"Five Who Took Sanctuary After Jumping Ship Give Up," October 18, 1971, p. 40

"Sailors Who Fled War Duty Are Awaiting Discharge," December 5, 1971, p. 7

"General Discharge Given to 8 Sailors Who Avoided War," December 7, 1971, p. 10

"U.S. Churches Offer Sanctuary to Aliens Facing Deportation," April 8, 1983, pp. A1, A16

"More Churches Join in Offering Sanctuary for Latin Refugees," September 21, 1983, p. A18

"Ouster of Salvadorans Defended," January 26, 1984, p. A6

"Reporter is Arrested with Five in Texas in Aiding of Aliens," February 19, 1984, p. A39

"Refugee Center Operator Is Arrested in Texas," April 14, 1984, p. A8

"Social Worker Defends Actions on 2 Aliens," May 9, 1984, p. A19

"Sheltering of Salvadorans Is Debated," June 4, 1984, p. B3

"Church Members Back Sanctuary for Refugees," June 11, 1984, p. B2

"Churches and U.S. Clash on Alien Sanctuary," June 28, 1984

"Amid Charges, Immigration Bill Dies," October 12, 1984, p. A16

"16 Indicted by U.S. in Bid to End Church Smuggling of Latin Aliens," January 15, 1985, pp. 1, 7

"Activists to Persist in Assisting People Fleeing Latin Lands," January 16, 1985, pp. 1, 7

"Leader in Movement That Shelters Aliens Wins a Court Round," January 18, 1985, p. 6

"Despite a Crackdown, 7 Guatemalans Are Smuggled Into U.S.," January 20, 1985, p. 7

"Alien Movement Dealt Legal Blow," January 22, 1985

"U.S. Asks Curb on Sanctuary Case Testimony," January 27, 1985, p. 15

"Leaders of Alien Sanctuary Drive Say Indictments Pose Church-State Issue," February 3, 1985, p. 30

"Two Go on Trial in Houston For Illegally Helping Aliens," February 19, 1985, p. 7

"Salvadoran Says U.S. Traded for Testimony," February 20, 1985, p. 9

"Leader in Movement to Harbor Aliens Is Convicted," February 22, 1985, p. 8

"Clerics Denounce Curbs on Aiding Latin Aliens," March 1, 1985, p. 8

"Use of Informers Questioned in Inquiry on Aliens," March 2, 1985

"2 Sentenced in Aid to Illegal Aliens," March 28, 1985, p. 13

"Sanctuary Worker Given A Lighter Sentence," March 29, 1985, p. 8

Other Sources

Abbott, Walter M., ed. *The Documents of Vatican II*. (Chicago: Follett Publishing Company, 1966)

America Friends Service Committee, Church World Service Immigration and Refugee Program, Inter-Religious Task Force on El Salvador and Central America and Lutheran Immigration and Refugee Service, *Seeking Safe Haven: A Congregational Guide to Helping Central American Refugees in the United States*, undated [1984]

"Asylum, Right of," *New Catholic Encyclopedia*, vol. 1 (New York: McGraw-Hill Book Company, 1967) p. 994

"Basta!", Tucson edition, January 1985

"Basta!" Sanctuary Organizers' Nuts and Bolts Supplement No. 1" (Chicago: Chicago Religious Task Force on Central America, undated [Fall 1983])

"Basta!", National Newsletter of the Chicago Religious Task Force on Central America, April 1985

"Basta!" National Sanctuary Newsletter," July 1984 (Chicago: Chicago Religious Task Force on Central America, 1984)

"Basta!", Newsletter of the Chicago Religious Task Force on Central America, January 1985

Chicago Religious Task Force on Central America, the National Lawyers Guild, Proyecto Resistencia (Chicago) of the AFSC, and Travelers and Immigrants Aid Society (Chicago), *Sanctuary and the Law: A Guide for Congregations*, 1984

"City of Refuge," *Interpreter's Dictionary of the Bible* (Nashville: Abingdon Press, 1962) p. 638

Corbett, Jim, "A View From the Border," unpublished, September 8, 1984

Corbett, Jim, "Sanctuary and the Covenant Community," unpublished, June 1984

"De," 25A *Corpus Juris Secundum* (Brooklyn: West Publishing Co., 1966), pp. 481–483

"De facto," *Black's Law Dictionary*, 5th ed. (St. Paul, MN: West Publishing Co., 1979) p. 375

Gordon, Charles and Harry N. Rosenfield, *Immigration Law and Procedure*, rev. ed., vol. 1 (New York: Matthew Bender and Co., 1984)

"Government Crackdown on Sanctuary Movement," *Central America Refugee Defense Fund Newsletter* (San Francisco), June 1984, pp. 1, 5, 8

Immigration and Naturalization Service, "Our Immigration: A Brief Account of Immigration to the United States" (Washington, D.C.: U.S. Government Printing Office, 1980)

Interpreter's Bible, vol. II (Leviticus-Samuel) (New York: Abingdon Press, 1953) pp. 303–306, 360–361, 451–453, 648–650

Low, Sir Sidney and F. S. Pulling, *et al. The Dictionary of English History*, New Edition. (London: Cassell and Co., Ltd., 1928)

MacEoin, Gary and Nivita Riley. *No Promised Land: American Refugee Policies and the Rule of Law* (Boston: Oxfam America, 1982)

National Conference of Catholic Bishops, "First Draft of Pastoral Letter on Catholic Social Teaching and the U.S. Economy," November 11,

1984, reprinted in *National Catholic Reporter*, vol. 21, November 23, 1984, pp. 9–32

National Conference of Catholic Bishops, *The Challenge of Peace: God's Promise and Our Response* (Washington, D.C.: United States Catholic Conference, 1983)

"National Sanctuary Mailing," May 1984 (Chicago: Chicago Religious Task Force on Central America, 1984)

Office of the United Nations High Commissioner for Refugees, *Collection of International Instruments Concerning Refugees*, 2nd ed. (Geneva: UNHCR, 1979)

Office of the United Nations High Commissioner for Refugees, *Handbook on Procedures and Criteria for Determining Refugee Status* (Geneva: UNHCR, 1979)

Plaut, W. Gunther, Bernard J. Bamberger and William W. Hallo, *The Torah: A Modern Commentary*. (New York: Union of American Hebrew Congregations, 1981)

"Public Sanctuary for Salvadoran and Guatemalan Refugees: Organizers' Nuts and Bolts" (Chicago: Chicago Religious Task Force on Central America, undated)

Quinn, John R. "Pastoral Letter on Central America," published by Latin America Task Force, Commission on Social Justice, Archdiocese of San Francisco, November 1983

Quinn, John R. "When I Was A Stranger" (Pastoral Statement on our National Response to the Refugees of Central America), March 12, 1985

"Religious Leaders' Affirmation of Sanctuary Ministry" (unpublished), January 23, 1985

"Sanctuary," *Collier's Encyclopaedia*, vol. 20 (New York: Macmillan Educational Company, 1981) p. 390

"Sanctuary," *The Encyclopaedia Britannica*, 11th ed. (New York: Encyclopaedia Brittanica, Inc., 1911) pp. 129–131

"Sanctuary," *The New Encyclopaedia Britannica*, 15th ed., Micropaedia, vol. 8, (Chicago: Encyclopaedia Britannica, Inc., 1982) pp. 884–845

"Sanctuary: A Justice Ministry" (Chicago: Chicago Religious Task Force on Central America, undated)

"Sanctuary Defense," *Central American Refugee Defense Fund Newsletter* (Boston), December 1984, pp. 1, 2

Steinberg, S.H., ed., *A New Dictionary of British History* (New York: St. Martin's Press, Inc. 1963)

The Immigration Project of the National Lawyers Guild, *Immigration Law and Defense*, 2nd ed. (New York: Clark Boardman Company, 1981)

Tribe, Laurence H. *American Constitutional Law*, (Mineola, N.Y.: The Foundation Press, Inc., 1978)

United States Department of State, *Country Reports on the World Refugee Situation*, (Fiscal Year 1984) (Washington, D.C.: Department of State, August 1983)

2nd General Conference of Latin American Bishops, *The Church in the Present-Day Transformation of Latin America in Light of the Council*, English translation (Washington, D.C.: National Conference of Catholic Bishops, 1979)

3rd General Conference of Latin American Bishops, *Evangelization in Latin America's Present and Future*, English translation (Washington, D.C.: National Conference of Catholic Bishops, 1979)

EPILOGUE

On June 18, 1985, the United States Fifth Circuit Court of Appeals reversed the May 1984 conviction of Stacey Lynn Merkt, ruling that the trial judge had erred by refusing to instruct the jury to find Merkt not guilty of unlawful transportation if she was taking the refugees to the Immigration and Naturalization Service in San Antonio, Texas to apply for asylum. The Fifth Circuit remanded the case to the district court for a new trial. The prosecution has not yet decided whether to bring Merkt to trial again or to dismiss the charges.

Meanwhile, pre-trial hearings were held on May 21–24 and June 25–28 in the Phoenix, Arizona consolidated trial of the twelve sanctuary workers indicted in January 1985. The defense raised numerous motions: (1) a motion to suppress evidence illegally gathered during the search of defendant Sr. Darlene Nicgorski's apartment; (2) a motion to dismiss charges against Philip Willis-Conger and Katherina Flaherty because of evidence illegally obtained during their May 1984 arrest; (3) a motion to conduct discovery about the government informants; (4) a motion to dismiss all the charges based on international law obligations which supersede the INS' interpretation of domestic refugee law; (5) a motion to dismiss based on the guarantee of the free exercise of religion under the First Amendment; (6) a motion to dismiss based on the unconstitutionality of the government's investigation under the First, Fourth and Fifth Amendments; and (7) a motion to dismiss based on the Equal Protection clause of the Fifth Amendment since the relevant statute exempts employers but not churches from harboring charges. After extensive testimony and oral and written arguments, Judge Earl Carroll denied every defense motion except the discovery motion. Judge Carroll then considered the government's motion *in limine* and ruled that any evidence about the necessity of the sanctuary workers' actions in order to save the lives of the refugees or any evidence about their religious beliefs and motivations would be inadmissible at the trial. He delayed ruling on the rest of the motion *in limine*. Judge Carroll has also not ruled on the defense motion to change the venue of the proceedings from Phoenix to Tucson, where most of the remaining defendants reside. The trial is now scheduled to commence on October 15.

On May 7, 1985, over seventy national and local religious bodies and Central American refugee organizations, including the American Baptist Churches, the Unitarian Universalist Association, the United Methodist Church, the Presbyterian Church (U.S.A.) and Casa Oscar Romero, filed a lawsuit in the United States District Court for Northern California seeking to enjoin any future prosecutions of sanctuary workers and any future arrests or deportations of Central American refugees. The plaintiffs allege that the sanctuary workers are acting as persons of faith, with both a religious obligation and constitutional right to provide sanctuary to Salvadorans and Guatemalans. The plaintiffs also allege that the refugees are protected from deportation by the Refugee Act of 1980, the United Nations Convention and Protocol Relating to Refugees and the Geneva Conventions of 1949. The United States government has not yet answered the complaint.

Finally, the United States Supreme Court issued three decisions anticipated in the text above. In *Tony and Susan Alamo Foundation v. Secretary of Labor*, 53 U.S.L.W. 4489 (4/23/85), the Supreme Court ruled that the application of the Fair Labor Standards Act to workers engaged in the commercial activities of a religious foundation did not burden the workers' freedom to exercise religious rights. The Court reasoned that the workers could return any wages they received to the foundation if their religious convictions prevented them from accepting wages. In *Jensen v. Quaring*, 53 U.S.L.W. 4787 (6/17/85), an equally divided Court (with the ill Justice Lewis Powell absent) affirmed without decision the ruling of the Eighth Circuit Court of Appeals that a woman who believed that the requirement of a photograph on her driver's license would violate her religious beliefs about idolatry was entitled to an exemption. Thus, the Court did not change any of its Free Exercise of Religion doctrine. Finally, in *Jean v. Nelson*, 53 U.S.L.W. 4892 (6/26/85), the Supreme Court reversed the ruling of the en banc Eleventh Circuit Court of Appeals that inadmissible aliens are not protected from national origin discrimination under the Fifth Amendment. The Supreme Court held that the Eleventh Circuit had unnecessarily and improperly reached the constitutional issue and remanded the case to the district court. The due process issues in the case were not raised before the Supreme Court.